PRAISE FOR RAVI BATRA'S
GREENSPAN'S FRAUD

"The most thoroughgoing assault on the Maestro's legacy so far."

—*Fort Worth Star-Telegram*

"In this chilling exposé of one of the most powerful men of our time, Ravi Batra reveals Greenspan for who he secretly is: An ideologue who has waged war on the American Dream and imperiled the world economy. *Greenspan's Fraud* is a terrifying book."

—David Callahan, author of *The Cheating Culture: Why More Americans Are Doing Wrong to Get Ahead*

"As always, his economic arguments are expressed elegantly."

—*Publishers Weekly*

ALSO BY RAVI BATRA

Greenspan's Fraud
The Crash of the Millennium
The Great American Deception
The Myth of Free Trade
Japan: The Return to Prosperity
Surviving the Great Depression of 1990
The Great Depression of 1990
Muslim Civilization and the Crisis in Iran
The Downfall of Capitalism and Communism
The Pure Theory of International Trade
The Theory of International Trade under Uncertainty

THE NEW
GOLDEN AGE
*The Coming Revolution against
Political Corruption and Economic Chaos*

RAVI BATRA

palgrave
macmillan

First published in 2007 by
PALGRAVE MACMILLAN™
175 Fifth Avenue, New York, N.Y. 10010 and
Houndmills, Basingstoke, Hampshire, England RG21 6XS.
Companies and representatives throughout the world.

PALGRAVE MACMILLAN is the global academic imprint of the Palgrave
Macmillan division of St. Martin's Press, LLC and of Palgrave Macmillan Ltd.
Macmillan® is a registered trademark in the United States, United Kingdom and
other countries. Palgrave is a registered trademark in the European Union and
other countries.

ISBN-13: 978-1-4039-7579-9
ISBN-10: 1-4039-7579-5

Library of Congress Cataloging-in-Publication Data

Batra, Raveendra N.
   The new golden age : the coming revolution against political corruption and
economic chaos / Ravi Batra.
      p.   cm.
   Includes bibliographical references and index.
   ISBN 1-4039-7579-5
   1. Political corruption—Economic aspects.   2. Corruption—Economic
aspects.   3. United States—Economic policy—2001–   4. Poverty.
5. Business cycles.   6. Civilization, Islamic.   I. Title.

JF1081.B38   2007
330.'0511—dc22

                                                                      2006050324

A catalogue record of the book is available from the British Library.

Design by Letra Libre, Inc.

First edition: February 2007

10   9   8   7   6   5   4   3   2   1

Printed in the United States of America.

To Airie Stuart

CONTENTS

ACKNOWLEDGEMENTS

This book arose from my conversations with Airie Stuart, my editor at Palgrave Macmillan. I happened to call her in late 2005, at a time when rising American poverty was capturing headlines. Every year since the start of the new millennium, a million Americans had been joining the ranks of the poor with no end in sight even in an improving economy. Our conversation started on a light note as we exchanged pleasantries, but quickly turned serious. Airie expressed her profound concern for the growing social tumor of poverty afflicting not just the United States but also the entire globe and asked if I would be willing to write about the problem. Having edited my latest work, *Greenspan's Fraud*, she felt I was the right candidate to offer simple and practical solutions to ease the misery of the world's destitute.

My initial reaction was somewhat lukewarm, because I had been writing on world poverty for many, many years, and the cures I had offered conflicted with conventional wisdom coming from the economic establishment, which was and is busy appeasing the interests of the rich and powerful. "What's the point in me writing another book on the causes and cures of poverty," I asked, "when the real problem is worldwide corruption that creates and nurtures deprivation all over the globe?" "Then write on that," Airie exclaimed. "Prove to the people that it is corruption that creates poverty here and abroad."

As I pondered the assignment, I sought to expand the scope of the book proposal by incorporating the forecasting tools I had explored in the past, because they offer a mixed but bright message about the future. They indicate that the poor are about to multiply all over the globe, so much so that the oppressed masses will revolt and overthrow the ruling elite, culminating in a planetary golden age in which poverty will become a thing of the past. Like many abuses discarded in the dustbin of human history, hunger and deprivation would simply vanish. Airie accepted my augmented proposal, and the fruit of our conversations and cooperation is *The New Golden Age*. The final version of the manuscript has visibly improved because of her repeated but gentle prodding. To express my thanks and gratitude to her, I have decided to dedicate this work to a very fine lady, Airie Stuart, who feels for the suffering humanity and wants to do something practical about its agony.

Others who have been helpful in producing this book are my dear wife Sunita and research assistants, Amit Aggarwal, Jayant Sarkar and Huijun Wang. Some of the ideas developed here were first tested in a panel discussion organized by the McGuire Center for Ethics at Southern Methodist University in March 2006, and I am grateful to the center for selecting me as its teaching fellow for 2006 and for its moral support. Thanks are also due to Dick Alexander, Michael Blomquist, and Alan Bradshaw for discussions that came in handy while writing some chapters. Finally, I am thankful to my son Rishee for adding clarity to some graphs.

CHAPTER 1

GLOBAL POVERTY
AND
ECONOMIC CHAOS

I n spite of impressive economic strides made by some countries in recent years, a great mass of humanity around the world lives in
poverty, even destitution. A World Bank report estimates that nearly
3 billion people, about half the global population, were poor or lived on
less than $2 a day at the dawn of the new millennium. Another billion
people were destitute, subsisting daily on less than a dollar.[1] What is
worse, the situation changed little between 1980 and 2000,[2] while the
ranks of the $2-a-day poor actually swelled.[3]

Even in Asia, where the economies of China and India have been
growing at the exceptional rates of 8–10 percent per year for over a
decade, nearly 2 billion people are poor and 700 million are destitute.[4]
Thus, the impressive growth rates of some Asian economies have done
little to alleviate overall poverty in the East. Nor has penury eased in
Africa and Latin America.

Most experts blame the problem on our planet's population explosion. However, poverty is not just a Third World cancer; it also afflicts a
large swath of people in the First World, including the advanced
economies of North America, Europe, Australia and Japan. In fact, the
richest country, the United States, now resembles a banana republic,
with its poverty ranks swelling by a million every year. This book argues

that the main cause of poverty, anywhere and everywhere, is official corruption, which breeds economic policies that enrich the ruling elite and exacerbate income and wealth disparities. The poverty tumor is not the result of paltry growth in output, but of the growing monopoly power of big business, which in turn reflects government malfeasance. Global output has grown twice as fast as the global population since 1980, yet poverty stalks the world with increasing vehemence.[5]

Where is poverty headed? This is another question raised and tackled by this book, which goes on to explore the globe's future. My answer is that this future is very bright, although a few grim years are around the corner. By using some of the cycles that I have analyzed in the past, I come to the conclusion that, after a short interlude of intense economic chaos, the world will move into an era of unprecedented prosperity in which poverty will be mostly eradicated. No longer will there be hunger and deprivation.

Although this book focuses on the United States, which is at the center of the global economy, it offers lessons with universal applications. This is because in a U.S.-centric world, what transpires in America echoes around the planet. There is a well-known cliché that if the U.S. economy sneezes, the world catches pneumonia. Likewise, if the U.S. economy expands, the world booms.

American economic thought and policies now sway the globe. This economic thought is reckless, unethical and faulty, and stands in the way of eradicating poverty. In one form or another, U.S. economists espouse the well-known trickle-down economics, or what may be called tricklism, whereby prosperity is supposed to seep, drop by drop, from the top down to the bottom. Such thinking nurtures policies that worsen disparities in income and wealth. Since tricklism now dominates global thought, the gap between the rich and the poor is rocketing all over the world.

Here are some statistics about disparities in global income and wealth:

- 20 percent of the population in advanced economies consumes more than 80 percent of the world's output.
- Less than a thousand millionaires have as much wealth as the poorest 2.5 billion people of the planet.
- In 1999, the world's richest 200 people had a net worth of $1 trillion, while 582 million people earned an income of $146 billion.[6]

According to the Asian Development Bank, 93 percent of Asia's destitute live in India (357 million), China (203 million) and other South Asian nations (77 million).[7] Thus India, notwithstanding its superb economic performance since 2000, continues to be the ringleader in terms of hunger and deprivation. Yet a Bloomberg News report found that India's millionaires club swelled to 83,000 in 2005. Although this is still a small group, it grew by 19 percent, the fastest rate in the world. Similarly, China, with a population close to India's, had 320,000 millionaires. Not surprisingly, the United States topped the list with 2.7 million, followed by 448,000 in the United Kingdom.[8]

This book argues that trickle-down economics seeds poverty not only in America but also around the world. What used to be primarily a U.S. virus now infects the planet. Thus global poverty spews from the pandemic of tricklism. Furthermore, the virus also spawns yawning imbalances in terms of financial bubbles and growing budget and trade deficits, which in turn are a recipe for worldwide economic chaos.

Very briefly, my argument is this: In developed economies, tricklism keeps wages as low as possible while maximizing CEO incomes. This causes consumer demand to fall short of product supply, so that the demand-supply balance is maintained by the creation of more consumer and government debt. In developing economies, tricklism also means low—in fact, dirt-poor—wages, along with high CEO salaries, so that demand again trails supply. There the demand-supply balance is maintained by increased government debt and the creation of a trade surplus with the United States and Europe. Thus, in both cases, it is tricklism that maximizes CEO incomes and minimizes worker salaries. Clearly, there is only one cause of penury around the world. In order to eliminate global poverty, the U.S. economic thinking that espouses tricklism must change. Hence the primary focus of this book is on the American economy and intellectuals.

Once tricklism expires, the economic chaos, accelerating by the day, will vanish and give way to speedy and equitable prosperity. Poverty will then fade all over the world.

AMERICA IN THE NEW MILLENNIUM

The year 2000 was one of ultimate irony around the world, especially for the United States. It launched a new millennium, along with myriad new problems. The year began with a public euphoria, with share markets at their all-time highs and expected to vault higher. For some, money seemed to grow on trees. A vast wave of optimism swept the nation as millions of people basked in the glow of capital gains.

By midyear, however, it was clear that the millennium was off to a poor start. The Dow Jones Industrials index had begun to unravel, the NASDAQ was in a free fall. Although share prices stabilized quickly, their sudden and unexpected decline intimated that new troubles were about to emerge. By the end of the year, unprecedented events astonished the nation. The presidential election had been decided not by the electorate but by nine justices of the Supreme Court, in a vote of five to four. Al Gore was the choice of the people by a slim majority, but George W. Bush was the choice of the jurists, who ultimately prevailed.

As the year ended, people sensed that the new millennium did not augur well for the nation. If 2000 was bad, 2001 was worse. The share markets finally crashed and have yet to recover fully. Islamic terrorism struck the hearts of New York City and the capital, Washington, D.C., on September 11, stunning the country along with the world. Nearly 3,000 people perished in the 9/11 massacre, which also unleashed a string of events that ultimately spawned the quagmire known as the Iraq War. The economy, especially the job market, was shaken, with real family income in a free fall. September 11 and its offshoots continue to shape the thinking and the course of the United States.

Today Americans are apprehensive about their future. Poll after poll reveals public uncertainty and a sense of impending doom. The vast majority of people think that the nation is on the wrong track and stands on a precipice. We see before us all the problems that we must face: from political agendas that hinder the global fight against poverty, to corruption and chaos within the institutions and practices that fuel our economy. We wonder what is on the other side, or is yet to come. We face trillion-dollar debts and deficits; we borrow billions from the world every day and yet tout our economy as the best on the planet. Vast budget shortfalls loom in the near future—from Social Security to Medicare to pensions.

It's not an overstatement to say that there is a long history of corruption and incompetence in American administrations that periodically stir up the nation. Looking at some recent examples, we can conclude that the Nixon-Agnew team was corrupt but not incompetent; the Carter-Mondale team was incompetent but not corrupt; and the Bush-Cheney team is perennially accused of both corruption and incompetence. Under this latest team, corporate interests have been allowed to run amok as never before. In the past, corporations used to buy politicians mainly by offering junkets and donations for election campaigns. Now corporations are also invited to write legislation.

Who helped write the Bush-Cheney energy policy? The oil companies. Who coauthored their health-care policy? The pharmaceutical companies. Who ghostwrote their environmental policy? The industrial polluters. Who designed their tax policy? The CEOs. Who articulated their trade policy? The multinationals and the outsourcers. It's no secret that hefty campaign contributions are made with the hope that a candidate will influence policy. Did Bush-Cheney design anything themselves? Yes, the Iraq War, which sacrificed soldiers while helping the likes of Exxon-Mobil and Halliburton mint war profits. As Thomas Friedman, a *New York Times* columnist and the best-selling author of *The World Is Flat*, declares:

> President Bush has slipped in one recent poll to a 29 percent approval rating. Frankly, I can't believe that those polls can possibly be accurate. I mean, really, ask yourself: How could there still be 29 percent of the people who approve of this presidency? . . .
>
> Americans are slow to judgment about a president, very slow. And in times of war, in particular, they are willing to give him the benefit of the doubt. But I think a lot of Americans in recent months have simply lost confidence in this administration's competence and honesty.[9]

Why is a wartime president, one whose approval rating once vaulted above 80 percent, so unpopular today? An editorial from the *Athens News* nails down the reason:

> Bush is fundamentally pro-business. This isn't necessarily a bad thing, if leavened with common sense, compassion and independent thought. Bush's corporate reflex, however, never fails. On any given issue, if corporate interest is a factor, that's the way he's going to go. This explains his environmental and health-care policies, where energy companies, utilities, pharmaceutical companies and the insurance industry call the shots. He reflexively takes the corporate side, then roots around for a folksy-sounding rationale to explain why, once again, he's taken up against the public interest.[10]

Instead of being about compassion toward everyone, the Bush-Cheney mantra, compassionate conservatism, has turned out to be about rewarding government friends with tax cuts, no-bid contracts, authoritative jobs, environmental exemptions and lucrative sinecures.

In addition to bungling the war effort, Bush-Cheney appointed cronies to the Federal Emergency Management Agency (FEMA), created just 700,000 private-sector jobs in their first five years in office (about 6 percent of those created by the Clinton administration), gave important positions to their buddies in every department, messed up the Medicare prescription bill, and on and on. Do you remember Michael Brown, who from day one bungled the government relief effort for the victims of Hurricane Katrina? How did the president react? "Brownie, you're doing a heck of a job."[11] Hardly a week passes during which some administration official does not botch his assignment. As columnist Molly Ivins puts it:

> The great irony is that this was supposed to be the CEO administration. Bush was supposed to put people in charge of government who had track records in private industry, who did in fact know how to run a railroad. For just sheer incompetence, this administration sets new records daily. All those years the right wing sat around yammering about government incompetence, and it took this administration to make it true.[12]

That may be the crux of the problem. Major CEOs are often conduits of corruption. Their overwhelming greed and ruthlessness are becoming legendary. According to a recent poll, a whopping two percent of the public trusts them.[13] CEOs cut wages or fire people first and ask questions later, while awarding themselves perk after perk. Al Dunlap, the former CEO of Sunbeam, is nicknamed "Chainsaw Al" or "Rambo in Pinstripes" because of his ruthless approach to layoffs. As David Ploz of Slate.com describes him and the current corporate ethos: "The most cold-blooded businessman around, Dunlap personifies the relentless logic of Wall Street," which is to stuff one's own pockets regardless of how it stiffs the workers.[14]

Why is all this happening now when the world needs strong leadership to steer it through the minefield of terrorism and growing poverty? Where are we headed? What is on the other side?

Such are the queries I raise and strive to answer in this book, which focuses on three sets of diverse but interlinked questions:

- First, why is there so much economic corruption and incompetence today? How do we explain this rare affliction besetting our times? And what do we do about it?
- Second, what is corruption doing to the global living standard? How does it beget ever-growing poverty amid plenty?
- Third, when and how will we find a cure for poverty and corruption?

This book is an attempt to explain the present sorry state of affairs in terms of a variety of economic and political cycles, most of which turn out to be reliable forecasters and can be used with confidence to predict the future. I also offer a series of reforms that, if implemented, could possibly free us from official corruption and alleviate poverty.

Bizarre events, talismans of an impending crisis, occur every day. A company declares bankruptcy but rewards its executives with millions in bonuses and pensions. When the company fires workers, its share price soars. Just when oil companies are wallowing in profits, Congress showers them with subsidies. When officials bungle assignments, they get promotions. In 2002, Condoleezza Rice, Bush's national security adviser, was among the most vociferous about the existence of weapons of mass destruction (WMDs) in Iraq; she even warned the world about Iraq's nuclear ambitions and capabilities. However, no WMDs have ever been found. So, for all her failures, in his second term, the president promoted Rice to secretary of state.

By contrast, when someone tells the administration the truth about Iraq, he is mocked, and his advice is ignored. This is what happened to General Eric Shinseki, who warned the administration about sending too few troops to Iraq; subsequent events proved him right. He was ridiculed, and reportedly forced to retire, for offering valuable advice that the Pentagon did not like to hear.[15]

Our tax system has become a joke. When billionaires earn hefty dividends, the government lavishes them with tax breaks, but when a waiter earns tips, his tax bill jumps. The economy grows year after year, but so does poverty. The gross domestic product climbed a healthy 4.5 percent in 2005, yet another million people joined the ranks of the poor.

The incompetence and corruption of the administration are sur-passed only by the incompetence and corruption of Congress. Our law-makers, spearheaded by Republicans, are paralyzed by corporate cash; they simply rubber-stamp the administration's fiascos. Whenever Bush-Cheney are caught red handed—as in the Abu Ghraib torture scandal, domestic eavesdropping by the National Security Agency (NSA), out-right lying about weapons of mass destruction, and mismanagement of relief to hurricane victims, to name just a few peccadilloes—Republican lawmakers just change the subject (or the law) in order to absolve their fellow Republicans. See what two reputed journalists, Donald Barlett and James Steele, write in *Time:*

> In essence, campaign spending in America has divided all of us into two groups: first- and second-class citizens. This is what happens if you are in the latter group:
>   You pick up a disproportionate share of America's tax bill.
>   You pay higher prices for a broad range of products, from peanuts to prescription drugs . . .
>   In contrast, first-class citizens—the fortunate few who contribute to the right politicians and hire the right lobbyists—enjoy all the bene-fits of their special status. Among them:
>   If they make a bad business decision, the government bails them out . . .
>   If they want to kill legislation that is intended for the public good, it gets killed.
>   Call it government for the few at the expense of the many . . . al-most any time a citizen or a business gets what it wants through cam-paign contributions and lobbying, someone else pays the price for it. Sometimes it's a few people, sometimes millions.[16]

Another apt description of American politics today is as follows:

> The American government is corrupt. Those who have enough money can almost get anything they want from our government, whether it is tax breaks, or subsidies, or policies and laws changed, removed, or added. . . . Many have taken advantage of this, from Oil Companies, Utilities, HMOs, Pharmaceutical Companies, Prison Corporations, Defense Contractors, Logging Companies, and so on.[17]

It appears that the government can be bought and sold, and our Congress and the presidency are the best that money can buy. However, former Florida Congressman Mark Foley's X-rated scandal with child-like pages indicated that the 2006 Republican-dominated Congress was the worst that money can buy. The big question now is, what is in store for us as a result? My answer, coming in the midst of numerous omens and forebodings, will surprise you: we are headed toward a golden age, which will come after a tidal wave of public fact-finding and a subsequent voter's revolution. Unfortunately, there are rough times ahead as we battle the social, political and economic ills of our time, but then the electorate will vote for those who favor unprecedented economic and political reform. So good times will follow bad, but the end product will be so wonderful that we will gradually forget the bad. We will come to view our struggle as the price we had to pay to rid the nation of the malaise, corruption and injustices that plague us today.

SOME PREVIOUS FORECASTS

Today, we live in a time when anything and everything goes. These are the times that try our souls. The daily drumbeat of mayhem in Iraq is compounded by rocketing oil prices and surging inflation and interest rates. However, today's bizarre events do not surprise me. I anticipated them as early as 1978 in a book called *The Downfall of Capitalism and Communism: A New Study of History*. In spite of its novel title, my book attracted little attention at the time. The reviewers did not criticize my theory but were unprepared to accept my forecasts about the impending fall of the two systems. I predicted that Soviet communism would vanish around 2000, possibly before the end of the century, and that monopoly capitalism would expire around 2010, give or take a decade.

Soviet communism is no more. It fell before your eyes around 1995. Is capitalism next? My answer, as before, is yes, especially because most of what I had anticipated in 1978 about the Western world, especially the United States, has come to pass.

Twenty-five years ago, I began to fear that by 2000 or soon thereafter vast numbers of people in our society would become dirt poor while CEOs and business executives remained wealthy. In a recent book, *Greenspan's Fraud*, I discuss how this trend accelerated in the

United States after 1981, when Ronald Reagan became president and Alan Greenspan became his multifanged adviser (although the damage began under Jimmy Carter).[18] Greenspan is now gone, but the multiple ills of his legacy remain. Greenspan's contribution can be read in the dismal decline of the living standard for American production, or nonmanagerial, workers, who make up as much as 80 percent of the labor force. According to the *Economic Report of the President*, prepared by the president's own economic advisers, workers' weekly real wage, which is the purchasing power of one's salary, was $310 in 1978 but fell to $277 by 2005.[19] This decline was further aggravated by rising sales, payroll and gasoline taxes. Today, as many as 39 million Americans subsist below the poverty line, compared to just 23 million in 1973, which was the first year since World War II in which the ranks of the poor grew.[20]

As noted before, at present the destitute grow by a million a year in the United States. Others are burdened by a heavy debt load. The national savings rate is a stunning zero percent, if not negative; Americans are consuming their home equity to maintain their lifestyle, as if there is no tomorrow. The concentration of wealth is at an all-time high, with just one percent of families owning more than 40 percent of the collective net worth. U.S. Census data reveal that in 2004, *for the first time ever,* more than half of America's income went into the pockets of just 20 percent of income earners, whereas the lowest 20 percent earned a record low 3.4 percent of income. Such destitution and disparity did not exist even during the Roaring Twenties, an era often derided for excess. In the 1920s the lowest 20 percent of the populace lived on 3.6 percent of the income.[21]

FORECASTS ABOUT SOCIAL CONDITIONS

My 1978 book was not just about economics and the downfall of Soviet communism and monopoly capitalism; it was also about an overhaul of world history. It examined a wide swath of human conditions and problems. It dealt with politics, the rise of religions and the priesthood, and many other institutions. Because of my writings, people would ask me all sorts of questions not only about the economy but also about politics, religion and philosophy in my lectures and conversations. They were especially interested in understanding the events in Iran, a country in the midst of turmoil at the time, and making headlines again today. In response to such questions, I would say that the priesthood would soon replace the reigning regime headed by the shah of Iran, most likely by mid-1979. Indeed, in February 1979 the shah was replaced by Ayatollah Khomeini, and the clergy came to power, where it still remains.

I published the results of my ongoing research on Islam in 1980 in a book entitled *Muslim Civilization and the Crisis in Iran*. In it, I made some more forecasts and also dealt further with the idea of the fall of capitalism and communism.[22] In 1978, I had believed that both systems would vanish at about the same time; but in 1980, I concluded that the Soviet Union could collapse before the end of the twentieth century, and in fact the Soviet empire broke up during the 1990s. I also predicted that an intense conflict would ensue between Islamic fundamentalists and the West around 2000.

HISTORICAL CYCLES

Unlike other economists and writers, I was able to foresee these events because, during my doctoral studies in economics in the 1960s, I explored historical cycles rather than the more conventional economic technique, econometrics—which, though sophisticated, is dubious. Cyclical study is a method of analysis and forecasting that has been recently popularized by Pulitzer Prize–winning historian Arthur Schlesinger Jr.[23] Other prominent exponents of cyclical analysis in the past include Aristotle and Arnold Toynbee.

In *Downfall* I focused on an idea called the law of social cycle, which is similar to some of Aristotle's and Toynbee's ideas. Later, I explored some more cycles and described them in books written in 1980, 1985 and 1999. In all, I examined six historical patterns or cycles, which will be explained in the coming chapters:

1. The law of social cycle
2. The law of reverse justice
3. The cycle of inflation
4. The cycle of money growth
5. The cycle of depression
6. The final-year syndrome

These cycles enabled me to make a variety of forecasts not only about inflation, oil prices, share markets and interest rates for the 1980s and the 1990s, but also about the rise of some new institutions, such as the priesthood in Iran. Most of the forecasts came true, and, of course, some did not.

Of the six cycles listed above, the cycle of depression has misfired. But all the others have held up so far—in fact, they have been impeccable forecasters. They have proved vastly superior to the forecasting techniques used by celebrity economists like Greenspan who did not foresee the stock market crash of 2000—which, incidentally, was mentioned in my 1999 book, *The Crash of the Millennium*.[24]

In the forecasts made in this book, I ignore the cycle of depression and rely on the other cycles, which have been accurate so far. I have used the cycles to make about thirty-six predictions since 1978, and three or four of the predictions have been wrong. I continue to have confidence in the five cycles or historical patterns that I have used successfully. What follows is a foretaste of what this book is about.

First, we need an understanding of the kind of economic problems that we face as a nation. Chapter 2 examines what may be called the twin bubbles—one in the housing market and the other in the oil industry. Next, chapter 3 explores inflation, which seems to be heating up of late.

Second, the five successful cycles need to be updated in the light of all that has transpired since 1978, especially in the new millennium. Without updating the cycles, I cannot explain new forecasts, short term or long term. That said, the next six chapters study two of these cycles, adjust them in light of new data and information, and make them ready for use in chapter 10, which deals with our common future. Thus chapters 4 and 5 describe the law of social cycle and apply it to Western society, ancient and modern. In chapter 6, entitled "The U.S. Business Empire," I explain why Americans are all drowning in a sea of official corruption and incompetence, and why poverty coexists with plenty. Chapter 7 examines why and how our celebrity economists have missed all the monumental changes that have happened in the world since 1978; how these economists are, in fact, responsible for the nation's plight and the mushrooming poverty. Chapters 8 and 9 apply the social cycle to Muslim society and explore the contemporary world of Islam. My analysis helps explain the current conflict between Muslim fundamentalists and the West, especially the United States.

All these ideas are a prelude to the pivotal chapter 10, in which I try to anticipate the future. The chapter is entitled "Our Common Future," the idea being that we are all floating in one boat, and it is our responsibility to do something about what will happen in the next few years. Also in chapter 10, I explore what can and should be done about the Iraq War. Finally, in chapter 11, I consider economic reforms needed to end poverty around the world and to steer us toward fairness and ethics in society so that we will be free from the affliction of official incompetence and corruption.

Thus the central message of this book is that we are heading toward a time of still greater poverty, problems and chaos that could climax in a social revolution. The first decade of the new millennium started off poorly and could end in a jolt, but it will be followed by a golden age the likes of which the globe has never seen.

The Soviet Union, as I predicted in 1978, has fallen right before our eyes; the downfall of monopoly capitalism could also materialize soon. So we need to act as "We the People" did at the time of the framing of our Constitution. We need to unite, and not remain divided as Democrats and Republicans; we need to vote for honest politicians. It is this division that enables corporate interests to use the world's resources for personal gain while impoverishing others. Workable theories to alleviate poverty exist, and proper ideas are available; what is missing is a political apparatus able to effect these ideas and implement an ethical economic policy, which could end destitution around the globe. If we act in time, we could bring about this golden age without excessive suffering; if we do not, we are doomed to repeat the same mistakes that led to the fall of the Soviet empire and to the revolution in Iran. For such is the dictum of history: when the elite become ruthless and neglect the downtrodden to build their own nests, natural laws are set into motion to replace the elite with a better system. The choice is ours.

Thus the crux of this book is that poverty in America today arises from the prevailing orgy of official incompetence and corruption. But what explains this orgy? It occurs because we're in the last phase of what may be called the age of acquisitors or money-grubbers, and a monumental change is due soon. It is our duty to act, to turn the current and forthcoming adversity into opportunity and bring about a better system through a ballot-box revolution.

CHAPTER 2

THE TWIN BUBBLES: HOUSING AND OIL

The year 1973 marks a watershed in the economic and social annals of the United States. That's when, for the first time ever, the real wage began a steady decline for the vast majority of American workers, in spite of rising productivity. That is also the year when an Arab cartel, the Organization of Petroleum Exporting Countries (OPEC), imposed an oil embargo on the United States and the rest of the world. The oil price jumped fourfold, never to fall back to old levels again. Thus started a long, and nearly relentless, period of asset-market bubbles, which need to be explored in depth, because they play a crucial role in steering an economy toward chaos. For instance, every depression in the past was preceded by an asset bubble or balloons. The agony of the 1930s was seeded in the stock market euphoria of the 1920s.

For a while, bubbles disappeared under the onslaught of economic reforms introduced by President Roosevelt in the New Deal. However, they returned in 1973, and ever since then the United States, along with the rest of the planet, has been hopping from one financial bubble to another. Prices of a variety of goods have surged, sunk and then surged again. Oil, stocks, bonds, gold, silver, platinum and occasionally housing all seem to have moved in an up-and-down rhythm, generating uncertainty and chaos in the process. For when a bubble bursts, millions of people suffer.

The bubble used to be a rare species; it would arrive once, at most twice, in a century, burst open and then disappear for a while. The first balloon of the twentieth century occurred during the so-called Roaring Twenties, when the stock market first scaled to unprecedented heights, before crashing in 1929. The next crash did not arrive for 44 years. However, something has changed since the early 1970s, so much so that now bubbles appear, disappear and then reappear with much more frequency than ever before.

Economic or financial bubbles normally refer to sharply inflated prices moving at exceptional speeds. Most of them arise because of irrationality among buyers of a product or an asset, but they may also emerge because of some other reason, such as the formation of monopolizing trusts or cartels. Occasionally, they arise in product markets, including producible goods such as oil, copper and gold (even tulips), that are marked by rising prices. In this case, investors treat the product as an asset, and seek to profit not from its expanding production but from its price appreciation.

Bubbles occur primarily in asset markets involving land, stocks and bonds that attract funds from wealthy investors, in which the act of producing is not as important as value appreciation. However, regardless of their origin and nature, all bubbles burst in the end. In fact, if an item's swollen prices fail to burst, we may not even consider the case a bubble. Quite often a balloon is recognized not when it is inflating, but when it punctures.

Most bubbles are associated with irrational buyers; however, they may spring from the greedy actions of suppliers as well. The enormous oil price jump during the 1970s was not the result of consumer euphoria. In fact, global demand for oil began to fall soon after 1973, but the oil supplies kept shrinking, so the oil price climbed throughout the 1970s. By 1981, the price had jumped to as much as $42 per barrel, about 1,600 percent higher than its base price of $2.50 in mid 1973.

The oil balloon resulted from the monopolistic actions of OPEC, the international oil cartel, which, to its surprise, discovered that oil prices could be raised sharply by trimming output. Once the bubble formed, it kept swelling. It lasted nine years; after 1982 the oil price began a precipitous fall. By 1986, a barrel of oil that once fetched $42 in the U.S. market sold for less than $10. By any reckoning, the OPEC-generated bubble had ruptured.

DEMAND VERSUS SUPPLY-SIDE BUBBLES

Since prices are determined by the interplay of demand and supply, bubbles are formed in two ways: the price of an asset keeps rising when its demand continually outpaces supply, or when its supply recurrently falls short of demand. Such a distinction is crucial to understanding the true cause of the bubble. It is also crucial in initiating any remedial action against the perpetrators of price hikes. In demand-side bubbles, asset demand continually exceeds its supply; in supply-side bubbles, supply periodically trails demand. Bubbles of the first type stem from the obsession of buyers with some assets, whereas those of the second type usually spring from market concentration or producers' manipulation.

Since prices are determined by the dual action of demand and supply, all bubbles, regardless of how they originate, burst in the end. This is because price jumps invite a response from both buyers and sellers. In the case of the demand-side bubble, high prices can be sustained only if demand stays ahead of supply, whereas in the polar supply-side case, price maintenance requires that supply continues to lag behind demand. These are the conditions necessary for price balloons to persist, and since buyers and sellers are independent entities, a time comes when such requirements no longer hold. The interplay of the market forces guarantees that all balloons rupture in the end. Thus a bubble has a three-part life cycle: it forms, usually abruptly and unexpectedly, then expands swiftly over several years, and finally bursts.

The oil price hike from 1973 to 1982 is a good example. It started in 1973 with the sudden jump in oil price; then it expanded when the price rose further over the next eight years, and finally it exploded in 1982 and thereafter.

Conventional wisdom is unclear about the dual nature of balloon generation. It argues that the bubbles are formed primarily when an asset's demand abruptly jumps and keeps jumping for a few years, so that the price continues to climb.[1] This is only partially true. The other side of the picture is that supply must be slow to respond to price hikes. The oil bubble of the 1970s and the early 1980s was one balloon that inflated fast and sharp without the assistance of irrational buying from consumers. This was then a supply-side bubble, because it arose from the production cuts of oil exporters. Even though oil demand slowly sank, the supply sank even faster. While oil exporters were single-minded in their pursuit of ever-rising prices, politics also had something to do with their success.

As described earlier, initially the bubble started as an oil embargo, which lasted only six months, from October 1973 to March 1974. It created a huge shortage of petroleum products around the world. Most price balloons, however, are demand-side bubbles; they arise from the concerted actions of buyers who expect further jumps in asset prices. Such were the share-price bubbles of the 1920s and the dot-com bubble of the 1990s that started as early as 1982. They were triggered by sharply rising profits, and were made worse by rising wealth concentration and the government's easy credit policy. They started out rationally, with investors parking their old and new savings into profitable industries. Others jumped into the share markets, as companies continued to earn ever-larger incomes. Finally, when stocks moved upward for several years at a heightened pace, men and women in the street also came rushing into Wall Street, hoping to make quick money and possibly become millionaires. When the initial stock hoopla turned into a mania, the share markets crashed, reminding people that irrationality always exacts a hefty price.

The share market balloons were demand-side bubbles, because demand for stocks continually outran their supply. Companies did respond periodically by issuing more stock, but not adequately to stabilize the share prices, which eventually collapsed.

By the same token, the stock, land and housing bubbles in Japan from 1975 to 1990 were demand-side bubbles. So were similar balloons in the economies of the Asian Tigers during the 1990s. Thus most bubbles arise from buyers' frenzied actions rather than sellers' monopolistic control.

This was certainly the case with America's latest share-price bubble, which burst toward the end of 2000. It started out with an outburst of activity at the New York Stock Exchange (NYSE) in 1982, as the Dow Jones Industrial index (the Dow in short) registered large gains. The Dow had been depressed throughout the 1970s, mostly because of the oil bubble, and remained subdued in 1980 and 1981. But then it started to take off, catching most investors off guard. When the oil bubble also began to rupture, few restraints remained on the markets. Shares appreciated nearly in a straight line until Black Monday, that fateful day in October 1987 when the Dow suffered its worst crash in history.

The share-price appreciation of the 1980s itself was known as a bubble, which burst with a bang. Barely had this balloon popped than another, much bigger monster took its place. Within a year of Black Monday, investors dared to be manic again. Share prices now fired from two barrels; the Dow was joined by a feisty stalwart, the NAS-DAQ composite index, which included stocks traded over the counter. Both indexes peaked in the year 2000. The Dow started around a low of 780 in August 1982 and crested at 11,720 in January 2000, whereas the NASDAQ, starting from a base of 165, peaked at 5,049 in March 2000. In retrospect, the U.S. bubble that began in 1982 punctured in 1987, only to resume its advance the next year. Finally it burst again toward the end of 2000, and spiralled downward almost to the end of 2002, by which time the NASDAQ had dropped nearly 80 percent and the Dow nearly 40 percent.[2]

Thus, ever since 1973, the character of the world economy seems to have changed permanently, with bubbles becoming more frequent than ever. One way or another, the buyer's irrationality or the seller's greed has affected real wages, economic growth and the living standards around the globe. Not surprisingly, a wide variety of imbalances have developed globally in the form of high government debt, trade deficits and consumer borrowing, all of which slowly but steadily contribute to economic chaos. In this new economy, government efforts to contain the aftershocks of one bubble, as explained below, spawn another.

THE HOUSING BUBBLE

When Black Monday struck in 1987, Alan Greenspan headed the Federal Reserve. He successfully restrained the aftereffects of that crash through swift action, which brought interest rates down around the world. His timely moves quickly made credit available to financial markets and prevented the fiery crash from turning into a conflagration. Nearly 14 years later, in January 2001, when the share markets would not respond to his soothing words, Greenspan swung into action again. He followed the same recipe for disaster control and began trimming the federal funds rate. The federal funds rate is an interest fee that banks charge each other for overnight loans, and its drop signals the Fed's willingness to open the money pump. When this rate falls, other interest rates usually follow.

However, unlike in 1987, this time the stock market crash led to a recession, with falling output and rising unemployment. So the Fed chairman trimmed the funds rate several times during 2001, and then again the next year. The rate actually fell from 6.5 percent to barely 1 percent in 2002. This was the lowest level since the early 1950s.

However, the drop in the rate this time was even faster than in the 1950s. Nothing like this had occurred since the Great Depression, when the economy was in a free fall. The share-market crash of 2000 was similar to the crash of 1929, and Greenspan did not want a repeat of that tragedy. But his prescription proved to be an overdose to the economy and produced a side effect.

All those cuts in interest rates eventually spawned a housing bubble. Ever since 2001, when George W. Bush took over the presidency, home prices have been rising at a dizzy pace. They had started to outpace inflation as early as 1996, but picked up speed in the new millennium. Eventually Greenspan became aware of the phenomenon but dismissed it as "a little froth in this market."[3]

Why do low interest rates spark a housing rally? This is one question that is a no-brainer. Most homes are bought on credit, not for cash, and mortgage loans last anywhere from 15 to 30 years. The lower the rates, the lower the monthly payment, and the greater the demand for homes.

When demand for something rises, its price goes up. So interest rate cuts normally spur home values not just by stimulating home demand, but also because the buyers can afford to purchase expensive homes. The housing bubble that started in 2001 was an inevitable by-product of Greenspan's panic and rush to trim the federal funds rate sharply.

A number of books have recently appeared on this subject, but real estate developer Michael Blomquist's is by far the most comprehensive and enlightening.[4] His work offers a good deal of housing data and a penetrating analysis of what has transpired in the housing market in recent years. Between 2001 and 2005, home values appreciated 53 percent nationally in a slow-growth economy. But regionally they appreciated much faster than the nationwide figure. The Office of Federal Housing Enterprise Oversight reported that during 2005 alone home prices jumped 13.5 percent, the fastest annual pace since 1979.

Historically the average home has sold for 2.6 times the median family income, versus the current figure of 3.2, which is 25 percent above the historical norm. This may not sound abnormal in these days of mega bubbles, but given the vastness of the housing market, even a small uptick can have widespread consequences. This is because the housing market is largely regional in character, and in some states and cities the bubble is gargantuan. The median home price in places like Los Angeles, San Francisco, Orange County, San Diego and New York City is roughly 9 times the median family income. According to Dean Baker, the codirector of the Centre for Economic Policy and Research and an authority on the housing market, "Every week, approximately 140,000 U.S. families buy a house, a majority of them at bubble-inflated prices."[5]

Some economists suggest that the housing bubble is invulnerable to a meltdown, because, unlike other assets, people buy residences not just for their value appreciation but also to live in them. Following this logic, therefore, there is never going to be a fire sale of homes, prices will not collapse, and there is no bubble. For, as mentioned above, a bubble is recognized definitively only after it bursts open.

This argument does make a good point; in fact, nationally, home prices have not fallen since the Great Depression. But regionally they can and have occasionally dropped sharply in the past. The current housing bubble, though, is exceptional in many ways. Take a look at figure 2.1, which plots the U.S. home price index from 1975 to 2005. From 1975 to 1995, the index appreciated in virtually a straight line; it began to rise faster from 1996 on, but after 2000 moved up at a torrid pace. This is clear from the steeper curvature of the home-price path after 2000.

In the 20 years from 1975 to 1995, home prices jumped 204 percent, which is not far from the overall inflation rate of 183 percent during that period. Housing appreciation thus surpassed the Consumer Price Index (CPI) inflation rate by about 1 percent a year, which was thus too slow to be noticeable. Between 1995 and 2000, the inflation-adjusted rise in home prices was 3 percent per year, but soared to 9 percent per year from 2000 to 2005. Clearly, home values have substantially accelerated in the new millennium. This is precisely the stuff of which bubbles are made. They pick up speed after they are formed, and keep expanding for a while, until they can expand no more; at that point they burst.

Figure 2.1. The U.S. Home Price Index: 1975–2005

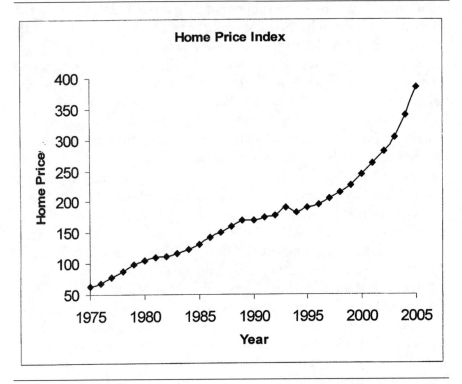

Source: Office of Federal Housing Enterprise Oversight, 2006, www.ofheo.gov

According to Dean Baker, real home prices have climbed 60 percent from 1998 to 2005, after being nearly flat in the 1980s and the 1990s. Nothing like this has been recorded in U.S. history. Note that the real home price is the same as the inflation-adjusted price.[6]

As stated above, the current housing bubble is exceptional. There are some other aspects of the housing market that are also new and very disturbing. In record numbers, people have been using their home appreciation as vehicles for maintaining their lifestyle. They have refinanced their mortgages, taken equity out of their homes and used the money primarily for consumption. Consequently, the nation is sinking in an ocean of debt. In the past, people would treat their home like a castle; now they treat it like an ATM. They don't care if they own it outright and have a debt-free retirement. Homes are now mortgaged to the hilt. The national equity to home value ratio is at a record low.

The use of housing for improved consumption is something new and is now the primary prop for U.S. economic growth. By some estimates, as much as half of the annual increase in GDP and job creation in the new millennium has come from the construction industry. This does not bode well for our economy or our future. Because of sinking interest rates, home demand has expanded smartly since 2001, and residential output has grown accordingly. In 2004 and 2005, 2 million housing units were built, and a similar number was expected in 2006. However, the population increase can only support an increase of 1.5 million units, which means that almost half a million homes a year were being snapped up by speculators, who bought them not to live in but to make money from speculation. This phenomenon also points to the presence of a bubble, which is nothing if not speculative.

The housing price and production boom took place while family income fell. Median household income shrank more than $1,500 between 2000 and 2005. Logically speaking, how is it possible that household incomes fall, and the general public moves into pricier homes? When something like this happens, something else has to give. Weak growth and sinking incomes add another distorted dimension to the housing market, fueling the perception that we are in the midst of an unprecedented bubble.

Blomquist offers a palpable explanation of how people were able to buy expensive homes in spite of stagnant incomes:

> In addition to the proliferation of exotic and misleading loans, lenders have promoted and our government has allowed fraud to become commonplace in the lending industry. The most prevalent fraud is the little white lie that inflates annual incomes by 10 percent or more. These lies are used in conjunction with stated income documentation loans. Instead of providing income documentation (W-2s, pay-stubs, tax returns, and so on), you just state how much you earn or more likely what you need to qualify. If your income looks in line with your stated and verified profession there should be no further questions.
>
> There are other types of loan documentation that do not require you to state your income or employment. Perhaps borrowers that elect to use these guidelines may not have to lie to lenders to get approved, but if they are buying or borrowing beyond their means, they are still lying to themselves.[7]

The banks and savings associations have been making inflated loans to some borrowers without asking for any income documentation or employment verification. In return, they earn hefty commissions, but in the process they make their industry vulnerable to financial collapse. Blomquist's information is shocking. The secret of the housing bubble's durability is now out: the mortgage loan industry's outright fraud. Such fraud is the main reason why the housing bubble persists even though interest rates have been ratcheting up since 2004.

Another worrisome development—also pinpointed by Blomquist among others—is that foreign investors are involved hugely in our housing market. Mortgage loans have broken record after record in recent years, and the bulk of this money has been provided by foreign individuals and institutions. They have been buying mortgage-backed security (MBS) assets, which have exposed them to the whims of the housing industry. In the past, foreign investors bought U.S. government bonds, which are among the safest of investments. But the purchase of trillions of dollars of MBS assets has exposed foreign investors to an unprecedented level of risk. If the housing market collapses, or even slows down, these investors could suffer unacceptable losses due to homebuyers' defaults. At that point, the entire global financial system could unravel in a hurry. The foreign investors would then stampede out of U.S. asset markets, and trigger a worldwide meltdown. At present this scenario seems rather far-fetched, but the rate at which Americans are borrowing money from abroad could make it possible in the near future. I will return to this point in chapter 10, which deals with our common future.

The housing bubble, just like the earlier share-market balloon, has a global dimension. The world economy is now a colony of what may be called the American business empire. Therefore, few phenomena or economic events remain localized today, especially if they spring from the United States. Thus the housing bubble has global proportions. Even *The Economist* is worried: "The worldwide rise in home prices is the biggest bubble in history. Prepare for the economic pain when it pops. NEVER before have real house prices risen so fast, for so long, in so many countries. Property markets have been frothing from America, Britain and Australia to France, Spain and China."[8] Believe it or not, home property values in the advanced economies of Europe and North America have already climbed more than $30 trillion in the new millennium; stated differently, property values surpassed the combined GDPs of these nations in a matter of five years. The much ballyhooed global stock market bubble of the late 1990s pales before the housing bubble. Table 2.1 details how home prices have soared in some nations in recent years.

Clearly, the British balloon is the largest, involving a home value jump of 154 percent between 1997 and 2005. Britain is followed by France with a rise of 87 percent, and then the Netherlands with an increase of 76 percent. The United States is next with a jump of 73 percent. Germany and Japan are the sole exceptions to the property euphoria, as home prices in these countries have actually declined. Yet these exceptions did not prevent the emergence of history's biggest bubble. It certainly appears to be far more than Greenspan's "little froth."

THE OIL BUBBLE

This perhaps is the first time in history when the world is afflicted not by one but by two potentially hazardous bubbles at the same time. In addition to housing, the global oil market is also bubbly. The international price of raw crude has been climbing since 2002, and so has the retail price of gasoline in the United States and around the world. This much is clear from figure 2.2, which charts the paths of gasoline and the West Texas crude oil prices from 1984 to the end of 2004. The graph (reproduced from an energy report prepared by the Federal Trade Commis-

Table 2.1: Home-Price Indexes in Selected Countries (Percent Change)

Nation	2004	2005	1997–2005
United States	12.5	8.4	73
Britain	5.5	16.9	154
Canada	5.2	5.7	47
France	15.0	14.7	87
Germany	−1.3	−0.8	−0.2
Italy	9.7	10.8	69
Japan	−9.4	−6.4	−28
Netherlands	1.9	5.5	76
New Zealand	12.5	23.3	66

Source: The Economist, June 16, 2005.

Figure 2.2. Comparison of the National Average Price of Gasoline and the Price of West Texas Intermediate Crude (1984–Jan. 2005)

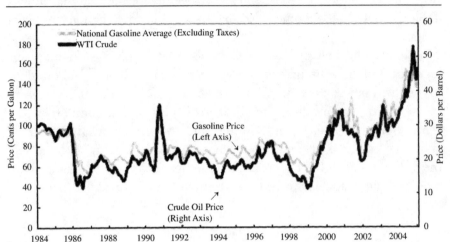

sion in 2005) displays a big rise in both prices since 2002. It also shows that gasoline and crude oil prices move together.

The obvious question is, are we really facing another oil bubble? In quest of an answer, we need to examine in greater detail the stages in the formation of a bubble:

1. Virtually no one recognizes a bubble when it is first formed. History shows that financial balloons always appear abruptly, catching people by surprise as an asset's price bursts out. Once the price jump has persisted for some years, then rational explanations appear in droves, denying the phenomenon as an artificial bubble. This is how the oil balloon was formed in 1973; this is also how the share-price bubble started out in the 1920s and then during the years between 1982 to 2000. Likewise, the oil price jump caught the public napping in 2003, and investors kept shaking their heads as the gas price kept exploding. I remember the days in 2003 and 2004 when a friend of mine, Satish Gupta, chairman and CEO of SB International, Inc., an oil servicing firm, constantly wanted to short the oil market, expecting its price to drop any month, if not any moment. Fortunately my friend

heeded my contrary advice. Keeping in mind the three-decade cycle of inflation explored in the next chapter, I kept telling him that oil will meet the same fate it did in the 1970s. I also remember the days when expert after expert would appear on CNN, CNBC and Fox News and predict the drop in oil prices. Clearly, the big oil price climb was totally unexpected.

2. Once the bubble is formed and has persisted for a while, few expect the related price to drop. In other words, once a bubble has persisted, and appears durable, people think it is permanent and will go on forever, that is, it's not a bubble at all. This is what happened with the share price balloon during the 1990s, when experts convinced investors that we were in the midst of a "new economy" of growth that would never slow nor cease. That is where we are now (mid 2006), as far as raw crude is concerned. Analysts envision the asset crossing $100 per barrel in a few years.

3. Once the price is predicted to rise, speculators move in and the prophecy becomes self-fulfilling. That is what hedge funds are currently doing in the market for oil futures.

4. A time comes when experts expect no fall in the price as far as the eye can see. For oil, that time is here now. Billionaire investor T. Boone Pickens, for example, sees oil hitting ever new heights in the foreseeable future.[9]

By 2006, the oil market had experienced all four of the initial stages of a bubble. There is some froth in the oil industry, to say the least.

OIL: PRIMARILY A SUPPLY-SIDE BUBBLE

What kind of balloon is this? As in the 1970s, the current oil bubble is primarily a supply-side bubble. However, this time the monopolistic trigger has not come from OPEC but from our own oil companies, such as Exxon-Mobil, Chevron, Shell and so on. This view contradicts conventional wisdom, which never foresaw the oil explosion of 2005. Conventional wisdom holds that soaring gas demand from China and India, along with the behavior of OPEC, is primarily responsible for the persistence of expensive oil. This wisdom, as usual, serves the interests of the paymasters who finance it. For instance, the FTC has conducted an extensive study on the oil market. As expected, its report absolves the oil companies of all responsibility for rocketing fuel prices and puts the blame on OPEC and the rising world demand for gasoline:

> OPEC's influence has been an important determinant of higher prices since 1973, but other factors also contribute. Significantly increased long-run demand from industrializing countries has exacerbated the price-increasing effects of OPEC's production cutbacks.[10]

Since the OPEC cartel fostered the oil bubble from 1973 to 1982, it is all too easy to make it the culprit again, even if it is now an innocent by-stander and sees its self-interest in stable, not escalating, energy prices. Let's closely examine the words of the FTC report, whose argument proceeds along the various steps presented below:

1. The world price of crude oil is the most important factor in the price of gasoline.
2. In 2004 . . . steep increases in world prices for crude oil caused steep increases in gasoline prices.
3. Over the past two decades, the demand for crude oil has grown significantly. . . . Overall, however, the long-run trend is toward significantly increased demand for crude oil—particularly demand from developing economies such as China and India.
4. OPEC still produces a large enough share of world crude oil to exert market power and strongly influence the price of crude oil when OPEC members adhere to their assigned production quotas.
5. Larger-than-predicted increases in world demand for crude oil caught producers off guard. In addition to increased demand, unexpected production difficulties reduced some producers' crude output.

The FTC argument, in a nutshell, is this: The U.S. gasoline price is chiefly linked to the world price for crude oil, which is partly set by OPEC and partly by global demand and supply conditions. The sudden jump in American gasoline prices in 2004 arose from a sharp increase in the price of crude, which in turn sprang from larger than expected increase in crude demand from India, China as well as the United States. Hence the conclusion: global demand pressures are largely responsible for recent steep increases in U.S. gasoline prices.

Before I find holes in this argument, however, let's see how the FTC's own words, appearing elsewhere in the report, contradict its principal conclusion: "Throughout most of the 1990s, however, crude prices remained relatively stable, suggesting that crude producers increased production to meet increased demand." These lines say it all. They contradict the FTC's findings, because they say that increased demand need not cause a rise in price if supply goes up at the same time. The global demand for oil indeed grew in 2004, but so did supply. The same thing happened in 2005 as well, in spite of the hurricane's destruction of some oil rigs in the Gulf of Mexico. There is plenty of crude available around the world. Unlike the 1970s, there are no gas lines anywhere in the globe; there is no shortage. So why are gasoline and crude superexpensive?

The FTC argument implies that crude oil inventories must have declined in the United States from 2003 to 2005. If supply falls short of demand, then inventory must fall. This point should be obvious, that is, if a nation uses more oil than it can acquire through import or production, then its crude oil stock must decline. Let's look at figure 2.3, which is another graph supplied by the FTC. The figure deals with oil stocks in OECD countries, a group composed of 24 advanced economies, including those in North America and western Europe. Figure 2.3 does not exhibit a fall in oil inventories from 2003 to 2005; in fact, it only delineates a rise in such inventories.

Figure 2.3. OECD Stocks, End of Month, October 2003 – 2005

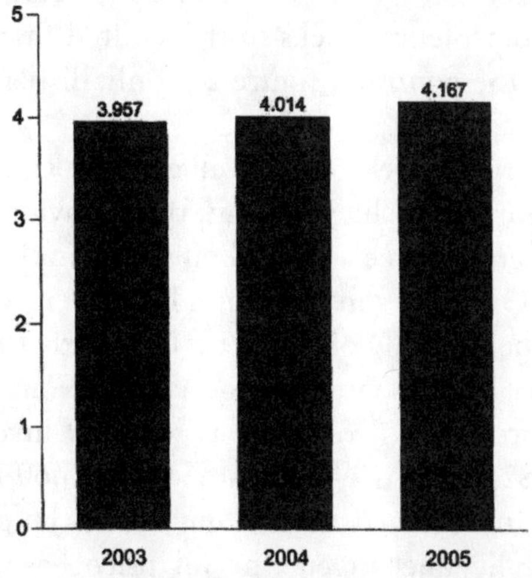

Source: Energy Information Administration/Monthly Energy Review, February 2006; FTC Report, www.ftc.gov

Figure 2.4. Petroleum Stocks in OECD Countries (Billions of Barrels):
        2004–2005

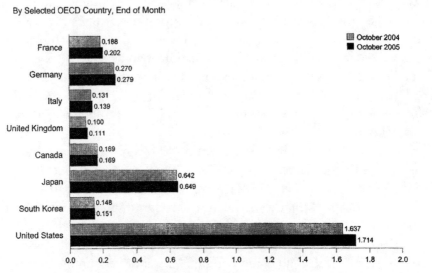

By Selected OECD Country, End of Month

France: 0.188 / 0.202
Germany: 0.270 / 0.279
Italy: 0.131 / 0.139
United Kingdom: 0.100 / 0.111
Canada: 0.169 / 0.169
Japan: 0.642 / 0.649
South Korea: 0.148 / 0.151
United States: 1.637 / 1.714

October 2004
October 2005

Source: Energy Information Administration/Monthly Energy Review, February 2006

The next FTC graph, figure 2.4, examines petroleum stocks in individual OECD nations from 2004 to 2005. As in figure 2.3, this figure fails to show a fall in petroleum stocks in the United States or in other OECD nations. On the contrary, figure 2.4 only displays a rise in such stocks.

In fact, the oil inventory has been rising, albeit very slowly, ever since 1990, as shown in figure 2.5, which displays the behavior of West Texas Intermediate (WTI) crude price and total oil stocks in the United States from 1990 to 2005. Oil figures in the graph have been converted into an index by dividing the monthly oil stock by 100, so that both the price and stock figures can be presented in one chart. From 1990 to 2001 the oil price was more or less constant, as were oil inventories. The per-barrel price was $24.50 in 1990 and stood at $25.60 in 2001. But since 2002, while the inventory behavior, and hence the demand-supply situation, are basically unchanged, the oil price has shot up, which clearly demonstrates that the global supply-demand balance has absolutely nothing to do with the spike.

Figure 2.5. Oil Price and the Oil Stock Index in the United States: 1990 – 2005

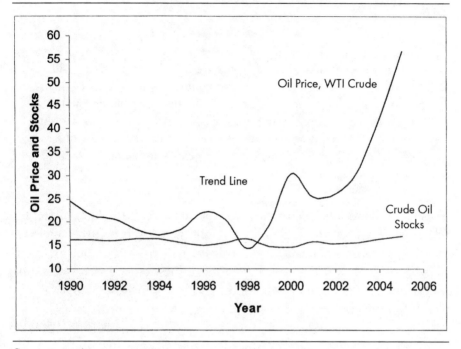

Source: www.eia.gov

Even Lord Browne of Madingly, the chief executive of British Petroleum, concedes: "There has been no shortage and in fact inventories of crude oil and products have continued to rise." *At the end of 2005, U.S. crude oil stocks stood at their all-time high at 1.7 billion barrels.* (See figures 2.4 and 2.5.)[11] This means that oil should be around $30 a barrel.

So there is no dearth of crude on earth. As yet there has been no decline in oil inventories around the world. In 1973, and then from 1980 to 1982, there indeed were crude shortages, which were reflected in gas lines and shrinking oil inventories in OECD countries. Have you seen any gas lines in recent years? I haven't. So why are analysts and the government (FTC) blaming the oil price jump on the big increase in demand from India and China? In an age and a political system dominated by the rich, who are the intellectuals and economists going to blame? The giant oil companies? No. In fact, the FTC went through the charade of issuing a 165-page report to defend Big Oil's gargantuan profits:

> Profits play necessary and important roles in a well-functioning market economy. Recent oil company profits are high but have varied widely over time, over industry segments, and among firms. Profits compensate owners of capital for the use of the funds they have invested in a firm. Profits also compensate firms for taking risks, such as the risks in the oil industry that war or terrorism may destroy crude production assets or that new environmental requirements may require substantial new refinery capital investments.

This passage is a joke. When was the last time the Bush Administration asked anybody, let alone an oil corporation, to improve the environment? Yes indeed, oil profits have varied widely over time, but for every year of low profits, there are four years of high ones. In 2005, Exxon-Mobil alone earned $36 billion in profits, and then took out ads in newspapers to defend them.

If there is no gas shortage, then why is oil so expensive? Let's take a close look at what has transpired in the oil industry and on Wall Street since the early 1990s. In May 2004, the General Accounting Office, a bipartisan government body, issued a scathing report, concluding that 2,600 mergers had occurred in the oil industry since the early 1990s.[12] So many mergers could not but generate monopolistic conditions in the oil market, which is now cornered by five major companies—Exxon-Mobil, Chevron-Texaco, British Petroleum-Amoco-Arco, Royal Dutch Shell and Conoco-Phillips. Their names tell it all. Each of these five oil giants has been formed through the merger of highly profitable firms. They are the bullies profiteering from the self-generated oil bubble. Another nonpartisan report issued by the General Accounting Office in September 2004 said that oil mergers had raised the pump price at least 10 cents a gallon, and the crude price as much as $10 per barrel.

These reports are more credible than the FTC's apologia for Big Oil. When competition declines and an industry becomes concentrated, the product price usually rises to generate monopoly profits. OPEC is no longer what it used to be; it supplies only 38 percent of global oil output, but Big Oil controls over 60 percent of gasoline production and distribution in the United States. However, Big Oil controls only 21 percent of natural gas production, which makes gas more competitive than oil.

During September and October 2005, the Gulf of Mexico was hit by Hurricanes Katrina and Rita; several refineries and natural gas platforms were battered, oil and gas production fell sharply, and, not surprisingly, energy prices soared, with gasoline galloping to $3 per gallon and natural gas to as much as $14 per million cubic feet. Crude oil also jumped as high as $70 per barrel.

The post-Katrina behavior of energy prices speaks volumes about the nature of the oil industry. By March 2006, the crude price was down to $63 per barrel, gasoline averaged $2.30 per gallon, and natural gas had plummeted below $7. This is because energy demand fell due to a warmer-than-expected winter. Now the question is, why did natural gas prices sink more than 50 percent, while petroleum prices, especially crude oil, barely budged? You don't have to labor hard to find the answer. Put simply, economic power is not nearly as concentrated in natural gas production as in petroleum production. In view of the figures presented above, the relative concentration power is 21 percent versus 60 percent. The natural gas market, as stated above, is more competitive than its petroleum counterpart. Therefore, when energy demand fell, natural gas prices fell much faster than petroleum prices. Such is the potent force of competition. Where there is little competition or excessive concentration, as in the oil industry, the laws of supply and demand still work, but very sluggishly. The price then falls in response to sinking demand, but only slightly.

In a competitive environment, a rise in demand, when matched by the rise in supply, generates no price hike. In a monopoly milieu, by contrast, increased demand makes prices skyrocket, especially when the product sold is a necessity like gasoline with few short-term substitutes, because the producers have a ready scapegoat for the price rise. Rising oil demand and supply during the 1980s and the 1990s generated few price hikes, because the global oil market was far more competitive. In fact, figure 2.2 shows that gasoline prices plummeted in 1998 and 1999. In the new millennium, however, oil costs escalated even though supply jumped with demand, because by 2000 the oil industry had cornered the market, with the Five Bullies controlling over 60 percent of refinery output.

When a monopolist finds an easy scapegoat and raises prices substantially, without a similar rise in its costs, the phenomenon is known as price gouging. The September 2005 Senate testimony of Tyson Slocum, the research director of Public Citizen's energy program, provides a wealth of interesting but shocking facts about the oil industry and its financial muscle that commands our lawmakers' obedience. Here are some excerpts:

> . . . recent mergers in the domestic oil refining industry have consolidated control over gasoline, making it easier for a handful of companies to price-gouge consumers.
>
> This price-gouging has not only been *officially documented*, but it is also evident in the record profits enjoyed by large oil companies. Since 2001, the five largest oil refining companies operating in America . . . have recorded $228 *billion* in profits. While of course America's tremendous appetite for gasoline plays a role, uncompetitive practices by oil corporations are a cause—and not OPEC or environmental laws—of high gasoline prices around the country.[13]

Here's an interesting fact: the price-gouging has been officially recognized; in other words the government knows about it, but has not seen fit to punish the perpetrators by enforcing antitrust laws. But as consumer advocate Ralph Nader lamented in July 2006: "The Senate Judiciary Committee passed a bill a few months ago to authorize prosecution of the oil-producing countries under the antitrust laws. Imagine, Bush suing the countries whose oil powers our cars and economy."[14]

So finally the government decided to stand up to Big Oil—and sue OPEC. I wonder if we should cry or laugh at this affront to our intelligence. The oil mafia is openly robbing your bank in broad day light, and all our lawmakers can do is to offer a toothless gesture with a threat to take oil exporting countries to court rather than cut the criminals down to their size. Similarly, Slocum sees clearly that the hurricanes were only temporary phenomena and should not be blamed for enduring oil price hikes:

> Oil and gasoline prices were rising long before Hurricane Katrina wreaked havoc. U.S. gasoline prices jumped 14 percent from July 25 to Aug. 22. Indeed, profits for U.S. oil refiners have been at record highs.

In 1999, U.S. oil refiners made 22.8 cents for every gallon of gasoline refined from crude oil. By 2004, they were making 40.8 cents for every gallon of gasoline refined, a 79 percent jump.

Now comes the really shocking material from Slocum:

> Although federal investigators found ample evidence of oil companies intentionally withholding supplies from the market in the summer of 2000, the government has not taken any action to prevent recurrence.
>
> A congressional investigation uncovered internal memos written by major oil companies operating in the U.S. discussing their successful strategies to maximize profits by forcing independent refineries out of business, resulting in tighter refinery capacity. From 1995–2002, 97 percent of the more than 920,000 barrels of oil per day of capacity that has been shut down were owned by smaller, independent refiners. An internal Mobil document helps explain . . . the need to prevent the independent refiner from operating.

So we now know what the operating strategy of the Five Bullies such as Exxon-Mobil is. It is to force independent refiners out of business, tighten gasoline supplies, and then jack up the price. Finally, when the profit skyrockets, take ads in newspapers to claim that the profit is reasonable. In 2005, Katrina provided an excuse to oil firms to raise the crude price to as high as $70 per barrel; but why did crude hit $78 in July 2006 without a devastating hurricane? The answer comes from the monopolized oil industry along with another factor examined below.

HEDGE FUNDS

Big Oil is not the only reason for gargantuan energy price increases despite the absence of an oil shortage. The other factor is Wall Street and its overwhelmingly avaricious behavior. During the stock market mania of the 1990s, Wall Street bankers and companies earned huge commissions, fees and bonuses. They developed a get-rich-quick mentality. Then came the share-market crash, hefty losses and stagnant stock prices. But the quick-buck mentality did not die. Ever since 2000 big money has targeted the oil market, which is cornered by just a few corporations that can be counted on to ensure lofty crude and gasoline prices. Energy investments are now high on the list of hedge funds, which speculate profusely in the energy futures market. The oil price has stayed up for so long that it is now moving into the realm of superspeculation. This is another reason oil is becoming a bubble.

Whenever a quick buck can be made, speculators appear like vultures to take advantage of the situation. It matters little to them that their activities create financial instability or enhance the price of necessities. In fact they love instability, though it can render a lot of people poor. This is because fluctuations allow them to play ups and downs, that is, buy low, sell high, or even, sell high, then turn around and buy low.

Hedge funds are now generating artificial demand for oil. They spend billions every day to buy up oil futures, hoping the price will go up in the near term. Their purchases add to the normal global demand for petroleum products and tend to inflate the cost of energy. In his Senate testimony, Slocum also described the activities of these funds:

> Contracts representing hundreds of millions of barrels of oil are traded every day on the London and New York trading exchanges. An increasing share of this trading, however, has been moving off regulated exchanges such as the New York Mercantile Exchange (NYMEX) and into unregulated Over-the-Counter (OTC) exchanges. The Bank of International Settlements estimates that in 2004, the global OTC market has grown to over $248 *trillion*. Growth in global OTC derivatives markets has averaged 31.6 percent since 1990. Traders operating on exchanges like NYMEX are required to disclose significant details of their trades to federal regulators. But traders in OTC exchanges are not required to disclose such information, allowing companies like Goldman Sachs, Morgan Stanley and hedge funds to escape federal oversight and more easily engage in manipulation strategies. . . .
>
> The Commodity Futures Trading Commission has a troublesome streak of "revolving door" appointments and hiring that may further hamper the ability of the agency to effectively regulate the energy trading industry. In August 2004, CFTC chairman James Newsome left the Commission to accept a $1 million yearly salary as president of NYMEX, the world's largest energy futures marketplace. Just weeks later, Scott Parsons, the CFTC's chief operating officer, resigned to become executive vice president for government affairs at the Managed Funds Association, a hedge fund industry group that figures promi-

nently in energy derivatives markets. Such prominent defections hamper the CFTC's ability to protect consumers.[15]

Are big fund managers manipulating the futures markets? From what we have seen in the past, the answer must be yes. This is because many of the financial brokers involved in the hedge funds are the same as those who cheated investors in the past, and even paid fines for their illegal activities. All those shenanigans perpetrated during the share-market bubble of the 1990s leave little cause for confidence that our financial experts play fair.

Hedge funds are one reason that crude is now so expensive even though there is no physical shortage of oil anywhere in the world. How does this process work? In the past, OPEC was a major factor setting the crude oil price, which in turn determined the price of gasoline and other energy ingredients such as heating oil and airplane fuel. But now prices reflect mutual dependence. With increased monopoly power in the market, gasoline price often sets the crude price, and vice versa. Anytime gas becomes expensive, the crude price rises immediately. This is because those who control gasoline also control the crude. As noted, Big Oil produces 48 percent of U.S. crude output and over 60 percent of refined products.

The hedge fund managers, smart as they are, are aware of this fact. They can count on the Five Bullies to keep gasoline expensive. They know that if the pump prices decline only sluggishly in spite of a major fall in energy demand, crude price will also decline slowly. This way they buy ever more gasoline futures and crude oil futures, and ensure that these prices stay high. That is why during the warmer-than-expected winter of 2005–2006, natural gas prices operating in a competitive market plummeted, but crude prices, linked to gas prices operating in a monopolized market, fell only a little.

If the gasoline market were as competitive as natural gas, the hedge funds would not be sure of the staying power of gasoline. They would then dump their oil futures contracts as fast as they dumped their natural gas contracts. Then both crude and gasoline prices would have fallen proportionately to the price of natural gas.

See, for instance, what the Associated Press wrote in early 2006, during the mild winter:

> Many analysts say the quick rise in oil prices at the start of 2006 has little to do with any change in the fundamental balance between supply and demand. Instead, they point to a 7 percent surge in the number of

NYMEX crude oil contracts opened in the first two trading days of the year as a sign that hedge funds and other speculators continue to pour money into the market.[16]

Even the oil companies themselves are speculating and manipulating the futures market. This is what Bill O'Reilly reported on his show, *The O'Reilly Factor,* on the Fox News Network, on January 13, 2006: "A few months ago, I received some criticism for telling you that the big American oil companies are price gouging. You should have seen my mail. Well, I was right, and here's the proof. The U.S. Commodity Futures Trading Commission just fined Shell Oil $300,000 for manipulating crude oil markets." So now the oil bullies have found another way to stiff the people—speculation.[17]

O'Reilly's guest that day was Tyson Slocum, who said, "And what I see consistently here, Bill, whether it's Hurricane Katrina, whether it's political unrest in Iran, whether it's supposed economic growth in China or India, I see it all as excuses by a fairly small group of energy traders who are really in control of determining what the price of oil is."[18]

Thus it is clear that the oil market is now bubbly. All the elements that make up a bubble—sudden jump in price, increasing bullishness, escalating speculation—are present in the global oil industry. During the 1970s OPEC generated the oil balloon by withholding supplies; the oil behemoths are now doing the same by restraining competition. The bubble displays a mixture of both supply-side and demand-side factors. That is what makes it novel and potentially hazardous.

Anytime there is an asset bubble, there is a danger that it will rupture and slam the investors hard. But when there are twin bubbles, a rare phenomenon, the rupture's perils are magnified. That is the crucial juncture where we stand today, and the resulting explosion could be brutal in the near future, which I explore toward the end of this work.

CHAPTER 3

THE CYCLES
OF INFLATION
AND MONEY

M any economists view the rate of inflation as a crucial determi-
nant of a variety of economic activities. Much of their analysis
and forecasts rest on the behavior of prices. A remarkable feature of American economic history is that inflation actually moves in a
rhythmic cycle, which in turn is linked to another pattern that may be
called the money cycle. I have frequently used these cycles to make
forecasts about oil prices, inflation rates and the rate of interest in the
United States, and so far they have proved very reliable. Because of the
vastness of the American business empire, which has essentially colonized the world economy, the message of these cycles, at least for now,
has far-flung economic implications, which I will explore in the for-
ward-looking chapter 10.

A careful examination of U.S. statistics about product prices reveals an incredible pattern that exists as far back as the data go. A
straightforward plotting of the price figures for the eighteenth and
nineteenth centuries shows a regular and uneventful up-and-down
movement; prices rise and fall, until as late as 1940. After that year,
however, product prices go up and up, declining in rare circumstances. Thus a great chasm exists between price behavior before and
after 1940.[1]

There is an *apparent* discontinuity in the price data that separates the behavior of the U.S. economy prior to the start of World War II. However, it turns out that the discontinuity is more apparent than real. If we transform the data into the rate of inflation, which is simply a percentage change in a price index, the chasm disappears. The economy no longer seems to have diverged significantly, at least as far as the behavior of inflation goes.

What is so special about historical inflation rates? Ever since the 1750s—that is as far back as the data take us—every third decade in the United States has been a peak of inflation, with the one exception following the 1860s, due to the Civil War. It is well known that inflation springs primarily from excessive state printing of money over many years. There may be other causes for the price sizzle, but they are all generally temporary and cannot sustain the spiral of inflation. When too many dollars chase too few goods, the cost of living jumps. The link between the two is so powerful that a cycle of inflation cannot exist without an almost parallel cycle of money growth. In today's global economy, however, the chief spark for inflation has come from expensive oil, although money growth continues to play a supporting role.

THE CYCLE OF MONEY GROWTH

Why are we talking about money growth instead of money supply? The reason is that growing population, capital accumulation and improving technology tend to raise national output year after year. People need more cash in order to purchase the new output; they can also increase the use of credit cards that lead to borrowing, which is also part of money. If new money is not forthcoming, through the printing press or credit, then prices will fall, creating economic turmoil. This is because the same amount of money can buy increased production only at lower prices.

No business can properly make production plans without the stability of future prices. Therefore, just to keep prices fairly stable, money supply has to increase in step with the increase in real GDP. In other words, product prices remain constant as long as money growth approximates output growth. Thus if output jumps 5 percent, then money supply must also rise 5 percent to escape a prolonged price fall or deflation. Prices will rise and generate inflation only if money growth outpaces the growth of production, and exceeds 5 percent. Since output generally grows annually, we have to examine the behavior of money growth over time, and not just that of money supply, to understand inflation. A persistent jump in prices requires a sustained surge in money growth.

Let's now explore the empirical evidence.[2] Consistent estimates of money supply are available from the birth of the American nation in 1776. The data used is for every tenth year, which is also a natural way to examine information extending over two or three centuries. A simple transformation of these figures into rates of change yields a vivid cycle, presented in figure 3.1. Here money growth is defined as a percentage change in money supply estimated as currency in the hands of the public plus demand and time deposits with commercial banks.

The first peak of money growth is in the 1770s, when the American Revolution occurred. The provisional government had to print a lot of money to finance the conflict with England. Money growth at the time, according to historians, dwarfed any preceding level in colonial America. Once the revolution was over, money growth declined over two decades, soaring again in the first decade of the 1800s. In this way a cyclical pattern emerged over three centuries, with money growth peaking every third decade, except during the aftermath of the Civil War.

The Civil War was the most destructive event in U.S. history. It devastated the economy, especially in the South. So it is not surprising that the normal pattern of money growth was disrupted at that time. In two decades, the economy, as well as society, recovered, and then the money cycle rediscovered its normal course. The rhythm of the three-decade pattern returned after the 1880s, as the cycle crested in the 1910s, the 1940s and then the 1970s. The 1970s, not surprisingly, were followed by two decades of declining growth of money. The data for 2000 to 2010 is not complete yet, but if the money growth of the first five years of this decade is repeated over the rest of the decade, then there is another peak in the making.

Clearly, the money cycle is resilient. Even a cataclysm such as the Civil War could not disrupt the money pattern for long. *Thus figure 3.1 shows that, except for the post–Civil War interlude, the rate of money growth crested every third decade over more than two centuries.* This is an amazing feature of the U.S. economy, and comes in handy in the matter of forecasting.

Figure 3.1. The Long-Run Cycle of Money Growth in the United States:
    1760s–2000s

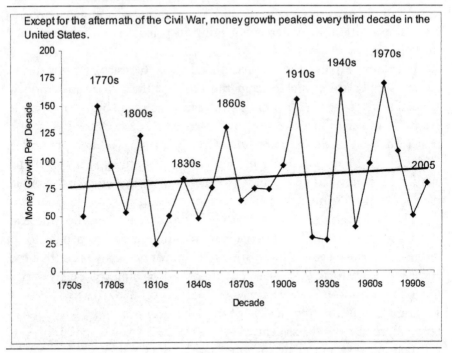

Source: The Historical Statistics of the United States, 1975; The Economic Report of the President, 2006; Ravi Batra, Common Sense Macroeconomics

The middle portion of the figure displays a trend line that shows the behavior of the average rate of money growth. The trend is nearly horizontal, revealing that U.S. money growth, on average, has been more or less the same over more than two centuries. The trend is indeed positive, signifying that while money growth has picked up over time, especially during the twentieth century, it is still fairly flat. Such stability points to the inherent stability of the U.S. economy and the political system that guides it.

THE CYCLE OF INFLATION

When average prices rise persistently for a while, inflation is said to occur. A one-shot upsurge is not enough for the situation to be described as inflationary. Furthermore, it's not necessary that all goods become pricey over time. If the average price level, estimated by an index, increases persistently, there is inflation. Computers and cell phones have become cheaper recently, while overall prices keep rising. So inflation exists, even though some goods face sinking prices.

The cycle of inflation, unlike the money cycle, is not self-evident. First, it is visible only in the wholesale price index, although in the twentieth century the consumer price index displayed the same pattern. Second, we need to transform the annual wholesale price index into a decennial figure. We can do this either by adding up annual prices to obtain the aggregate price level in each decade or by taking an average of the aggregate by dividing it by eleven, the number of years in each decade, including the first and the last year. Either figure may be used as the price level per decade.

Some economic historians look at ten observations during a decade, while others examine eleven. For the purpose of the cycles explored here, we look at eleven observations. Next we transform the average price level into rates of price change or inflation, and then plot them in figure 3.2.

What emerges is the long-run cycle of inflation, elegantly displayed by several lines systematically moving up and down through 25 decades, beginning in the 1750s. This cycle is yet another testimony to the resilience of the U.S. economy. Its message is basically the same as that of the money cycle. Except in the immediate aftermath of the Civil War, figure 3.2 reveals *that over the last 250 years the decennial rate of inflation crested every third decade and then usually fell over the next two decades.*

Inflation first peaked in the 1770s, then declined over the next two decades, and peaked again in the 1800s. Again it fell over the two subsequent decades, rising to its pinnacle in the 1830s. This time inflation declined for only one decade, but still the next peak did not appear for 30 years. At this point, following the 1860s, the cycle, as expected, was disturbed, but it began anew with the 1880s, because the peak reappeared in the 1910s. Thirty years later the cycle crested in the 1940s, and then again three decades later in the 1970s. In the 1980s and the 1990s, the rates of inflation tumbled.

The inflationary peak of the 1830s is somewhat puzzling, for it occurs virtually on the zero line. But the decades immediately preceding and following the 1830s display deflation or negative rates of inflation. The zero rate of inflation then represents at least relative inflation,

Figure 3.2. The Long-Run Cycle of Inflation in the United States: 1750s–2000s

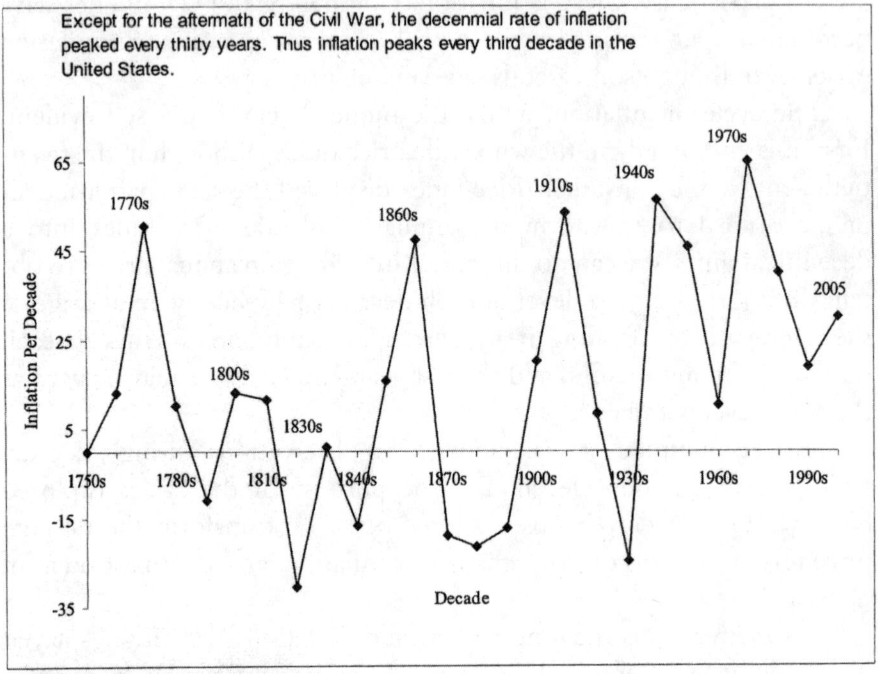

Except for the aftermath of the Civil War, the decennial rate of inflation peaked every thirty years. Thus inflation peaks every third decade in the United States.

Source: The Historical Statistics of the United States,1975; The Economic Report of the President, 2006; Ravi Batra, Common Sense Macroeconomics

though not inflation in the absolute sense. Thus, the 1830s may be properly regarded as the peak of the inflation (or deflation) cycle of the 30 years between 1820 and 1850.

The behavior of inflation in the United States is one of the most interesting features of its economy; it can be used to make a variety of forecasts about oil, commodities, interest rates and economic growth. While other nations display no such rhythm, the U.S. cycle can be used to foresee changes around the world, which, as explained in chapter 6, is a part of the U.S. business empire.

INFLATION AND MONEY SUPPLY

While excessive printing of money is now recognized as the main cause of inflation, this notion was hotly debated until the late 1970s. The experience of that decade settled the issue, once and for all. There is now a consensus among economists that high inflation springs chiefly from prolonged monetary expansion. There may be other contributory factors, but they cannot feed the price spiral without enhanced growth in the supply of dollars. Thus, a persistent rise in the growth of money is a prerequisite for the rise of inflation.

Figure 3.3 combines the previous two graphs, bringing together the paths traveled by money growth and inflation. You can see that the two cycles are almost parallel. Both have matching peaks and troughs, and both are disrupted by the Civil War. Figure 3.3 thus clearly reveals that a surfeit of dollar bills is the main spark behind inflation.

The money-growth and inflation cycles have survived phenomenal changes in the economy and society. They have continued through industrial revolutions, breathtaking technological change, two world wars, waves of regulations and business mergers, the Great Depression, the New Deal, discovery of the atom, the hydrogen bomb, the computer revolution, the fall of the Berlin Wall and numerous social movements.

What determines the amount of money sloshing through the economy? Since money is anything that society accepts to carry out the exchange of goods and services, money supply depends on myriad factors. Cash and coins are not its only components; they may not even be its primary components. People can carry out transactions using checks, credit cards, sometimes even precious metals. Furthermore, checks are issued by thousands of banks and financial institutions. Many new innovations, such as ATM machines, mutual funds and money market accounts have entered the arenas of banking and finance. When you recognize that dozens of unrelated and constantly evolving factors determine the supply of money, the observed pattern of money growth is simply astounding.

Since the 1760s, when our data begin, numerous changes have occurred in the concept and shape of money. Money existed in a variety of forms in the early nineteenth century, as paper bills circulated along with gold and silver coins. At that time, the federal government was not the sole provider of printed money. It issued the greenback; but state banks as well as the U.S. banks were also authorized to issue notes. Thus the money bills were issued by three sources—the federal government, federally chartered U.S. banks and state banks.

Figure 3.3. Money and Inflation Cycles

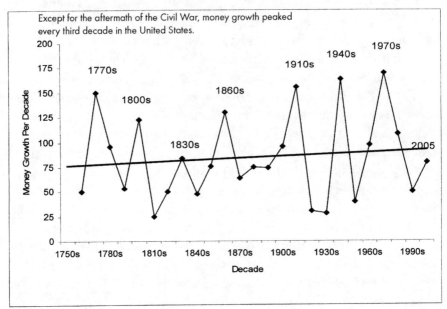

Except for the aftermath of the Civil War, money growth peaked every third decade in the United States.

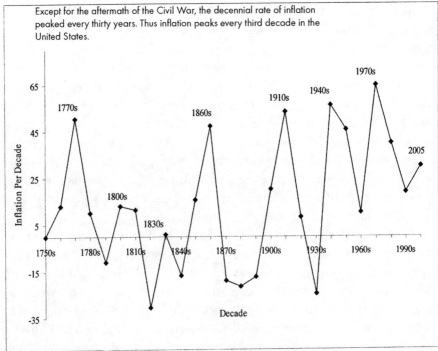

Except for the aftermath of the Civil War, the decennial rate of inflation peaked every thirty years. Thus inflation peaks every third decade in the United States.

Unlike today, however, the bulk of the currency was issued by the state institutions, which changed dramatically following the Civil War, when a federal tax on state notes chased them out of circulation, and only bills issued by the national treasury and nationally chartered banks remained. At the same time, businesses increasingly began to use checks, so much so that by the end of the nineteenth century, currency was no longer the primary form of money. Thus the Civil War and its aftermath constitute major watersheds in the history of money and banking in the United States; no wonder both the inflation and money cycles were disrupted for about 20 years during this period.

Another watershed in the annals of money occurred in 1914 with the establishment of the Federal Reserve System (the Fed), which serves as a central bank for the United States. The Federal Reserve System was established to counter a number of flaws that had plagued the economy since the birth of the Republic. Prior to the establishment of the Fed, money supply responded only to changing conditions in money and bond markets. As the Fed was created precisely to control the supply of money, one would assume that the central bank would have at least tamed, if not eliminated, the money cycle. Instead, it had just the opposite effect. Figure 3.1 reveals that the decade-long fluctuations in monetary growth were of a smaller magnitude in the nineteenth century than in the twentieth. Thus the creation of the Fed simply augmented the long-run oscillations of monetary growth without disrupting the cycle. Such fluctuations may be attributed to the intensity of the two world wars, which, as explained later, strongly impacted the growth of credit.

Yet it is true that annual fluctuations in the growth of money have declined since the 1940s. This suggests that the Fed can leash the supply of money in the short run, but not in the long run. The creation of the Fed caused nary a ripple in the rhythm of money growth, which continued to peak every third decade. Nor could anything else make a difference. The world in which the United States lives and operates has changed dramatically over the past two hundred years, but the money cycle endures.

WARFARE AND THE TWO CYCLES

The money cycle spans more than three centuries. The cycle displays seven peaks, of which as many as five occurred during periods of a major domestic or global war. The 1770s saw the American Revolution, the 1800s the Napoleonic wars in Europe, the 1860s the Civil War, the 1910s World War I and the 1940s World War II. During each conflict the warring states, confronted with grave danger, chose to finance the escalating cost of their operations by printing copious amounts of money, which in turn sparked a round of booming prices.

How did Napoleon's myriad battles, in which America was not militarily involved, affect the U.S. monetary growth and inflation? Napoleon came to power in 1799 and almost immediately plunged into the task of glorifying France at the cost of its neighbors. With war raging in Europe, the United States exported large quantities of foodstuffs and raw materials for which the Europeans paid with precious metals, which in turn swelled monetary growth and prices in the United States. It was due to these circumstances that the first decade of the nineteenth century became a peak period of the monetary and inflationary cycles.

Even though the wars themselves were over by 1815, their aftershocks were potent enough to affect two full decades. Like the 1800s, the decade of 1810 also encountered inflation, although the price surge during the 1810s was relatively subdued. Once inflation takes hold for a few years, it leaves a lasting impression on the human psyche. People adjust their behavior so as not to be caught again by price surprises. They shun money, especially paper money that depreciates over time, and start hoarding goods. Thus inflation fuels further inflation, as the increased hoarding of products propels their demand and hence prices. Of course, the process has to end at some point as the state shuts down its money mint at the end of the war, but not before it has plagued society for a decade or more.

What about other periods in which the cycles peaked, the 1830s and the 1970s, during which most nations largely escaped bloody conflicts? Although these periods were free from major conflagrations, even during times of relative peace warfare plays a role in the surge of money and prices.

During the 1820s, the economy experienced serious deflation; monetary growth was extremely shallow and the cost of living fell sharply. In the following decade, there were minor though perennial battles between the U.S. government and Native Americans. The needed expense was significant enough to escalate government spending, necessitating the printing of money in the form of treasury notes. From 1835 to

1842, there was a seven-year conflict known as the Second Seminole War, which cost the federal government $50 million. Since the entire federal budget between 1830 and 1840 varied annually from a mere $15 million to $24 million, hostilities with the Seminoles consumed a large chunk of government spending.[3] As a result, even though the conflict didn't cost too many lives, it did generate larger money growth and halted the deflation in prices. The inflation rate during the 1830s was no longer negative.

Warfare was also involved in inflationary peaks during the 1970s, though much more indirectly than in any other peak decade. The so-called Yom Kippur War began in October 1973, as Syria and Egypt launched a surprise attack against Israel. The United States backed Israel and Russia backed the Arabs. In response, OPEC, dominated by the Arab nations, imposed an oil embargo against the West, and effectively the rest of the world. Oil prices skyrocketed.

OPEC learned that oil prices could be raised substantially by trimming production. Even after the hostilities ended in less than a month, the cost of gasoline actually climbed. The war by itself should have had no lasting impact on U.S. monetary growth and inflation; product prices would have surged for a couple of years due to costlier energy, but then returned to their normal level of stability. But the U.S. administration chose to fight the recessionary and inflationary consequences of the oil surge with monetary expansion. Money growth jumped and a temporary problem of inflation swelled into a decade-long spiral.

The discussion I've presented above should give us pause. Except for the singular exception of the aftermath of the Civil War, U.S. monetary growth and inflation have peaked every third decade since the 1750s. Furthermore, some kind of war, directly or indirectly, was involved in generating these cycles. Of course, how the authorities respond to war is the stuff of which the cycles are made. Frequently governments print money when trouble flares on the battlefront or the economic front. And if an economic slump is triggered by inflationary pressures, monetary expansion begets escalating inflation without curing the recession.

However, none of this means that there is a three-decade cycle of warfare as well. Nor does it imply that in modern times major wars have usually occurred at the interval of three decades. There were certainly bloody conflicts in other decades as well. The United States fought a war with Britain from 1812 to 1815, with Mexico from 1846 to 1847 and with Spain in 1898. The three-decade cycles merely signify that the U.S. response to warfare fits with its three-decade pattern of money and inflation. There were also conflicts in the 1950s and 1960s that fell outside the realm of the three-decade pattern. Both the Korean War and the Vietnam War were costly in terms of defense spending and lost lives. However, in both cases the money spigots were kept closed, and inflation was moderate.

Warfare is a perennial human activity, but its financing has varied somewhat over time, and these variations have generated regular economic cycles. For example, the 1973 Arab-Israeli battles were short lived and didn't involve the United States militarily. Yet in the aftermath the United States responded by printing oodles of money, and in the process generated the highest peaks of the money and inflation cycles. Thus it is not warfare that has been following a regular pattern, but the U.S. government response to it.

What accounts for the three-decade periodicity of these cycles? It is hard to explain why certain events can occur with such regularity. The answer must lie in the relative stability of the mental and psychological processes of the people involved in these events. It is human nature alone that can possibly generate rhythmic patterns.

It is usually observed that each generation is active for about thirty years. Whenever a crisis occurs, the easiest way out for the government is to print money. Thus every generation succumbs to the temptation of pump priming to solve its problems, and inevitably encounters inflation. Then it learns its lesson, curbs money growth and hence the spiral of prices. But the hard-earned lessons of the past are forgotten, because the old generation has been displaced even as new problems occur. Every generation apparently finds a way to make the same mistake. This way there are three-decade cycles of money growth and inflation.

Such cycles may be called generational cycles of money and prices. They resemble the generational cycles of Arthur Schlesinger Jr., who uses them to forecast trends in American government and politics. He writes: "Each generation spends its first fifteen years after coming of political age in challenging the generation already entrenched in power. Then the new generation comes to power itself for another fifteen years, after which its policies pale and the generation coming up behind claims the succession."[4]

Schlesinger goes on: "Each new generation when it attains power, tends to repudiate the work of the generation it has displaced and to reenact the ideals of its own formative days of thirty years before."[5] This way Schlesinger explores two cycles—one lasting thirty years and the other fifteen years—to examine social and political events. However, I have observed that there is also a cycle of seven and a half years. It all depends on the momentum behind any event. Thus the shortest cycle implies that a major event or trend lasts for seven to eight years and then perishes. World War II, for instance, started in 1939 and ended in 1945, thus lasting seven years. A fifteen-year cycle, on the other hand, means that a momentous event, with an exceptionally strong start, dies fourteen to sixteen years later. Historians call the period 1930 to 1945 a time of troubles for much of the world. It included the Great Depression and World War II, enduring for fifteen long years. Here "the time of troubles" is one complete episode and, from start to finish, it has a fifteen-year cycle.

By contrast, the three-decade cycle signifies that similar events repeat themselves roughly every thirty years. Cyclical analysis does not imply that there is nothing new in history. While the events tend to repeat themselves, their intensity need not be the same. Thus a great depression started in the world in 1930; thirty years later, there was also an economic slump, but it was not as intense as the one in the 1930s; in 1990 also there was a downturn, which was similar to the slump of 1960.

OIL AND INFLATION

In recent years, however, the trigger for U.S. inflation has come mainly from the high cost of imported oil. Monetary growth is still an important inflationary factor, but because of growing international commerce that restrains prices, such growth has not provided the initial spark behind giant price hikes; its role has been more supportive than instigative. A quick and sharp climb in oil prices would normally spawn a recession, which in turn would lower oil demand and reverse the rise in the price as well as the rate of inflation. However, if high monetary growth accompanies the high cost of oil, the recession is prevented. So both expensive oil and inflation persist for a long time. Thus money growth is still important in generating long-term inflation but only after product prices have jumped from the rise in oil.

In fact, during the 1970s when oil prices surged, the rate of inflation was at its highest level in U.S. history. The oil price began to soar in 1973, and kept rising until 1981. Inflation followed the same path. Then came the steep recession of 1982; oil demand fell, as did its price, along with general inflation. The price of oil shot up again in 1991, as did the cost of living. It plummeted in 1997 and 1998, along with the growth in prices. Thus ever since the early 1970s, oil and inflation rates have generally moved in tandem. This symbiosis enables me to predict the price of oil by analyzing the cycle of inflation, which I will do, as mentioned before, in chapter 10.

CHAPTER 4

THE LAW OF
SOCIAL CYCLE

The two cycles studied thus far have unique characteristics in that they are rhythmic patterns, which are unlike business cycles analyzed by other economists. The economic literature offers a Mitchel cycle, a Kuznets cycle, a Kondratief cycle, a Jugular cycle, and so on. All these have varying periodicity and are not rhythmical. Now I will explore a much broader cycle, which is also unconventional, and, like the cycles of money and inflation, can be used to make a variety of forecasts. It is called the law of social cycle, and was discovered by my late teacher, P. R. Sarkar.

Sarkar was a great historian, philosopher and spiritualist. He authored many books with uncanny originality in a wide variety of disciplines. I have frequently used some of his hypotheses to make forecasts that have come true.

According to Milton Friedman, a theory is known for its predictive ability. He argues that since the primary goals of positive, value-free science are predictions, any thesis that forecasts well is a good theory.[1] Friedman, a Nobel Laureate, is a well-known economist, and has critics, but few have contradicted this argument and rightly so, because the future is unknown, and if someone can prognosticate the unknown, then they must have a pretty good understanding of the workings of society. Friedman's argument has the support of another Nobel laureate, Gary Becker, among many others. Mark Twain once quipped that it is very difficult to make predictions, especially about the future. A theory that proposes to explain social events on the basis of logic, not morality or values, must pass the hardy test of predictive ability. But first we must understand the idea itself. In ensuing chapters, I will apply the social cycle to various societies, before examining its predictive content in chapter 10.

Let's start with a simple question. What is the main source of political power in different countries? Stated differently, if we carefully explore the political landscape of our world, what do we see? In places like the United States, western Europe, Canada, India, Australia and Japan, money rules society and an ethos of supermaterialism prevails. In places like Iran, the priesthood is dominant, and religion is a strong influence in people's lives, whereas in Russia former intelligence officers, such as ex-KGB chief Vladimir Putin among others, hold the reigns. In China, the Communist Party is supreme but the ultimate source of political power is the military, which established the party's rule in the 1949 Marxist revolution. Remember the Tiananmen Square massacre of 1989 when the Chinese government faced a serious challenge to its authority: Who restored order in the country at the time and crushed the opposition to communist rule? The army. The army is also the source of power in North Korea, Syria, Libya and Egypt.

Another source of political power is organized labor; but labor generally has to share the honors with the military, commerce and religious institutions. Take Britain, France and Germany, for instance: workers there are organized in unions and are strong enough to command wage increases even in times of high unemployment. They also have a say in elections because of their large numbers and the union campaign contributions that finance their favorite candidates. When their representatives are elected to form a government, however, hardly any cabinet officers are selected from their ranks. Britain's Labour Party has ruled for over a decade, but it is hard to find a laborer as a minister in Prime Minister Tony Blair's cabinet. Thus all through history laborers have been generally deprived of political influence, and even when they do play a role in politics, they normally share power with others.

Nevertheless, laborers do wield some authority, especially when they are well organized. Even in the United States, where unions have become feeble in recent years, organized labor has some impact on the electoral process. Labor unions have a modicum of influence on legislation, especially when workplace conditions are in question.

What does this all tell us? A close look at any society reveals that, broadly speaking, there are four possible sources of political power—the military, human intellect, organized labor and, of course, money or wealth. Religion may also yield social and governmental prominence, but priests dominate society through their mastery of scriptures and rituals. In other words, they also use their intellect to control or influence people. Thus, ultimately political power or societal dominance stems from four avenues—physical strength or skills, human intellect or analytical skills, business acumen or acquisitive skills that arise from and lead to the hoarding of wealth, and labor organizations. As a result, throughout history, we find that societies are sometimes dominated by warriors, sometimes by intellectuals (including priests), sometimes by the wealthy, and sometimes by combinations of the wealthy and laborers, wherein the opulent reign supreme but workers also have some authority.

THE FOUR SOCIAL CLASSES

In fact, we could go a step further and say that each of the ruling elites belongs to a certain class. Normally classes have been defined on the basis of their incomes and wealth. Karl Marx, for instance, divides society between capitalists and the proletariat; others talk of the rich gentry and the rest. Still others describe class divisions in terms of various occupations. Sarkar, however, offers an alternative way to classify society. In his view, class divisions derive from people's own nature. People's inner qualities generally lead them into certain occupations that in turn define various classes.

According to Sarkar, there are basically four types of human minds. He argues that while people generally have common goals and ambitions, their methods of achieving these goals may differ, depending on their internal qualities. Most of us want creature comforts, respect from friends and relatives, and, possibly, name and fame. But we may try to accomplish these objectives by developing physical skills, intellectual power or entrepreneurial abilities (which normally require saving a good deal of money and starting a business). Following Sarkar's logic, people can be categorized as warriors, intellectuals or acquisitors. Finally, those who do not acquire such higher-valued skills are physical laborers. Thus, in Sarkar's view, society basically includes four types of people, each with a different frame of mind. He defines people's qualities in such a broad way that almost everyone is covered by a classification.

Stated differently, people have common objectives but they pursue different occupations because of sharp differences in their inherent abilities and qualities. Some people, born with muscles and strong physiques, try to develop their physical skills requiring stamina, courage and vigor. Such people usually work in occupations that carry physical risks. Sarkar considers them warriors in the sense that they all have a warrior mentality that is not averse to taking bodily risk. Thus soldiers, police officers, fire fighters, professional athletes, skilled blue-collar workers, and so on, all belong to the class of warriors. Their job descriptions differ but they have one thing in common, namely, their occupations require muscular strength and may cause them physical injuries or even death. Developing such skills requires a good deal of physical exercise, which may be difficult and tedious for others. In general, anyone who tries to do well in society with the help of their muscles and valor belongs to the class of warriors or has a warriorlike mind.

There are those who lack the sinews of a warrior but are endowed with relatively superior intellects. Naturally, such persons will try to develop analytical skills to accomplish their goals. According to Sarkar, anyone who tries to do well with the help of their brains rather than brawn is an intellectual. This is a much broader usage of the term than is commonly recognized. Thus, in his view intellectuals include not only authors, professors, scholars and scientists but also lawyers, engineers, white-collar workers, physicians and, above all, priests, because they all use their brain power rather than muscle power to achieve their goals in life. All these people have an intellectual or analytical mentality.

The third type of person, according to Sarkar, tends to accumulate wealth to obtain the amenities of life. Though not as smart as the intellectuals, such persons are often brighter than warriors and possess entrepreneurial abilities and business skills. They too may be risk takers but not of the physical variety. They are generally wealthier than the other classes, and money is the principal, if not the only, goal in their life. Sarkar calls them acquisitors, because almost all of their actions and thinking run after money. Mammon is all that matters to them. Those belonging to the class of acquisitors generally include merchants, bankers, businessmen, capitalists and landlords. While other classes

chase money for enhanced consumption of goods and services, acquisitors covet money for the sake of money. They feel good thinking about
their bank balance.

Finally, there is a fourth type of person who is altogether different
from the others. As a group, they may lack the others' marketable skills.
That doesn't mean their contribution is insignificant or their wages
should be low; quite often their work is indispensable to society's well-
being, but their large numbers may preclude them from making a decent
living. Without the skills in demand, they are exploited by the rest of society. Their only hope is in forming organizations; when they get united,
they can become a formidable force and earn decent wages. Sarkar ex-
horts society to do everything possible to enhance their education, income and social status.

Peasants, "serfs," and unskilled farm and factory workers generally
belong to the class of physical laborers. There may be exceptions among
those engaged in unskilled occupations. Some peasants and factory
workers may be quite intelligent; others may be employed in these jobs
not by choice but by the force of circumstances. They were perhaps born
to poverty or have never had the educational opportunities available to
the well-to-do. Such persons do not belong to the laboring class but to
other groups.

In the past, almost all societies forced some people to become
slaves, who had to perform physical labor for their masters. Such a situation does not mean that the slaves belonged to the class of laborers.
The laboring class consists primarily of those who perform unskilled or
low-tech work by choice or are unable to acquire other technical or oc-
cupational skills.

These then are the four social classes that generally exist in every society and have existed since antiquity. Sarkar dubs this the quadri-divisional social system. He differs sharply from others such as Marx who
defines classes along economic grounds, basing them on people's incomes
or wealth. Sarkar does not overlook the economic aspect, but it is only
one entity among the four that describe the totality of society. To Sarkar
class differences derive from inherent differences in human nature. Most
of us are simply born to be warriors, intellectuals, acquisitors and laborers, although a major change in our environment may alter our grouping.

Although Sarkar describes human mind in terms of broad generalizations, he recognizes the effect of the environment on human psychology.

His classes are not static, but dynamic, which creates the possibility of social mobility; in fact, Sarkar's class system is quite flexible, especially over time. People change through concerted effort or through prolonged contact with others; intentionally or unintentionally they may move into another class. A laborer recruited into an army may become a fine officer through long drills and training. He or she may also become an intellectual with tutoring and hard work. Similarly, an intellectual, in the company of acquisitors, may actually join their class, or an acquisitor may turn into a laborer. Thus class distinctions are not rigid and don't have to be hereditary. Yet such social mobility is rather limited. While a person can go against his nature and circumstances to acquire skills unsuited to his temperament, it is not easy. A wrestler, for instance, will find it very difficult to be a scientist, and vice versa. An acquisitor will generally have a tough time becoming an intellectual.

Hybrids, individuals who display two or more personalities, are also possible. A person may be a warrior as well as an intellectual. General Dwight D. Eisenhower was one case of an author and a first-rate warrior in one; President John F. Kennedy was yet another. But they are exceptions to the singular categories offered by Sarkar. In general, even if some people reveal two mentalities, only one predominates.

Personally, I think I belong to the class of intellectuals, although my critics may have their doubts about it. I am a professor and an author, and writing comes easy to me. I don't think I can become a warrior like Mohammad Ali, the legendary boxer, even if I am reborn a hundred times. Nor can I become an entrepreneur like Bill Gates, no matter how hard I try. Thus while social mobility is possible, it is generally not that easy, with one exception. It is easy to acquire an acquisitive mentality, though not the business skills. In fact, when money rules society, the vast majority of people, as I argue later, turn into acquisitors.

THE LAW OF SOCIAL CYCLE

Sarkar's mental categories are broad enough to cover the entire gamut of a society. The history of civilization reveals the existence of the quadridivisional social system described above. To reiterate the point for clarity and emphasis, according to Sarkar, every civilization, or mature society, is made up of four classes, each consisting of people whose behavior and predilections reflect the predominance of a certain type of mind. There is a bit of the acquisitive instinct in most of us, but only a few constantly chase money and make it their life's goal. We all covet living comforts and social respect, but some of us pursue them through physical skills, some through intellectual excellence and some by starting a business after saving a good deal of money.

In every society, warriors generally defend the nation against foreign attacks and maintain law and order; intellectuals develop religion, ideas and inventions; acquisitors manage farms, factories, financial institutions and retail stores; while laborers do routine work and perform low-tech jobs. Each and every class is crucial to social progress, but unfortunately not everyone, especially labor, is rewarded in accordance with their national contributions. Also in every society, the ruling elite are usually rich, but wealth need not be their original source of power. How the elite rise to the top of the social hierarchy is the crucial question.

In formulating a theory, most social scientists focus on concepts that they think apply to the general public and ignore the exceptions to their definitions. It is not that the exceptions are unimportant, only that they are immaterial to the forecasts provided by the theory. Sarkar's modus operandi is the same. He defines human personality in terms of four broad generalizations, notes the exceptions to his concepts and then goes on to frame his thesis in terms of his class system.

Once we understand the quadri-divisional social system, we can grasp the philosophy of history offered by Sarkar, who argues that while all four classes exist in every civilization, only one of them dominates society at any point of time. A civilization, he says, evolves in terms of four distinct eras. Sometimes warriors, sometimes intellectuals, sometimes acquisitors and sometimes a combination of acquisitors and laborers dominate the sociopolitical order. Laborers rarely top the social hierarchy, although at times they become united enough to earn decent wages and sway the government. These are also the times when the ruling elite become so corrupt and self-centered that a vast majority of society lives in poverty or in debt. The general public then has to spend most of its waking hours in making ends meet; it has little time left to pursue the finer aspects of life—music, art, adventure, poetry, spirituality. A lot of people then have to labor hard just to survive. Such a time period may be called the era of laborers.

Thus, in Sarkar's philosophy no single group remains atop society's pecking order forever. What is most interesting, as well as fascinating, is that the movement of society from one age to another follows a specific pattern. In the annals of every civilization, modern or ancient, eastern or western, early medieval or postmedieval, Sarkar posits that "The era of laborers is followed by the era of warriors, the era of warriors by the era of intellectuals, and the era of intellectuals by the era of acquisitors, culminating in a social revolution—such a social evolution is the infallible Law of Nature."[2]

This is Sarkar's law of social cycle that describes social evolution. The emphasis on change is noteworthy, because social change goes hand in hand with human evolution. The social cycle thus becomes an inevitable natural phenomenon, wherein societal hegemony shifts from one class to another.

Peering into the eons of history, we read about myriad kings, queens, generals, poets, artists, prime ministers, chancellors, presidents, pharaohs, prophets, religions, jobs and occupations. But according to Sarkar, history's seemingly random and unrelated events, vast, complex and unfathomable, have all followed a singular pattern determined by natural laws; furthermore, such societal happenings will continue to follow that pattern into the future. This type of social evolution is displayed in figures 4.1 and 4.2.

Figure 4.1 depicts the social cycle as a circular pattern; while the figure provides no new information, it does demonstrate how societies change over time, how they move along this circle and how, according to Sarkar, they will keep changing in the future. The figure has some powerful policy implications for a country's politics and government that will be discussed in chapter 11. The chief message of the circular pattern is that no age lasts forever and that each particular era is followed by another.

Figure 4.2 uses the information of figure 4.1 and presents it in terms of a cyclical graph. Here again a civilization starts out in the age of laborers, where there is no state or any kind of government, and then moves up into the age of warriors. In the figure, the vertical axis displays the influence and respect of the dominant class. In other words, in the age of warriors, in the ascending phase of the cycle (line 1), the martial class consolidates its power and expands its influence over the years; people's respect for the warriors also gradually rises at that time. Around the peak, the warrior rule is more or less unchallenged; most people then covet a career in the army. All this will become clear in the next chapter, where I apply the social cycle to Western history.

Figure 4.1. Sarkar's Social Cycle as a Circular Pattern

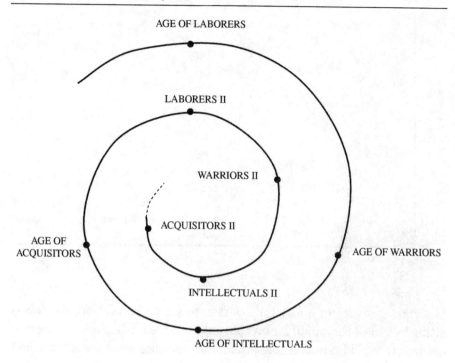

Following the peak, warriors' influence and social respect begin to decline, and move into the descending phase of the cycle. At the bottom of this age, near anarchy prevails again, and the warrior rule is overthrown by society's scholars, who then start the age of intellectuals. Their power and influence follow the path of the cycle along line 2, then peak and decline thereafter. The intellectuals are dethroned by acquisitors, who then win over the hearts and minds of the populace. Acquisitors in turn ascend to their peak along line 3, and move downhill like other classes thereafter. However, in the downward phase of the acquisitive era, acquisitors have to share power with laborers, thereby starting the laborer or the acquisitive-cum-labor age. In the second age of laborers, civilization does not revert to the primitiveness of the first such era; it only displays the integral features of that age, without completely dismantling the state. Acquisitors still hold the reigns of power, and the elite flout the laws.

In figure 4.2, the "A & L" age stands for the acquisitive-cum-labor age, which at the bottom point ends in the flames of a social revolution.

Figure 4.2. Sarkar's Social Cycle over Time

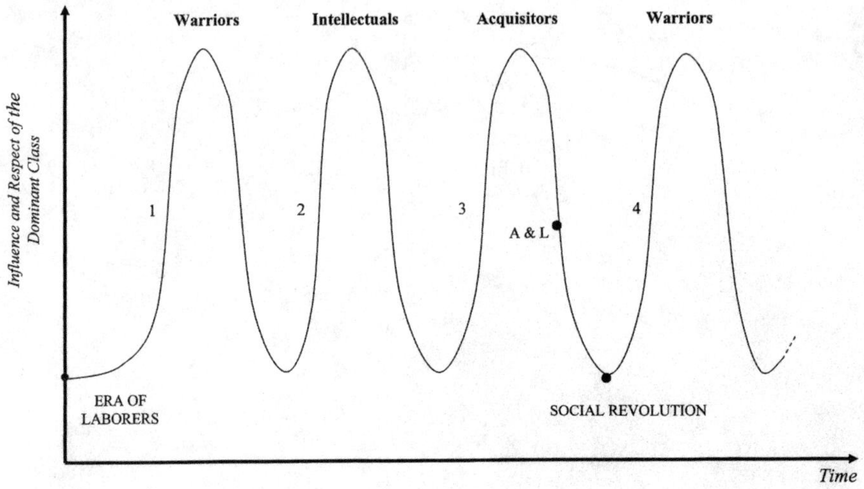

Since it takes a lot of effort and courage to start a revolution, the rebels display a warrior mentality, of which valor and fearlessness are the principal features. The new leaders then start another age of warriors, and the social cycle marches on along line 4, and so on.

THE AGE OF LABORERS

Since I have discussed Sarkar's social cycle in detail in two previous books, I will only briefly describe the features of the more recent age of laborers here.[3] If all or most of these traits are present, then society is passing though the laborer age, or, in view of the discussion above, the acquisitive-cum-labor age. Features of the more recent era of laborers include the following:

1. Family breakdown resulting in large number of divorces
2. Rampant crime and official arrogance, disregard for the rule of law
3. Extremely loose morals accompanied by high rates of prostitution and dissemination of pornography
4. Neglect of children and the elderly
5. General aversion toward physical and mental discipline

6. Supermaterialism and greed of the elite leading to a thriving drug culture
7. Commercialization of everything, including religion, art, music, sports, adventure and so on
8. Religion of fear, and educational decline
9. Intellectual dishonesty and the spread of dogmas
10. Low status for women because of the prevalence of divorce, prostitution and pornography
11. Divided and decentralized government
12. Acquisitive intellectuals dominating politics but sharing power with laborers.

These are various features of an acquisitive-cum-labor age. They are self-explanatory and need not be explored in detail, especially since most of them are prevalent today.

THE ERA OF WARRIORS

In almost every respect, the age of warriors is just the opposite of the age of laborers. When warriors dominate society, they create a highly centralized government with almost all authority vested in their own person. Initially, or in their ascending phase, they are compassionate, just and magnanimous, but after tasting luxury for a while, they become corrupt and autocratic. They turn into dictators and generate fear among all other classes. Some of them even turn out to be tyrants. But even when they are not tyrannical, people are afraid to cross these warriors because of their absolute powers and complete control over the army.

Let me clarify the role of the military in every age. There were no armies in the first era of laborers; they emerged when warriors came to control the polity and then have remained more or less intact in all subsequent eras. They obey whatever class comes to be dominant, and then maintain order and stability in society. During the warrior age, the ruling warriors control the army. In the ensuing era, such control passes into the hands of intellectuals, and when the acquisitors come to power, they dominate the military. The question is why army warriors ever accept the rule of the intellectuals and acquisitors. The answer to this all-important question will become clear later. For now, let me say that the army generally obeys its commander in chief. In the age of warriors, an accomplished warrior himself is the commanding general. In the age of intellectuals, such an officer is under the thumb of the ruling intellectuals, and in the age of acquisitors as well as laborers, the commander in chief is generally a member of the acquisitive class regardless of whether he has any fighting skills. The main features of the warrior era include the following:

1. Strong family bonds and relationships resulting in good care for children and the elderly
2. Low levels of crime
3. Low levels of prostitution and pornography
4. Joint family system that takes good care of the children and the elderly
5. General inclination toward physical discipline
6. Low level of materialism; people are interested in art and adventure, not so much in money
7. Religion exalting gods of beauty and power
8. High status for women, especially motherhood
9. Absolute and centralized government
10. Prosperous economy
11. Constant warfare for territorial conquest and personal honor
12. At the end of this era, tyranny and near anarchy take over.

THE ERA OF INTELLECTUALS

Warriors are good at warfare and in expanding the realm of their kingdoms, but they are inept in managing their domains. They need experts in administering the territories that they capture on the battlefield. Such experts come from the class of intellectuals, and when the intellectuals come to power, society generally displays the following features:

1. Strong family ties resulting in good care of children and the elderly
2. The lowest crime level of all eras
3. A high level of prostitution
4. A general inclination toward mental discipline
5. Low levels of materialism; people are interested in otherworldly pursuits, not so much in money
6. A monotheistic religion

7. A very low status for women
8. Power sharing and a decentralized government
9. A poor economy
10. Occasional warfare based on religion or ideas
11. Excessive rules and regulations governing public behavior
12. At the end, the intellectuals' tyranny and near anarchy signal the need for a major change.

THE ERA OF ACQUISITORS

When the intellectual mentality comes to dominate society there is a great shift in many aspects of life. People's love of fun, adventure and sports may give way to asceticism, austerity and the quest for a good afterlife; or it may be replaced by new-found interest in scholarship and analytical pursuits in which theories are debated and mastered for their own sake. Women are subordinated, and poverty stalks the land. In the same way, when the acquisitors come to power, the public's lifestyle cannot but change in numerous ways. Since the era of acquisitors dominates the world today, we will study its features in detail.

Even during the era of intellectuals, good scholars oppose the parochial doctrines of the ruling elite, often at the risk of their freedoms and lives. They preach individual rights and denounce absolutism of all forms—monarchical as well ecclesiastical. As a result of their efforts and sacrifice, the public begins to see through the shaky ideas, which may be theological or secular. People also question the lavish lifestyle of the priesthood and scholars. As a result political power slowly passes into the hands of wealthy landlords or businessmen. Thus begins the age of acquisitors in which the principal power source is land or wealth. In other words, the era of acquisitors arises either as feudalism or as capitalism in every society.

Acquisitors differ from intellectuals in the way they use their intellect. While interested in creature comforts as well as money, an intellectual is also inclined toward analytical pursuits for their own sake; such people like to write theories for the sake of theories; they have a prolific pen that can be used for good as well as evil. The acquisitor, however, will have none of this; such persons are obsessed with amassing, not just enjoying, wealth. Yet the intellectuals have a crucial role to play. As in any era, most of them do what comes naturally to them—that is, they invent dogmas rationalizing the hegemony of the dominant class. They devise new slogans that fool the gullible. In this case, they justify the supremacy of the acquisitive class behind the cloak of individual rights, liberty and social justice. In reality, however, such lofty principles are overtly flouted, and are usually observed only when the nation faces a crisis or when it serves the interests of the acquisitors.

In return, the wealthy offer patronage to the intellectuals; in our age, this takes the form of research grants, distinguished professorships and consulting jobs. Once the intellectuals submit to the affluent, classes that had already come under the control of the intellectuals also serve the interests of the rich.

Thus, in the age of acquisitors, most, if not all, sections perform services for the wealthy, with the intellectual class justifying the acquisitors' rule, the warrior class entertaining them in sports and fighting their wars, and the laborer doing physical labor for them. In all civilizations, the acquisitive class has consisted of such disparate groups as money lenders, merchants, landlords and businessmen. No longer does a keen intellect, by itself, bring political power and the attendant perks; instead the power base shifts to the money-chasing intellect.

Salient features of the era of acquisitors include the following:

1. Family ties loosening with the rise of individualism
2. Rising crime rates
3. Increasing prostitution and pornography
4. Growing aversion toward mental and physical discipline
5. Rising materialism and interest in money
6. Rising atheism and disrespect for religion
7. Continued low status of women
8. Highly decentralized government
9. The rise of reason, science and technology
10. Rising standard of living and rising wealth concentration
11. Frequent warfare based on competition for resources and markets
12. At the end, acquisitors' tyranny, poverty, general malaise and the near anarchy of the laborer age.

As usual, with the change in society's dominant mentality comes a major change in the public's thinking and lifestyle. As the intellectuals lose power, their old theories go down the drain with them. New theories, offered by a different group of scholars, are born. Once the theocratic age of intellectuals ends, religion no longer has the same hold on people as before. Individualism begins to replace the earlier communal thinking. As a result, family bonds begin to weaken. Parents, who had tremendous power over their offspring in the past, begin to lose the loyalty of their children. Families split up, replacing the old joint family system with smaller families.

With family fragmentation and weakening religion, materialism begins to rise. During the era of intellectuals people are oppressed by myriad rules and regulations, and money lending and profit are looked down upon. All that disappears as the era of acquistors dawns. In this new era men and women of affluence are respected. Similarly, the inclination toward physical and mental discipline begins to wane; gods and goddesses, especially the deities of wealth, return to religion. While most people continue to believe in one almighty God, they now generally pray for material things from him. The interest in the afterlife gives way to an interest in the present, and as time passes the ranks of atheists swell.

Women's lowly status in the intellectual age generally deteriorates in the acquisitive age, even though affluent ladies are admired. Women begin to work in factories, but they put in long hours at low pay. As the profit motive is no longer denounced, some entrepreneurs invest money in the sex industry and sharply expand the business of prostitution. Thus, the so-called oldest profession expands manifold. Once the ruling elite discard moral scruples, other groups generally follow. Consequently, moral degradation gradually spreads. A number of factors such as the lewdness of men, loose family ties and the declining influence of religion abet this process.

The government of the acquisitive age differs sharply from that of previous eras. Political authority was highly centralized during the age of warriors and somewhat centralized in the age of the intellectuals, as absolutist kings or authoritarian priests dominated the social order. The acquisitors fear a centralized rule, because such a system can force them to share their wealth with the state and the poor (such incidents are not that uncommon in the eras of warriors and intellectuals). So whenever acquisitors come to power, political authority is gradually decentralized; there is no single, absolute or unchallenged source of power any more. And the degree of decentralization only increases over time, leading to the rise of many localized power groups.

The chief hallmark of the acquisitive age is a sharp improvement in the economy relative to the previous age. As the noose of rules and regulations loosens, and as people become more interested in the present life, they start thinking about bettering their living standard. The quest for money leads to new inventions and technologies, which raise worker productivity as well as profits. In the beginning everyone benefits from technological discoveries, and the public is very happy with the new system. People have greater freedom, enjoy a better lifestyle and welcome an end to warrior and intellectual tyranny. The living standard remains high for a long time, and the other classes make a living by working for the affluent.

In every class, there are good and bad people; so there are nice as well as mean acquisitors. The good ones offer safe working conditions and wages proportionate to worker productivity; they are as much interested in the welfare of their employees as in profits. They are honest, pay their fair share of taxes and are philanthropic. Unfortunately, such people are few and far between.

But there is a vast army of bad acquisitors, whose minds constantly chase money. They exploit their workers through poor working conditions, low wages and long working hours. They also exploit people's baser instincts by offering pornography, addictive drugs and dangerous weapons. They patronize dishonest intellectuals, who in return justify the rule of money in society.

As time passes, increasing levels of wealth become concentrated in the hands of the elite, and the general living standard starts to decline. The ruling elite are indeed the wealthiest in every age, but when acquisitors are on top national wealth gets even more concentrated in fewer hands. This is because the acquisitive class, by its very nature, seeks to hoard money. It is never enough for them. A millionaire wants to become a centi-millionaire, a centi-millionaire a billionaire, a billionaire a mega-billionaire. Toward the end of this age, the entire state machinery seems to be working to make the rich richer, and the poor poorer.

Going back to figure 4.2, we find that in every age the dominant class passes through two phases—one ascending, the other descending. The influence and social respect for the dominant class gradually grows over time in the first phase and slowly declines during the second phase. However, unlike in other eras, the declining phase of the era of acquisitors undergoes an almost complete overhaul. Figure 4.3 displays the so-

cial pyramid in the ascending period of the acquisitive age, where acquisitors are on top, followed, in order, by intellectuals, warriors and laborers. However, the acquisitive mentality virus spreads potently and
quickly; it rapidly infects the intellectual mind, and some intellectuals
turn into intellectual acquisitors, who then dominate society during the
descending phase of this age.

In spite of major differences in their inherent qualities, all classes
make roughly equal contributions to the well-being of society. Without
the warriors there would be no law and order, which is crucial to happiness and prosperity; without the intellectuals there would be no con-
ceptualization of human rights, liberty and justice, and we would all
still be oppressed by dictators; without acquisitors the economy would
be in a poor state; and without laborers there would not be much production. Every good person is crucial to social welfare, and every bad
person is ultimately a societal parasite regardless of their innate qualities and achievements.

Once certain intellectuals discover that hoarding money and starting
a business are keys to social prestige and political influence, they quickly
learn the art of entrepreneurship from the acquisitors, and with their superior intellect eventually come to dominate the arteries of government.

Figure 4.3: Social Pyramid in the Ascending Phase of the Age of Acquisitors

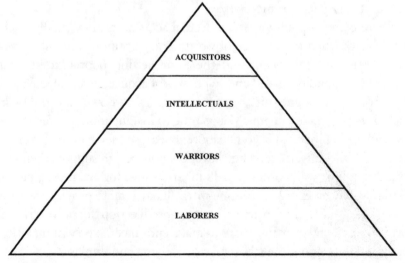

This usually happens after the acquisitors have caused a major economic crisis, and then the baton of leadership passes into the hands of intellectual acquisitors. That is when the engine of exploitation runs full speed. This is because the intellectual acquisitor combines in one brain the cunning of the bad intellectual and the greed of the acquisitor.

Thus in the descending phase of the acquisitive age, as shown in figure 4.4, the intellectual acquisitor is atop the social hierarchy, followed by acquisitors, a small number of remaining intellectuals (that is, those who love theories for the sake of theories), warriors and laborers.

SOCIAL REVOLUTION

The salient feature of the era of intellectual acquisitors is that the ruling elite amass wealth but make people believe that such an endeavor is good for society. For instance, they cut taxes for themselves while raising taxes for other classes, and yet are able to convince the public that such economic policies are in society's best interest. Or they may persuade you that God has blessed them with opulence so that they can take care of the indigent. They have the intellect to make you feel better even as they hit you, at least for a while. Dogmas proliferate at this point, and the laborer bears the maximum burden of exploitation.

Once the majority of intellectuals become acquisitive, materialism degenerates into supermaterialism. There are no more religious or ethical restraints on the avarice of the elite, and as the public follows its leaders, everything gets commercialized.

There comes a point when intellectual acquisitors are virtually unchallenged; that's when the process of wealth concentration runs full throttle, with the rich getting richer and the poor getting poorer at incredible speeds. The boundless greed and hypocrisy of acquisitive intellectuals ultimately torments the majority of people. Salaries go down, and the bulk of society is forced to devote much of its time to making money. Warriors and intellectuals then have to become laborers because they have little time left for the finer pursuits of life. They have to labor hard to support themselves and their children. The intellectual's inherent love for art, music, painting and philosophy gives way to routine work all day long to provide the means for family survival. The warrior's innate predilection for adventure and sport is replaced by overtime work to make ends meet. The vast majority of society comes to adopt the laborers' way of living and thinking.

Figure 4.4: Social Pyramid in the Descending Phase of the Age of Acquisitors

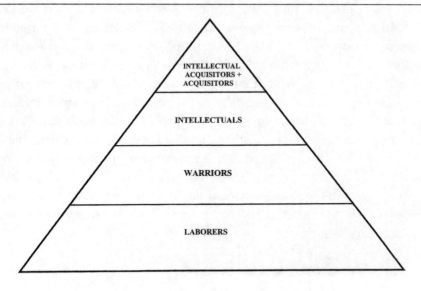

Only two classes then remain—acquisitors and laborers, or the haves and have-nots. The age of acquisitors eventually turns into the age of laborers, which may now be called the acquisitive-cum-labor age, in which the acquisitive intellectual is dominant. But many traits of the first era of laborers come to afflict society, which essentially gets divided into two groups, one consisting of all the wealthy acquisitors, and the other comprising the destitute and the middle class. The poor include the physical workers, and the middle class includes those erstwhile warriors and intellectuals now forced into toiling long hours for their survival.

For a while, people suffer through the deceit and exploitation of the reigning class. They maintain their lifestyle by increasingly getting into debt. Acquisitors now have a field day. They make money left and right. They enrich themselves through their control over businesses, farms and factories, and through lending money to the other classes.

This is the time that creates a group of disgruntled laborers from the former warriors and intellectuals. New leaders emerge from this group. Fed up with the status quo, one day they overthrow the ruling elite with the help of the masses, culminating in a social revolution of workers. It is through this process that the social cycle starts anew.

If the leaders of this revolution were formerly intellectuals, the change is peaceful; if they were formerly warriors, there is much bloodshed. In any case, rebelling against the elite is not easy; it takes immense courage to oppose a regime and become revolutionary. So those who muster such courage, no matter what their initial grouping, are the true soldiers, who then start another warrior age, which begins with an ascending or magnanimous phase. With the return of the warrior mentality, many features of the first eras of warriors make a comeback, but some novel and progressive institutions also appear because of inevitable social evolution through time. Once again the acquisitors, having lost their credibility, go back to a lower status. The public remembers their acts of oppression and imposes restraints on their acquisitiveness. This way the social cycle goes on and on, as we shall see starting with the next chapter.

CHAPTER 5

WESTERN SOCIETY

Western society, defined normally by its Judeo-Christian ethic, is by far the most dominant culture in the world today. In the past when the tiny island of England amassed the largest empire on our planet, it was often said that the sun would never set on the British Empire; yet today, England has lost its colonies, is back to its tiny size, and is ironically called Great Britain. Still, Western influence over the world's culture is perhaps greater than ever before. This is because while the British Empire is gone, something else from the West, which may be called the American business empire, has taken its place. The American version has no colonies, but, because of its vast economy, the Internet and the computer revolution, its clout and business practices are perhaps the most pervasive ever in the world.

How does the law of social cycle apply to Western culture and civilization? That is what I now explore. Many historians begin their study of the West from the Roman era, which will be our starting point as well. Much more has been written about Europe and the United States than about any other society. With so much information available, Western civilization best proves the assertions made by Sarkar and myself regarding the inevitability of the social pattern.

The ancient history of the West can be studied very briefly in terms of the law of social cycle. If we start from the Roman Empire, it is clear that the age of warriors then prevailed in Western society, lasting from just before the time of Christ to nearly the end of the fifth century, when the last Western emperor was overthrown by warlords from the colonies. Then came the rule of intellectuals represented by the priest-hood of the Catholic Church, which was headed by a pope. At that time priests dominated society with the help of their ideas and theories. This period lasted until the end of the tenth century, and was followed by the rule of the wealthy, represented by rich landlords. Their dominion is known as feudalism, which thus established the age of acquisitors. Land was the main form of wealth at the time, and many landed magnates were richer than their king. They displayed a highly acquisitive mental-ity, always striving to expand their domains.[1]

THE FEUDALISTIC AGE OF ACQUISITORS

Since today much of the world lives in another era of acquisitors, we should study the previous acquisitive age in detail, so that we can com-prehend what is happening in our times. This way we can compare our lifestyles and mores with those that prevailed when landed barons were at the peak of the social hierarchy. We will find that there are a lot of similarities between feudalism and capitalism, at least in terms of the ac-quisitive tendencies of the elite and their followers.

As I outlined in chapter 4, an acquisitor is someone whose intellect runs mostly after money or wealth, and when the wealthy become politi-cally prominent by purchasing the services of the other three classes, the acquisitive era begins. Most of the intellectuals then change their tune and offer ideas that justify the primacy of the rich, while the warriors fight wars and anarchy to protect the wealth of the opulent.

Such an age came to prevail in western Europe at the beginning of the tenth century, although its foundation had been laid in the previous century, which saw the vanishing of what is known as the Carolingian dynasty or Charlemagne's empire. Following the emperor's death in 814, the central government of the kings became so weak that a large number of nobles, possessing vast estates, declared independence and assumed the powers of administration. Just as Germanic barbarians had helped bring the priesthood (or intellectuals) to power in the sixth century, so did the invading Northmen hordes help the landlords or acquisitors at the end of the ninth century. The Northmen, also known as the Vikings, were based in the northernmost nations of Scandinavia—that is, today's Norway, Sweden and Denmark. The rough Baltic Sea had cut them off from the influence of Christianity. Their invasions began in 793 and became frequent in the next century. They destroyed much that came in their way, including villages, towns, crops and monasteries. Their ax fell equally on everyone. It was only toward the end of the ninth century that they were repulsed by powerful nobles, who by then had built impregnable castles.

With their monasteries destroyed, the priests took refuge with the nobles. It was through this sequence of events that the main task of the state, defending people from invaders, passed into the hands of the landed nobility. After maintaining law and order, the nobles assumed other functions of government—namely, the provision of justice, collection of taxes and management of the economy. At the same time, the Vikings settled in different parts of Europe, which was then divided into small kingdoms—one each in Italy, Germany and France, and two each in Burgundy and England, while Spain was under the rule of the Muslims.

The chief hallmark of the new kingdoms was their essentially feudal character, which European scholars define as a society in which the political and economic power is primarily in the hands of rich landlords, while people serve them in terms of well-defined contractual obligations. Everyone is a vassal to someone, including the overlord, who is a vassal to his king. According to historians E. M. Burns and P. L. Ralph:

> Feudalism may be defined as a structure of society in which the powers of government are exercised by private barons over persons economically dependent on them. It is a system of overlordship and vassalage in which the right to govern is a contractual relationship involving reciprocal obligations.[2]

In other words, feudal nobles enjoy the power of government simply because their people are economically dependent on them. This is precisely what defines an age of acquisitors, who rule not because of their superior intellect or physical strength but because of their command over the means of production, which in those days was based primarily on land. Thus the second half of the Middle Ages, lasting from the tenth to the fourteenth century, was an acquisitive age.

It goes without saying that feudalism was not the same everywhere in Europe. Even democracy today is not the same everywhere in the Western world. While Britain has a prime minister as its chief, the United

States has a president. In the same way, feudalism differed from place to place. In some places kings were powerful and the central authority was strong, but such scenarios were more exceptions than rules. Even powerful kings had to appease their landlords, such as dukes, barons, earls and margraves. Indeed some of the landlords had more land and property than their king. Similarly today the U.S. president has to defer to his wealthy supporters.

Once acquisitors came to power, the popular theory of government could not but change its tune. No longer did scholars rationalize the absolute rule of the king or the pope. On the contrary, in the later Middle Ages the popular idea was that man should not yield to the tyranny of any sovereign—a viewpoint that collided with the early preachings of the church, which asserted that the state had been created by God to help man expiate his sin, so the ruler must always be obeyed. No longer was the ruler a maker of the law; he was merely an administrator of the law. So just as the ruling mentality changes, popular theories also change to appeal to the interests of the dominant class.

At this juncture, the jurisprudence of the early Roman Republic (before the empire), when the wealthy ruled, was now back in vogue.[3] This was the case because in both times the acquisitive age prevailed. The scholars and philosophers were different, but the mentality underlying the written word was the same. Thus, historically, whenever the acquisitive era has appeared in the West, the government has been decentralized and in their self-interest the intellectuals have offered new theories to rationalize the social supremacy of the wealthy.

Once land holdings became the principal source of power and perks, the elite sought to expand their domains through matrimony and petty feuds. So small-scale battles among the barons were common, and the losers had to give up a parcel of their property. Occasionally kings warred with each other over land. At that time the nobles provided armies and money to their king.

Thus most regions in Europe were organized in this segmentary way. A region usually had a king at the top of the hierarchy, but his power was limited; the real authority belonged to his vassals—the dukes and barons—who in turn provided protection to their vassals, including the priests and army officers, commonly called knights. The knights in turn were obligated to take care of their vassals, the peasants and the serfs.

In feudal society, therefore, kings and nobles were the dominating acquisitors, priests and philosophers the intellectuals, knights the warriors, and peasants and serfs the laborers. As the ruling mentality changed, the rest of society along with various institutions changed as well.

Who were these serfs? They were freed slaves or peasants facing harsh times, who needed land to plow and farm. They leased land from the landlord, and paid him by toiling on his other farms. The landlord also had the right to impose fees on his serfs. Both the lords and churchmen treated serfs as virtual slaves.

In terms of living standard, the acquisitive age that began toward the end of the tenth century dwarfed anything that had come before. The prosperous European economy had been shattered by the fall of the Roman Empire. Farming, industry and cities had all been blighted, and famines and pestilence were common.

Once the church monopoly on education eroded, modern universities and embryonic sciences developed new inventions, and technology began to improve. The impact of these developments was first felt in the farm economy, which was the primary source of livelihood at the time. Agricultural productivity went up sharply, as much as 50 percent above the level common in the previous era of intellectuals, benefiting mostly the landlord but also his serfs.[4]

There were improvements in transportation as well—modest by today's standards, but they revolutionized the late medieval economy. They helped the agricultural surplus move to towns and cities, and laid the foundation for new industries. They increased consumer demand and large-scale production in factories. Industry and commerce prospered, as did international trade.

Until the economy revived, the serfs chafed under the crushing burden of hard physical labor and the myriad fees they owed to their lord, who obtained the fees in kind, not cash. But with the growth in population, farm prices increased and the peasants earned larger incomes from their portion of farm production. They found it more convenient to pay rent to their lord in terms of a fixed sum of money rather than in physical labor. This way they freed themselves from serfdom. This development is known as commutation, which did a lot to ease the plight of the serfs. Relieved from their obligations to perform free labor for the lord, they began to live as free citizens. Their living standard improved immensely.[5]

Thus, although the acquisitive era began with serfs ground under the wheels of poverty and oppression, by the thirteenth century many of them had gained economic freedom. Clearly all sections of society had benefited from the general advance in the economy. With prosperity came the surge of cities, which were initially run by the landed nobility, but in time became free from feudal control. They were administered by councils of elected merchants, and thus still dominated by acquisitors. Some labor unions also came into being in the form of craft guilds that set product prices and wage rates.

Women fared better in the cities as well. Many engaged in an assortment of trades and even dominated some industries. However, economic discrimination was commonplace; then as now, female wages, for the same kind of work, were lower than those of men. Historian V. L. Bullough describes the city life of women in this way:

> Throughout Europe they dominated the manufacture of beer and much of the processes of textile manufacture. In fact, the very word "spinster" would indicate that spinning was not only the regular occupation of all women but also the habitual means of support for many of the unmarried. Still many craft regulations excluded females, and when they did work they often did so at wages lower than those of the men.[6]

But despite gains by women and by landless peasants, wealth was still concentrated in the hands of the clergy and the aristocracy. Two economic historians, E. K. Hunt and H. G. Sherman, observe:

> Thus the manor might be secular or religious (many times secular lords had religious overlords), but the essential relationships between lords and serfs were not significantly affected by this distinction. There is little evidence that serfs were treated any less harshly by religious lords than by secular ones. The religious lords and the secular nobility were joint ruling classes; *they controlled the land and the power that went with it.*[7] [my emphasis]

In other words the main source of social domination for both religious and secular overlords was their control over wealth. The Church's holdings and wealth concentration continued to grow, and led to a gradual economic decline for the masses toward the end of the thirteenth century. Many knights and serfs mortgaged their homes and went into debt. They borrowed money from city and village merchants to try to maintain their lifestyles. Yet the Church would not relent on collecting its tithe.

The rise of the West was catastrophically interrupted by the bubonic plague of 1348. Over a third of the population succumbed, giving rise to a tremendous shortage of labor. The so-called Black Death was the worst pandemic in European history. This episode could not but shake the very foundations of feudalism, which had all along rested on the slippery slope of an excess labor supply.

The population blight doubly hurt the landlords. Rents sank for their surplus land, while wages soared. The nobles responded by rescinding the freedoms they had granted the serfs under commutation and tried to reinstate the labor obligations as rental payments. The peasants, of course, resisted vigorously. Peasant revolts broke out all over Europe, with massive destruction of life and property. These rebellions were crushed with intense brutality, but the relatively cozy world of the overlords was irrevocably disrupted. It is not difficult to see parallels to the West of today, where the more equitable wealth distribution of a generation ago has vastly eroded, and economies are fragile enough to be shattered by a chance event such as a plague. Could we be on the verge of another cycle of chaos and disruption?[8]

SOCIAL REVOLUTIONS BY THE COMMANDERS

In addition to the plague and economic decline, the West suffered from centuries of warfare, including the Hundred Years War between England and France. The war led to the creation of large standing armies, as well as to greater centralization of power under the monarch—a development that foreshadowed the rise of absolute monarchs. A similar development occurred in Spain, which freed itself from the Muslim control after many years of warfare. New military technology also aided the rise of the state. For example, the discovery of gunpowder made the nobles' castles vulnerable. The king could now send an army and bring sense to a defiant vassal.

By the end of the fifteenth century, despotic nation-states had come into being in much of western Europe, each ruled by an all-powerful king or queen backed by the army. The wealthy nobles had been crushed and their functions of government taken over by royal appointees. An efficient, centralized state also favored the collection of taxes and control over the nation's wealth. Thus some military commanders such as Henry VII in England, Louis XI in France and the duo of Queen Isabella and Prince Ferdinand in Spain brought about social revolutions in their nations and put an end to the rule of wealth in society. They started a new age of warriors.

The great loser in these realignments of power was the Church. The words of W. K. Ferguson and G. Brunn make this clear:

> In a great many ways the fourteenth and fifteenth centuries were disastrous ones for the Catholic Church. The papacy, with its wide claims to supremacy over all Catholic Christians, had come into violent conflict with the growing power of the centralized territorial states and been defeated. National interests had combined with moral disapproval to break the vast authority that the church had wielded during High Middle Ages.[9]

Thus the rising power of the national monarchs had humbled the popes by the fifteenth century. The Protestant Reformation followed, and soon after church power was broken beyond repair by the wars of religion. Never again was the clergy to play an overwhelmingly dominant role in the lives of the people.

Economically, however, this blood-soaked era was a great success. In economist E. H. Tuma's words:

> The period extending roughly between A.D. 1500 and 1700 has been recognized as a critical one in the economic history of the western world. Some observers in fact suggest that the foundations of the economic upsurge of Europe and the West which occurred in the next two centuries were laid during this period.[10]

PRIME MINISTERS AND THE
SECULAR AGE OF INTELLECTUALS

The advent of new technology and commerce hastens human advance, and, with it, the speed of change in society. A new age came into being between 1460 and 1485, when feudal nobles were overthrown in France, Spain and England. These were the major centers of civilization in the

West, and what transpired there went on to determine the character of Western society.

England was the smallest of the three nations in size as well as population, but its economy and institutions developed much faster than those of the other two nations. England's technological advances surpassed those on the European continent. This may have partly resulted from the presence of the parliament that advised the Tudor kings and somewhat tempered the absolute rule.

The most illustrious Tudor monarch turned out to be a woman, Elizabeth I. The industrial revolution began in her reign, and the British economy made important strides. The queen never married and died in 1603 without naming an heir. The parliament then invited her cousin, James VI of Scotland, to wear the crown. This turned out to be a fortuitous development that had important consequences for social evolution.

First, a precedent had been set to show that the parliament could decide who sat on the British throne. Second, the influence and prestige of the legislature was greatly enhanced, so the king could no longer completely ignore its wishes. Third, the subsequent monarchs had none of the qualities that had distinguished the Tudors. It was therefore not surprising that the new king did not get along well with the legislature. But James died prematurely in 1625 and was succeeded by his equally mediocre son, Charles I. Eventually there was so much acrimony between the parliament and the king that England plunged into a virulent civil war that ended in the beheading of the monarch.

This was followed by a short interlude of what is known as the Protectorate, wherein monarchy was all but abolished. The Protectorate failed miserably, so the parliament invited Charles II, the son of the beheaded king, back to power. He was succeeded by his son James II, who wanted to restore the former power of the monarchy. Another conflict ensued, and ended in a bloodless coup of 1689, called the Glorious Revolution, in which James abdicated his throne and was replaced by William of Orange. British monarchy then emerged with much-diminished power relative to the parliament, which was headed by a prime minister. This started another era of intellectuals, a secular one, in Western society.

Other nations of Europe were not far behind. Not that the parliamentary style of government also emerged elsewhere, only that real power passed into the hands of highly educated advisers to the kings and queens. In France, the adviser was called the prime minister; in other nations like Prussia he was known as the chancellor. This was an age of shared power, in which the bureaucracy and the adviser shared authority with the king and his army. The theories that had exalted the absolute rule in the previous period were now replaced by those cherishing human dignity and people's rights and duties.

THE CAPITALISTIC AGE OF ACQUISITORS

In the nineteenth century, the capitalistic era, with money and wealth the primary sources of political power and social supremacy, assumed the general aspect it wears today.

At the end of the eighteenth century, the European economy was fettered by numerous rules, regulations and theories that exalted the economic interest of the state over that of individuals. In time, capitalists and their employees, who were beginning to join the middle class, became restless and objected to laws that restrained their behavior and growth. They joined the ranks of protesters who wanted to make elections more democratic. Thus the first Reform Bill was passed in England in 1832 to enhance the influence of the people in elections, but it increased the number of voters only slightly. The real power remained with the prime minister and his advisers, that is, with the peers of the House of Lords, who could still easily manipulate elections.

But in 1867 another Reform Bill was passed that added a significant number of new people to the list of voters. This was the beginning of the rise of democracy; with it came the rise of the might of money, which became necessary to win elections. Consequently, capitalists, with coffers full of cash, exerted the real power behind the prime minister and his advisers. The wealthy obtained laws that loosened regulations and made it easier to generate profits.

The development of the United States has been slightly different. At first, the new republic was dominated by landed magnates of great wealth, who controlled elections to legislative assemblies. After the Civil War, power passed into the hands of rich industrialists and bankers. From the country's birth, the wealthy have been supreme in American society in one form or another. Yet in terms of its population, economy and global influence, America's early stature in the West was decidedly secondary to that of Britain and France. How then did it evolve into the world's only superpower—and more important, for our purposes, into its dominant business empire? That is the subject of the next chapter.

In brief, the second rotation of the social cycle in the West, because of the development of science and technology, has been much faster than before. First, feudalism was overthrown during the fifteenth century by a number of army commanders in England, France and Spain, who thus launched a social revolution against the age of acquisitors and reestablished the age of warriors. Then toward the end of the seventeenth century, intellectuals came back to power, this time in the guise of prime ministers and advisers to the kings. Ever since the mid-nineteenth century, capitalists have been dominant in the Western world, and they represent yet another era of the wealthy, or acquisitors, which has found its fullest expression in the United States, whose history is explored next.

CHAPTER 6

THE U.S. BUSINESS EMPIRE

The United States is currently the nerve center of Western society and capitalism, and its history deserves a separate analysis. What transpires in America sways the world. Amazingly enough, the entire planet has been propping up the wobbly U.S. economy for a long time. Foreign money is coming into the country as if it grows on trees. Global investors, with trillions parked in the swollen U.S. housing industry, seem to care little about the safety of their investments. This is the kind of treatment that colonies used to accord their occupiers. They would send copious gifts of money, gold and diamonds to curry favor with their conquerors. In other words, the United States appears to be getting the respect of an imperial power from the world. Does America then have an empire? The answer is yes; but it's a business empire.

Normally when we use such words we think of colonies, captured territories and conquered people. We speak of gruesome battles among nations for supremacy, and of vanquished regions held captive inside a large kingdom.

But what about a business empire? A nation's business hegemony may appear to differ radically from its colonial counterpart, but in reality the two share many similarities. Although a business empire does not have statutory political dominance over other countries, it does have commercial dominance, which may in turn give it some political sway. In a colonial empire, the imperial power has the highest living standard; it collects gifts and taxes from its subjects; its ideas, values, language and culture spread to conquered areas; it obtains cheap labor from the people under its dominion, and above all, it has military supremacy over its colonies. In all these respects, today's U.S. business hegemony has the features of a colonial empire.

The archetypal empire is ancient Rome, a vast kingdom that stretched from western Europe to northern Africa and western Asia. The Romans extracted taxes, raw materials and labor from their subjects. This gave the Romans the highest living standard within their domains. Their language, culture, ideas and values spread throughout their territories.[1]

Rome did it all with the force of arms. No city and nation in the vicinity was safe from the Roman legions. The defeated lands helped build a rich economy for the victors. The living standard in Rome was almost as high as in some advanced economies today. Roman prosperity arose from the use of new technology, capital accumulation and the cheap labor of captured slaves. The slaves worked in farms, factories and homes in return for food, clothing and shelter. In other words, they worked for a subsistence wage.

Rome was the cultural and commercial hub of the empire, especially in the first two centuries. People from imperial provinces wished to emigrate to that city and acquire Roman citizenship. They were ready to do anything to that end, even work voluntarily as slaves. Thus, slave labor, forced as well as unforced, built a rich Roman economy that included prosperous sectors in agriculture, manufacturing and commerce.

Roman trade flourished with its colonies as well as its neighboring empires of India, Persia and China. Major industries included pottery, textiles, metals and glass. They provided goods for export, while imports consisted mainly of spices, silk, jewelry and the all-important grain from Egypt.

The development of crop rotation and soil fertilization led to advances in agriculture, which, of course, was aided by slave labor. Yet, in spite of great prosperity, the economy was far from perfect even in the first two centuries of the empire, because high salaries and wealth were confined to the upper classes, especially the military.

In general, the Romans disliked physical work, which was reserved for the slaves, whose supply fell over time, and eventually resulted in industrial decline.[2] Furthermore, the empire ran a persistent trade deficit with its provinces, which included the captive nations. The deficits were financed partly by taxes collected from the provinces and partly by the export of precious metals that drained the kingdom of gold and silver. The sinking Roman economy finally led to the fall of the imperial western government in 476.

There are two main reasons for the fall of Rome. The economic blight was one, and extreme militarism was the other. In order to subjugate its colonies, the government had to maintain a vast army and navy, which exacted a heavy price. The state had to impose huge taxes, which fell mostly on farmers and businesses in the provinces, and to some extent on the Romans. Heavy taxation in turn hurt industry and commerce. Large military expenditures and the loss of prosperity were linked to each other.

Another archetypal example of an empire is Britain. Unlike Rome, it built its empire through commercial interests, especially the East India Company, which secured a foothold in India in the late seventeenth century. By the middle of the eighteenth century, Britain had established colonies in the Caribbean, North America and India.

Britain lost its American colonies in the American Revolution of 1776, but renewed its territorial expansion elsewhere in the nineteenth century. By World War I, British dominion extended over one-fourth of the world's population and land area.

Although England's empire was started by commercial interests, which had their own militias, British military control over the colonies was as total as that of Rome. Inside England, parliamentary democracy had begun following the Glorious Revolution, in 1689, but in the colonies British governors and army officers ruled with an iron hand. The subject citizens, though not treated as slaves, were allowed few rights.

Early in the twentieth century, Britain permitted self-rule in some of its territories such, as India and Australia, but the colonies wanted more. They had elections and legislative assemblies, but their powers were limited to matters of local concern. India, in fact, erupted into a mass movement against British rule, and finally gained independence in 1947. Earlier, in 1942, Britain had granted complete autonomy to Australia, and other colonies were gradually freed after 1947. By 1960, the empire had all but disappeared. What is remarkable is that most former British colonies gained freedom in a peaceful way, for the first time in history.

Britain exploited its domains in a variety of ways. As usual, the colonies benefited the imperial nation and helped raise its living standard. Britain encouraged the policy of free trade inside its territories, but imposed tariffs on manufactured imports from them. Thus, the colonies supplied cheap raw materials for protected British industry, in which England had an early lead because of its industrial revolution, but the colonies' manufacturing exports were restrained.

The colonies, of course, were not permitted to impose tariffs on their manufactured imports. In this way, they provided markets and cheap raw materials for British industry, which grew manifold. Textiles, machine tools, iron and ship-building, among many other industries, grew apace, but colonial manufacturing was destroyed by mass-produced goods coming from Britain. The colonies also ran trade surpluses to pay for services imported from Britain at highly inflated prices. The surplus foreign exchange so earned paid for the high salaries that British governors and civil and army officers earned for their work in the colonies. Thus, British economic policy was for the sole benefit of the English at the expense of subject nations.[3]

Unlike Rome, Britain did not force its subjects into slavery, but it did obtain cheap labor from them in another way. The territories were used to recruit soldiers, who, while receiving subsistence wages, fought for Britain to defend its colonies in World War I and World War II. The British army benefited from cheap labor, which freed resources for Britain's own economic development.

However, the monopolistic control over colonial labor and product markets left British industry vulnerable to competition from other advanced economies. British firms were not as efficient as the firms in Germany and the United States. Consequently, following the dissolution of the empire, Britain suffered a rapid economic decline relative to other developed countries. The nation faced inflation, labor unrest, trade deficits and a persistently weak currency.

There is no doubt that Britain exploited its colonies for national gain, but it also made useful contributions to their social structure. It introduced them to democratic institutions, modern technology and some degree of industrialization. Democracy was alien to India before it was conquered by the East India Company. Indian intellectuals studying in England learned English, British law and the concept of parliamentary rule. As a result, after independence India did not revert to the monarchy and dictatorship that had been prevalent prior to its annexation into the empire.

The British also helped Indians free themselves from some of their worst parasites. For instance, the centuries-old practice of Sati, in which widows were burned alive along with their dead husbands, was banned and the culprits were sent to jails. British law, language and culture thrive in former colonies even today.

THE U.S. BUSINESS EMPIRE

The term "business empire" creates the impression of enormous wealth and opulence. It generates visions of multimillionaires and billionaires trotting across the globe to manage their corporations. We tend to think of business empires as private, the domain of famous tycoons; the term is rarely, if ever, used for a nation. In what sense, then, does the United States of America have a business empire?

The brief description of the two colonial empires presented above, one modern (the British) and the other ancient (the Roman), reveal four common traits. First, the empire is created through the force of arms, either by military officers or by commercial interests. Second, the ruling nation extracts cheap labor from its colonies. Third, the colonies run trade surpluses that raise the living standard of their rulers. Finally, the language, institutions and culture of the victors spread across imperial territories.

Of the four features just listed, three apply to the U.S. supremacy around the world today. The United States does not seek to conquer and colonize other nations, although it is militarily strong enough to do so. Yet its economic policies and multinational corporations have enabled the United States to enjoy benefits that in the past accrued only to imperial powers. What about today's Iraq? Is America an occupying power there? Not really, because, unlike the true colonists, the United States wants to leave the territory as soon as possible. (For more on Iraq, see chapter 10.)

Following World War II, America pursued a policy of free trade and liberalized foreign investment. It cut its own tariffs and persuaded many nations to trim theirs. This policy won the United States privileges that it could not have secured on the battlefield. In the Korean war, China and North Korea held America to a draw; in the Vietnam war, the

United States suffered a crushing defeat in spite of overwhelming military superiority. But what the United States failed to win militarily, it won through its economic and business policies. It eventually defeated communism, which, because of internal contradictions, has been more or less abandoned by the world.

Today, both China and Vietnam seek expanded economic ties with the United States. They want to export as many of their products as possible to the vast American market. Scores of Fortune 500 companies have started subsidiaries in China, as well as in Vietnam. The Chinese economy, in fact, has become dependent on U.S. trade, and the United States, as discussed later, is increasingly dependent on the Chinese holdings of American government bonds.

America does not dominate other nations politically, but it dominates them commercially. In fact, in this respect, U.S. dominance is far more pervasive than that of colonial empires. This is because colonial-era military conquests rarely covered more than a fourth of the world's land and population, but U.S. business and cultural influence now extends virtually over the whole planet.

The fall of the Berlin Wall in 1989 and the subsequent fall of Soviet communism left the United States as the world's sole superpower. Immediately after World War II, nations were divided into three blocs—the American bloc, the Soviet bloc and a group of nonaligned nations. The capitalist United States and the communist Soviet Union competed vigorously for influence in nonaligned countries.

Even though America offered them generous financial aid, the nonaligned group feared and respected the Soviet dictatorship and its vast army equipped with nuclear weapons. In many developing nations, the communist ideology was more popular than capitalist thought. Thus, although the Soviet Union could not match the United States economically, it strongly influenced the developing world.

All this changed abruptly after the disintegration of the Soviet Union in the early 1990s. Russian influence waned in the Soviet satellites of Poland, Hungary, East Germany, Czechoslovakia and Romania, while some of its former provinces such as Ukraine, Georgia and Azerbaijan seceded from the Soviet confederation. As a result, after 1991, Russia suffered an economic depression, which lasted throughout the 1990s.

Within a colonial empire, the ruling nation has the strongest army. America today does not own colonies, but its armed forces are the strongest in the world. This gives the country a level of political influence that others lack. For instance, the United States gets its way at the United Nations, at least more than any other country.

The second feature of a national empire is that the imperial state obtains cheap labor from its colonies. This trait certainly applies to the United States today. Cheap labor comes to America in two ways. Immigration to the country, legal and illegal, expands the U.S. labor supply and restrains domestic wages. Illegal immigrants coming mostly from Mexico and Latin America work for subsistence wages; were it not for their influx, American wages would be much higher. It should be mentioned here that immigration to America is voluntary and eagerly sought, for the country is perceived as the land of riches and freedom. Similarly, in their heydays Britain and Rome also attracted hordes of immigrants. In fact, they still do, but American citizenship is coveted most around the world.

Second, American multinationals employ thousands of workers in Latin America, Asia and Africa, paying local wages that are just a fraction of U.S. salaries. Products made by this labor force, which includes child labor forbidden in the United States, are then imported into the country, further depressing U.S. wages. However, this practice generates exorbitant profits for the multinationals and exceptionally high incomes for their executives.

Here again the United States gets these benefits voluntarily without the force of arms, but the benefits are substantial for the business elite. Businessmen are the richest group in America. Their income and wealth have skyrocketed since 1980, while the incomes of others have been stagnant or falling. The tax burden of the rich has declined while that of the poor and the middle class has risen significantly. Thus in the U.S. business empire, as in colonial empires of the past, cheap labor from abroad disproportionately benefits the elite.

The third and perhaps the most interesting feature of an empire is that the ruler forces trade surpluses on its colonies, while running trade deficits itself to raise its own level of consumption. Likewise, the United States has enjoyed a high level of trade deficit in relation to the rest of the world since 1983 without firing a single bullet.

In the ancient past, Rome obtained free goods from its provinces by imposing heavy taxes on them, and the revenue so collected financed a part of its trade shortfall. Britain also received goods freely from its territories by forcing them to pay for high-priced administrative services provided by its citizens. Now the United States gets some products from the world at virtually no cost. How is this possible?

The U.S. dollar is the single most sought after currency in the world, which needs increasing amounts of the greenback to finance growing international trade. A country's money is called a key currency, if it is globally acceptable to carry out commerce. The dollar is a key currency, and so are the yen, the pound and the euro. But the dollar is the most popular of them all.

The world does not want to hoard large amounts of pounds and yen, but it has been hoarding dollars since 1983. In other words, America pays for its import surplus, the excess of imports over exports, through paper dollars, and its only visible cost is the cost of printing the money, especially the large denomination $100 notes, which the world seems to love. Interestingly, more such bills are in circulation outside than within the United States.

Why the world is happy to accept paper money in exchange for solid goods will be discussed later. For now it may be noted that America has had a persistent import surplus relative to the rest of the world since the early 1980s at practically no cost.

Never before has a nation run an enduring and expanding trade deficit with free nations without exporting silver and gold. But America has somehow managed to do so. To be sure, the country also had a persistent import surplus in the nineteenth century, but at that time, the Europeans lent money for American investment projects from which they expected to earn profits. The size of their loans effectively determined the size of the U.S. deficit, which though persistent was rather small. But now there seems to be no constraint on American imports. The world simply exchanges its quality goods for paper dollars and then invests its dollars back into U.S. stocks and bonds.

In the past, a country's ability to borrow money from abroad limited its trade deficit. But now America simply imports as much as it wants, and the world pockets the dollars. Of course, other nations are still subject to the old-fashioned discipline imposed by the need to balance their trade.

Even other key-currency nations such as Britain and Japan cannot afford to run persistent import surpluses without suffering currency depreciations or rising interest rates needed to attract foreign money. But the United States is the one country today with a hefty trade deficit and a stable currency—all variegated fruits of its business empire.

The fourth and final feature of an empire concerns the spread of the ruler's language, customs and culture across imperial territories. Here also, the United States enjoys the same privilege. English is the language of the elite in most countries. For this, of course, Britain deserves as much credit as the United States. Books published by U.S. presses are the most popular around the world. They are avidly sought by youth, who love America's pop culture and music. The United States is the largest exporter of movies and television entertainment.

Teenagers around the globe know more about American film stars than about their own political leaders. Fast food from the likes of Mc-Donald's is not just an American craze; it is now becoming a worldwide craze. American materialism is also fast infecting the world's youth. Many foreign TV programs and movies display the same type of sex and violence that afflicts U.S. entertainment channels. In India, Bollywood mimics Hollywood.

Thanks to U.S. influence, capitalism has spread all over the world. Soviet communism and its ideology are gone; similarly, China is fast adopting American production techniques and methods. Most of its state enterprises are being dismantled or privatized to improve their efficiency. Today Chinese communism lingers in politics, but its economy is fast transforming into capitalistic modes of production.

It is no exaggeration to say that American global influence has reached new heights since the Persian Gulf conflict of 1991, towering even above its international status following World War II. Much of the world was annihilated in that war, while the U.S. economy emerged unchallenged and unscathed. American industry had practically no competitors, although left-wing philosophies successfully challenged the creed of capitalism in the postwar period. Soviet communism did not have much to show by way of economic success, but it had millions of believers.

The Soviet alliance with the Allies until 1946 brought Russia great prestige. This, combined with the subsequent Chinese revolution in 1949, gave communism an aura of moral superiority over capitalism. Capitalism appeared to be for the rich, communism for the masses. But that was then. Now America's former enemies or competitors—Russia, China, Vietnam—seek expanded economic ties with the United States.

Again, a major feature of an empire is that the ruler obtains free gifts of goods and services from the colonies through its trade deficit. America enjoys that privilege today and has ever since the early 1980s. So now the U.S. business empire is at its zenith.

GLOBALIZATION OF THE U.S. ECONOMY

How did the United States manage to amass the largest business empire ever built? The answer to this question illuminates how dozens of top American executives have succeeded in becoming billionaires.

Following World War II, the United States was the strongest economic power on earth. Its industrial might was unmatched, its technology envied and in demand all over the globe. What is interesting is that the country depended very little on foreign trade. In 1950, U.S. exports were just 5 percent of GDP, whereas U.S. imports were 4 percent of GDP. In the technical lingo of economics, the country was nearly a closed economy, impervious to foreign competition.

By contrast, the war had devastated other warring states—France, Britain, Russia, China, Japan, Germany and Italy. In order to contain the rising tide of communism, the United States launched what is known as the Marshall Plan, as well as an economic policy of globalization. The idea was to help western Europe grow rapidly through financial aid as well as freer trade. America also aided Japan through the export of technology and by opening its markets to Japanese goods. This way the United States hoped to shore up its allies to counter the communist menace from the Soviet Union and China—a matter of great American concern during the 1950s after Germany and Japan became free from Allied and U.S. occupation.

Powered by U.S. aid and trade, western Europe and especially Japan grew apace and turned into unexpectedly strong competitors. American businessmen failed to foresee the challenge that emerged from war-ravaged nations. By 1970, the enduring U.S. export surplus turned into a deficit. The world was awash in dollars.

Unlike today, other nations at the time were not ready to accumulate dollars indefinitely. The world wanted payment in gold, which was plentiful in the United States, but still not enough to finance a persistent trade deficit.

After protracted trade negotiations among the G–7 countries (the United States, Britain, France, Germany, Canada, Italy and Japan), the link between the dollar and gold was severed in 1973, and the world moved from fixed exchange rates to a flexible-rate system. Until then, the international price of gold had been fixed at $35 per ounce, and all other currencies were linked to the dollar. The yen, for instance, had been fixed at the rate of 360 to one, but in 1973 and thereafter, it began to rise, as a dollar bought fewer yen. Currency values were no longer fixed, but were determined by market forces of supply and demand.

The idea was that flexible exchange rates would eliminate the trade deficit and thus the U.S. need to export gold. In fact, this is what happened in the 1970s, and the U.S. import surplus all but vanished. This occurred in spite of the global turmoil caused by the rocketing price of oil, which raised the U.S. oil import bill manifold.

Economic winds, however, changed direction in the 1980s. High inflation and the need to curb it through restrained bank lending sharply raised American interest rates. Foreign money chasing high yields poured into the United States. This raised the global demand for dollars and caused an appreciation of the currency. Expensive currency meant pricey American goods abroad and cheaper foreign goods at home. Consequently, U.S. exports plummeted while imports soared, and the trade deficit made a return, this time to stay forever.

But such a trade deficit now required other nations to accept large piles of dollars, rather than gold. What had changed? The main change had occurred in Japan, where declining birth rates had caused a slowdown in the growth of consumer demand. In order to keep growing at the old high rates, Japanese companies began to ship increasing amounts of their production abroad, especially to the United States. This way, they earned more dollars while also maintaining their growth.

In the meantime, the U.S. government needed to borrow large sums of money to finance its growing red ink. Japanese companies and the Bank of Japan used part of their dollar hoard to buy U.S. government bonds. Another part went into the purchase of U.S. factories and real estate.

The reinvestment of Japan's surplus into American assets prevented the depreciation of the dollar, which normally would have accompanied the U.S. trade deficit. This suited Japan fine, but in the process it made the nation dependent on foreign, especially American, demand.

After 1985, the G-7 countries collectively adopted a policy of dollar devaluation to bring the U.S. deficit down. The dollar fell sharply relative to other currencies, but the deficit fell sluggishly, mainly because several years of increasing globalization had flooded America with manufactured imports. In the process the domestic industrial base had shriveled.

Many U.S. industries had been in retreat—autos, consumer electronics, machine tools, textiles, shoes and so on. In spite of the dollar depreciation, the home production of goods and services did not expand enough to match home demand. The difference between the two equaled the trade deficit.

The Japanese economic miracle became a role model for its neighbors. South Korea, Malaysia, Taiwan, Singapore, Hong Kong and even China began to emulate Japan. America was the export market they all coveted. If, in the process, they had to accumulate paper dollars and reinvest them in American assets, then so be it. Japan had done this with great success, and the other countries followed suit. In fact, China, which by 2005 had an export surplus of nearly $200 billion, now regularly bests Japan in this game.[4]

THE CENTER AND THE PERIPHERIES

At present, not just Asia but the entire planet is willing to pile up greenbacks. How do we explain this unprecedented behavior? As mentioned earlier, during the early 1970s, other nations, especially those in Europe, were reluctant to hoard American dollars indefinitely. Instead, they wanted gold for their trade surplus. But not anymore; now even Europe and OPEC are piling up dollars. It is hard to explain this phenomenon without comparing it to similar events in colonial empires.

We have already seen that colonial empires usually force trade deficits on their captive audiences. The United States has been enjoying a similar privilege since 1983, but not by force of arms. How did this happen? Asia, of course, wants dollars for its own industrialization, because its meager consumer demand cannot support large-scale factories. But why does the globe as a whole want dollars?

Every empire has a hub that is surrounded by other states. The center is under the direct control of the ruling people, more particularly their elite, while the states are under their indirect control. The appointees of the ruler run the colonies to further the interests of the imperial nation. They collect gifts and taxes and pass them on to the hub. Their own power and privileges stem from the stronghold of the ruling elite. Provincial elites strive to empower the central elite so that they themselves have the power and prestige to govern their own lands. Thus, the self-interest of territorial governors appointed by Rome aligned with the self-interest of the Roman generals. The two acted in unison to enrich themselves and stay in power.

In today's business empire, America is at the center, while most other countries are the surrounding provinces. The United States does not appoint the governors of these states, but the rulers of such states see their self-interest aligned with the interest of the American elite. Japan's ruling party wants a prosperous and stable America so it can keep its export machine alive, prevent a rise in joblessness, and thus maintain its power. Hence the Bank of Japan continues to pile up American bonds, keeping U.S. interest rates low and the economy strong; China, Europe, OPEC and others do the same. They help perpetuate their own power base and the power base of the elite in the United States.

The world already owns trillions of dollars of American assets, yet it keeps accumulating more. The export surplus nations have, in fact, become U.S. business colonies. You may call this the American colonization of the world economy. The interesting part is that all this is a purely voluntary arrangement.

As foreign individuals and central banks purchase U.S. bonds, they end up investing billions of dollars in the American economy every year. This is the secret of U.S. economic growth since the early 1980s. However, almost all the foreign money goes into American consumption, for which the bill has to come due someday, perhaps in the near future.

The interests of the rich in America are linked to those of the rich in other nations. The surplus goods and services from the rest of the world flow at little direct cost into the center, which is the United States. The foreigners accept dollars, which are cheap to print; but there could be high indirect costs related to this practice in the future, because it is now generating economic chaos in the form of financial imbalances around the globe. Thus the elite of all nations are trying to preserve the American business empire. In wishful thinking, this process could last forever; but, as will be shown in chapter 10, it is a corrupting process that keeps wages low and profits high all over the world. It is an artificial arrangement that magnifies income and wealth inequalities around the globe, and contains the seeds of self-destruction. It cannot go on and on.

AMERICA IN THE LABORER AGE

As described in the previous chapter, the United States and other Western nations are now in the age of laborers, in which the wealthy acquisitors pull economic strings and every other class supplies hard labor, effectively making the rich even richer. This acquisitive-cum-labor era actually started around 1973–1974, when the president and vice president, Richard Nixon and Spiro Agnew, were dethroned. Agnew resigned in 1973 after pleading no contest in federal court to charges of income tax evasion and bribery. A year later Nixon, mauled by the Watergate scandal, opted to quit rather than face certain impeachment by Congress.

These were unprecedented events in U.S. history. Both government leaders, not just one, had acted unethically and victimized their nation. This is precisely the kind of lawlessness and official arrogance that marks the laborer age, in which the dominant class increasingly turns to shoddy, even illegal, tactics in its pursuit of riches and power. Consequently, the moral fiber of the nation weakens, for the public consciously or unconsciously tends to follow its leaders. The end result is a steep jump in crime, duplicity and avarice, creating an "anything goes" atmosphere. It is not surprising that the 1970s were called the "Me generation," and the 1990s were known as the "decade of greed." Greed, and the use of fair means or foul in the pursuit of wealth, have become ubiquitous in today's America.

Following the Nixon-Agnew resignations, the abuse of power spread to lawmakers at the federal, state and local levels. Scandals have recently engulfed congressmen and state legislatures. Mayors, educators, senators, governors and police officers have been implicated in bribes and other illegal activities. Corruption seems endemic at every level of government. The scandals are too numerous to count, but to name a few: the accounting and bookkeeping fraud perpetrated by the likes of Enron, the analyst fraud committed by the nation's respected brokerage firms in the 1990s, the Tom Delay–Jack Abramoff scandal of the 2000s.[5]

The country faces a rising tide of crime, family breakdown, drug and alcohol addiction, divorce, pornography and child abuse, increasing destitution of the poor and the middle class, rapid expansion of debt, outrageous disparities in income and wealth, a massive economic hemorrhage brought about by enormous trade deficits and, above all, the dwindling real wage, as described in chapter 1. If there is a silver lining to these dark clouds, it is that such a tragic situation cannot last for long. A crisis is sure to erupt soon that will force the people to elect only responsible and honest leaders who will steer the nation, along with the world it leads, toward sanity in politics, economics and the general state of affairs.

THE CORRUPTION OF ECONOMIC POLICY

Any kind of corruption is bad; but the corruption of economic policy is perhaps the worst. Such malfeasance occurs when lawmakers not only enrich themselves but also deny just rewards to the downtrodden, that is, to those who have little bargaining power and are the weakest sections of society.

Consider, for instance, the behavior (or misbehavior) of the U.S. Congress since 1977 regarding its own salary increase. In the name of attracting high talent to the government, legislators have been awarding themselves with raises amounting to thousands of dollars a year. Parliamentary procedures have been so manipulated that no lawmaker is usually required to vote on the proposed income hike.

Finally, in 1987, the legislators voted to deny themselves a pay raise—but a day after the raise had already become law. Now this is duplicity and real chicanery. In January 1989, they sought to reward themselves with a raise of as much as 50 percent, again without casting a vote on the proposal. This time they failed, because the whole country was up in arms against such an open insult to our intelligence. However, you have to give high marks to the House of Representatives for diligence. In November 1989, barely ten months after the abortive effort for a pay rise, House members voted to grant themselves a salary increase of 40 percent spread over two years, although the Senate accepted only a 10 percent hike.

Another instance of the government's perfidy comes from the Social Security tax, which has been raised countless times since the 1970s. Everyone knows that the burden of this tax is heaviest on the poor and the middle class. The maximum Social Security tax on an individual was $374 in 1970, but soared to $6,885 by 2005, a whopping jump of 1,700 percent. The steepest climb in this tax occurred during the 1980s, when the payroll tax rate on the self-employed jumped from less than 10 percent to 14 percent. This was on top of the steep increase that had already occurred during the Carter administration. The payroll tax hike also occurred in the decade in which the Reagan-Bush administrations rewarded the rich by cutting top income tax rates in 1981 and 1986. As a result, those earning over $200,000 were taxed at a rate of 28 percent, whereas a couple with a taxable income of $72,000 paid a 33 percent rate. All this was done in the name of tax reform. Never before in U.S.

history has there been such a massive transfer of the tax burden from the affluent to the poor. But this is not all. With such heavy taxation of the worker, the Social Security program has been earning a growing surplus that has been used to finance the federal budget deficit, which was caused by the income tax cuts of the Reagan administration.[6]

The fundamental belief system that rationalizes such tax transformation is of course the well-known supply-side theory of economics, or tricklism, that contends that prosperity trickles down from the rich to the poor, something I first mentioned in chapter 1 and will discuss in detail in the next chapter.

The lawmakers, Democrats and Republicans alike, made sure that their annual pay hikes were subject to lower income taxes. Yet they could not bring themselves to maintain the meager lifestyle of the minimum-wage workers. For years they would not allow the minimum wage to catch up with inflation, while their own raises easily surpassed the growing cost of living. The Republicans were especially vicious in this matter. They took control of Congress in 1994; since 1997, the minimum wage has been constant at $5.15 per hour, while prices have jumped 30 percent. Such is our Congress; it is happy to pocket annual pay raises at puny tax rates, but it is reluctant to allow the destitute to live in an apartment and have three square meals a day. Minimum-wage workers today often cannot afford their housing and still be able to fill their stomachs; this is why we read about the working poor, and even about homeless people who have jobs, but can't afford a home and live in shelters.

Of course, the Republicans cry "joblessness" whenever a Democratic legislator tries to raise the minimum wage. This is simply the corruption of economic policy, because I have demonstrated elsewhere that whenever the minimum wage went up in the past—and this happened some 17 times—joblessness fell within 12 to 18 months. In fact, in 1969, when the nation had the highest minimum wage ever ($8 per hour in today's prices), the unemployment rate was the lowest in history, at barely 3.5 percent.[7]

The transformation of the tax burden and the plummeting minimum wage are two prime examples of corrupt economic policies. They create a double whammy: they are corrupt not only because they are unethical measures but also because they impoverish the country. Both the declining real minimum wage and regressive taxation, whereby the tax burden is transferred from the rich to the poor, raise unemployment and trim

GDP growth. Such is the testimony of history. Not only is congressional corruption unethical, it is also bad economic policy.

In spite of the growing public outcry against the state welfare for the rich, President George W. Bush proposed to cut the tax on capital gains and dividends, which is paid mostly by the affluent. This is heaping outrage upon outrage. There is thus a gaping chasm between the words and actions of the politicians; while their hearts bleed for the poor, their pockets overflow with money. While the rest of society toils hard to make ends meet, they don't shrink from extorting one perquisite after another.

MULTINATIONAL CORPORATIONS

Many countries, including developing ones like India and Mexico, have multinational corporations today. But U.S. multinationals are in a class of their own. Their top managers, the CEOs, have the highest salaries in the world. Japan, Germany, France and England also have global corporations, but managers there earn about a third of what their U.S. counterparts make. According to the Economic Policy Institute, "Not only are U.S. executives paid far better than U.S. workers, they also earn substantially more than CEOs in other advanced countries. U.S. CEOs earn three times the average of CEOs in the 13 other advanced countries for which there are comparable data. Only in one country, Switzerland, are CEOs paid even as much as 50 percent of what the average U.S. CEO makes."[8] Similarly, according to the Federal Reserve, while the CEO compensation in Britain was 22 times the pay of an average worker in 2004, in the United States it was 170 times, and in Japan only 11 times.[9]

Business privileges in America are simply outlandish. Even when some CEOs are fired, they get a huge package of benefits, known as golden parachutes. In reality, they are golden parasites, which are bad for company morale and promote a milieu of avarice and corruption. Stories of outsized CEO compensation abound. One prominent company awarded $300 million to a CEO's estate, to be paid after his death. Others have paid $10 million to $50 million in severance to departing executives after just a year's service. The most outlandish payment occurred in 2005, when James Simons, a hedge fund manager, earned $1.5 billion in just one year.[10]

Big business in America, as in other democracies, owns politicians. In fact both Democrats and Republicans are beholden to the wealthy. In the congressional and presidential elections of 2004, nearly $4 billion were spent. Of course, those who provide money reap rich rewards for their investment. In some cases, their rate of return is 100 times their donation; that is, for one dollar offered to a politician, they receive $100 in tax benefits or governmental business contracts.[11] After all, over 40 percent of the 2001 $1.35 trillion tax cut went to the rich, which is a handsome reward for a $4 billion investment in politicians.

The business elite in America are as greedy and ruthless as feudalistic barons. Even when they take their company into bankruptcy and extract large wage concessions from workers, they award themselves millions in salaries. The word "CEO" now is synonymous with crookedness. Money controls U.S. politics as never before. As a result, the tax burden has gradually shifted from the wealthy onto the backs of the poor and the middle class. From 1950 to 1980, the top-bracket income tax rate ranged from 70 to 90 percent, while the Social Security tax imposed on lower incomes varied from 4 to 9 percent. By 2005 the top income tax rate was down to 35 percent, but the Social Security tax had jumped to 15.3 percent. Such are the tangible benefits that moneyed donors receive from politicians.[12]

The transfer of the tax burden to the poor was justified in the name of promoting investment and growth. But as I demonstrated in *Greenspan's Fraud*, the growth rate fell sharply after the early 1980s, while the investment rate fell a little. All this happened just when businesses reaped huge rewards from their political investments. Thus political corruption, especially the corruption seeping into tax policies, shrinks economic growth and the nation's living standard. I will return to this point in chapter 11. First, we need to understand the role of contemporary economists in fostering corruption in society.

CHAPTER 7

LIES, DAMNED LIES, AND ECONOMISTS

The vast majority of intellectuals, concerned about their careers and comforts, act to justify the status quo and offer theories that promote the self-interest of the ruling class. Only a few mavericks dare go against the rising tide, oppose the elite and explore reforms that would improve the lifestyle of the masses. History is witness to the rise of countless dogmas that were false, illogical and self-serving, yet, drawing upon the zealous backing of established scholars, remained popular for centuries, until unmasked by a few brave souls.

Today CEOs and wealthy businessmen are the ruling elite in the Western world, especially the United States. Their donations finance elections and even education, which they are constantly saying has to adapt itself to the needs of the market (that is, be molded to inculcate their views). It should come as no surprise, therefore, that the theories offered by economists rationalize the self-interest of big business and the wealthy. Overtly, of course, such theories claim to benefit society and the public's well-being. But covertly, they do just the opposite: they make the great mass of people poorer while making the rich fabulously richer.

Mark Twain famously remarked that "there are lies, damned lies, and statistics." Ever since then the phrase "damned lies" has become a code word for the abuse of statistics, flip-flopping and deception. If Mark Twain were alive today, he might say, "There are lies, damned lies, and economists." Money rules; the vast majority of the public shares the acquisitive mentality of the intellectual elite, even if they prey upon the people. Greed dominates not only politicians but also scholars. Most experts want to amass as much money as the CEOs and lawmakers, so they offer ideas that please the affluent.

Where are such fawning ideas born? At elite universities, think tanks and schools. At last count, Harvard University had an endowment of some $25 billion, Yale had $15 billion and Stanford nearly $12 billion.[1] How did they get all this money? What did they promise to donors in return? Few people offer donations without strings attached; even if offers of charity are unconditional, recipients are not likely to criticize the actions of their benefactors, even though such actions may be reprehensible or harmful to society. Economists are known for their wobbly reasoning; they are always saying, "On the one hand this point is true; on the other hand, it could be wrong if something else happened." Even slight changes in circumstances can change their forecasts. Some 50 years ago, President Harry Truman sought to find a one-armed economist, who would not be able to say "on the one hand this, and then on the other hand that." Despite their legendary vacillations, elite economists are certainly not wobbly when it comes to their self-interest, which lies in winning the hearts of the rich through their theories and ideas.

Lately economists have made some forecasts that turned out to be ridiculously wrong. Their predictions looked dubious even at the time they were made, so much so that it was clear the experts were lying or were motivated by politics. Remember the well-known supply-side economics or what I have called tricklism? This theory holds that a tax cut for the wealthy induces the economy to save more, invest more and grow the GDP more. It was put into practice in 1981, 1986 and 2001, when income and corporate taxes were reduced in a big way. In 1981, Americans saved about 8 percent of their income; now they save practically nothing. Our current rate of savings is a hefty 1 percent and was negative in 2005.[2] The last time this happened was in 1933, during the dark days of the Great Depression. So much for that rise in savings promised by the supply-siders!

Our GDP growth has been about 3 percent per year over the last two decades, compared to more than 4 percent in the 1950s and the 1960s. So much for that rise in economic growth promised by the tricklists. Even though tricklism has been a dismal failure, the Ivy League and elite university professors keep singing its glories to the public. Republican politicians do the same thing, but that is understandable, because they are the party of big business. Taxes were cut for the wealthy again in 2002 and 2003. President Bush wants to make these cuts permanent, even though they are not giving Americans much benefit. In fact, as I have explained elsewhere, their economic impact on society is negative.[3]

Why don't elite economists ever want to reduce payroll, gasoline and sales taxes? Why do they always want to cut income and corporate taxes? Why do some Ivy League experts always want to slash tax rates on capital gains and dividends? Why is their theory silent about the beneficial effects of cuts for low-income people? The reason is simple: these other rate cuts won't offer much benefit to the rich, so well-paid economists working for the affluent see no investment and growth benefits from such reductions. If the experts urged consideration of tax cuts for the middle and lower classes, their colleges would likely starve for donations from the CEOs.

Economists also love outsourcing, which transfers work done by a multinational company's employees in America to those living abroad, who provide the same service at a fraction of the cost. During the 1990s, nearly 2 million jobs were transferred to other nations by big business, including IBM, Microsoft and Citigroup, among many others. The pace of outsourcing, also called offshoring, has picked up sharply in the new millennium. Newspapers are filled with such tales. In fact, outsourcing now afflicts most advanced economies, such as Canada, Western Europe, Australia.

I can't see what good outsourcing can do for our country. No matter what an expert says, this idea appears foolish, even disastrous. If a company offers an American's $100,000 job to someone in Asia for just $20,000, it is simply not possible that the company's profits will rise enough to provide more jobs to U.S. residents. If the Asian worker has already finished the work, why would the firm need another worker? Even the U.S. Department of Labor now admits that U.S. multinationals are creating mostly low-paying jobs at home. But why does the well-paid economist insist that outsourcing is good for America? Perhaps because his own job is not outsourced?

The economic arguments favoring outsourcing are phony. Economists tell you that when outsourcing raises corporate profits, more jobs will be created in America. When was the last time a business hired more people just because its profits went up? Nowadays, increased profits mean increased bonuses and payouts for company executives, not more American jobs. Take a look at the recent fiasco at Refco, which filed for bankruptcy in October 2005. There are reports that just before the bankruptcy filing the company's executives drained nearly a billion dollars from its cash reserves. Higher profits no longer create more jobs in America—they only stuff the pockets of the CEOs.

An example of such behavior is Exxon-Mobil, which earned $9.92 billion in the third quarter of 2005, and $36 billion for the year. Such a huge profit is hard to imagine. How many more American workers has the company hired? You can count them on your fingertips, because Exxon's new hiring has been close to zero. Economists keep telling you that when outsourcing raises corporate profits, firms hire more Americans; where is the evidence? The reality is that companies that outsource also give huge raises to their CEOs, who have often rigged the board of directors that "supervises" their activities. Hence even CEOs who lose money get fat bonuses. On outsourcing, analysts Lawrence Orlowski and Florian Lengyel write: "So far, outsourcing manufacturing and services has led to higher chief executive compensation, at the expense of shareholder profit. For example, I.B.M.'s chief executive, Samuel J. Palmisano . . . last year saw his total compensation rise 19 percent to $18.9 million—even as the total return for his company's stock fell 16 percent."[4]

The U.S. economy has recovered since 2001, and real GDP has been growing, but only low-paying jobs are being created. As a result, average family income has decreased by $1,500. This has rarely happened in the United States before: GDP growth coexisting with a declining living standard. Outsourcing is chiefly to blame. Yet elite economists keep touting the practice; they are in effect on the payrolls of multinational corporations whose CEOs earn millions in salaries and perks, and who offer their hirelings research grants, endowed chairs and lucrative consulting contracts. It is positively indecent that the hirelings then turn around, justify the mega fortunes of the CEOs and provide bogus rationales for outsourcing, thereby once again stabbing the American worker in the back.

Glenn Hubbard, President Bush's first chairman of the Council of Economic Advisers (CEA), is currently Dean and Russell L. Carson Professor of Finance and Economics at Columbia University; he pushed the president's tax cut on corporate dividends and capital gains to promote investment in America. Lo and behold, American companies are still not investing much in the United States, but they continue to invest plenty in China, Vietnam and other countries in Asia, chasing low wages.

N. Gregory Mankiw, Bush's second CEA chairman, is currently Robert M. Beren Professor of Economics at Harvard. His memorable contribution as CEA chief was his implicit argument that hamburger production should be counted as manufacturing activity in the United States. As David Johnston, a *New York Times* reporter and best-selling author, wrote: "Is cooking a hamburger patty and inserting the meat, lettuce and ketchup inside a bun a manufacturing job, like assembling automobiles? That question is posed in the new *Economic Report of the President*, a thick annual compendium of observations and statistics on the health of the United States economy."[5] The *Economic Report* did not give an answer to this all-important question, but asked further:

When a fast-food restaurant sells a hamburger, for example, is it providing a "service" or is it combining inputs to "manufacture" a product? . . . Sometimes, seemingly subtle differences can determine whether an industry is classified as manufacturing. For example, mixing water and concentrate to produce soft drinks is classified as manufacturing. However, if that activity is performed at a snack bar, it is considered a service.[6]

The *Report* did not stop there, but devoted more space to what it apparently considered a profound discussion of hamburgers and manufacturing. It added that the Census Bureau defines manufacturing firms as those "engaged in the mechanical, physical or chemical transformation of materials, substances or components into new products." I don't know whether we should laugh or cry at the ingenuity of our economists. The loss of manufacturing jobs under the Bush Administration has become so pathetic that his chief economist felt compelled to raise the question of reclassifying hamburger production as manufacturing activity. America could have regained its industrial prominence in a matter of minutes if the Harvard economist had had his way—a typical example of the manipulation of statistics to hoodwink the people.

Mankiw also regards outsourcing as just another positive effect of foreign trade, which will produce great benefits to the nation over the long run. According to him, "outsourcing is just a new way of doing international trade. More things are tradable than were tradable in the past and that's a good thing."[7]

Remember that famous remark usually attributed to Michael Boskin, "Potato chips, computer chips, what's the difference?" He denies saying it, but many give him credit for it. Who is he? He is currently T. M. Friedman Professor of Economics at Stanford University and a Senior Fellow at the Hoover Institution, and formerly the CEA chief of President George Bush senior. Not surprisingly, Boskin also supports outsourcing; he does not care if manufacturing disappears from America, and potato chips lead the way. Or maybe potato chips are also part of heavy manufacturing?

These big-shot economists have several things in common: they all hold prestigious positions and endowed chairs, and they all love outsourcing and tax cuts for the wealthy. Money talks loudly and the distinguished economists quietly listen, but in the process they offer ideas that are slowly killing the middle class. They sell the self-interest of the wealthy as sound economic policy, and in the process serve their own self-interest.

If these leading economists actually looked to see how many private sector jobs were created between 2001 and 2005, they might be shocked. Table 7.1 examines job creation under various presidents from 1981 to 2005. These are all rounded figures. Between 2003 and 2005, George W. Bush indeed created 3.5 million jobs, but overall his job creation was only 1.7 million from the time he took office, because at first many thousands were laid off. And his private sector job creation was only 0.7 million. Thus from 2001 to 2005, he created only 700,000 new jobs in the private economy.

Table 7.1 shows that President Bill Clinton had the best record, creating more than 23 million jobs overall and 21 million in the private sector in eight years. Note that the income tax rate went up during his tenure, contrary to the preaching of tricklism. President Ronald Reagan created nearly 14 million jobs in eight years, just 60% of Clinton's job creation; his private sector figures also pale before those of Clinton's. But then look at the achievements of the two President Bushes. In four years, Bush I generated just 3.4 million jobs, of which 2 million were in the private sector, whereas Bush II has the dismal record I have already mentioned. Yet the administration is always claiming how its policies

Table 7.1: Job Creation from Presidents Reagan to Bush II

President	Total Job Creation (millions)	Jobs Created in Private Sector (millions)
Reagan (1981–1988)	14.8	13.7
Bush I (1989–1992)	3.4	2.0
Clinton (1993–2000)	23.1	21.2
Bush II (2001–2005)	1.7	0.7

Source: Bureau of Labor Statistics, 2006, www.bls.gov; Dick Alexander, www.globalshop.com.

strengthen small business and the private sector. Barely 700,000 jobs is an interesting definition of strength.

Such is the subterfuge of supply-side economics. Free enterprise thrives on increased competition among firms, low taxes for the poor and the middle class, balanced budgets and balanced trade. It suffers grievous harm when policy after policy adds to the luxuries of the super-rich, while offering crumbs to the middle class and the destitute. This is what supply-side policies, practiced first by Reagan and now Bush II, have done.

OUTSOURCING'S DOUBLE JEOPARDY

Why was job creation, especially in the private sector, so weak from 2001 to 2005? Outsourcing, growing and expanding like wildfire, was the main culprit. But economists safe in their ivory towers won't budge. To them, since outsourcing is just another way of doing international trade, it has to be good. In reality, this practice inflicts a double-edged loss on high-wage economies like those of the United States, western Europe, Canada and Australia. One is a direct loss of jobs, the other is an indirect effect.

The direct loss, of course, occurs when someone's work previously done in America is awarded to a low-wage worker abroad. The fired American worker is either unemployed for a while, or has to accept another job at a lower salary. In both cases the worker's spending and thus consumer demand falls, which means some American-made goods will go unsold, causing further layoffs in the process. This is the indirect job loss from outsourcing. Who benefits? The company, its CEO and the

Ivy League economist! They all celebrate, but the American and the European worker mourns.

How does the economist benefit? He gets to keep his endowed chair, receives annual pay raises exceeding inflation, gets new research grants and consulting contracts from bigwig CEOs, and earns the respect of like-minded colleagues and the government for preaching something that contradicts common sense. His university is also effusive because the CEOs fatten its endowment. Many rich CEOs have donated money to elite universities to establish endowed chairs in their names. Outsourcing is not just another way of doing international trade; it's another way of destroying high-wage jobs in America.

DAMNED LIES BEHIND THE TAX CUTS

President Bush was first elected at the end of 2000 even though he lost the popular vote to Democrat Al Gore. As a result, he did not have a mandate from the public to bring about major changes in economic policy. That did not stop him, however, from cutting taxes in a big way. His economic advisers repeatedly announced that the federal government would have a surplus budget for years. They estimated the surplus to be $5 trillion over the next ten years, so the country could easily cut taxes, adequately finance Social Security and also pay off part of the federal debt.

Bush said to his audiences again and again: It is your money. Why should the government keep it? It was an appealing slogan, except that it was misleading. Much of the actual surplus of 1999 and 2000 had come from a surplus in the Social Security trust fund, which by law could not be spent by other branches of the government. Budget projections were bogus and phony. But economists turned statistics into damned lies. Chief among them was the world's most famous economist, Alan Greenspan. He also was once a CEA chairman, although to his credit he has never held an endowed chair—at least not yet. But he represented an extreme form of cronyism; he did not even have a PhD at the time of his CEA appointment in 1974, obtaining the high position because of his connections.

Bush's proposed tax cut was not going anywhere in 2001. People were afraid of the return of Reagan-style budget deficits. But Greenspan gave credibility to the budget projections of Bush economists. He said the government would not be able to manage the federal surplus that was expected well into the future. He forgot that the nation had faced a budget deficit every year between 1970 and 1998. He also forgot that he had advised Congress in 1999 not to cut taxes because budget projections could be wrong. But to win Bush's gratitude and a chance for another reappointment as the Fed chairman, he backed the president's tax cut, because the elite economists saw a huge surplus coming well into the future.

In March 2001, President Bush assured the people: "We can proceed with tax relief without fear of budget deficits, even if the economy softens. . . . The projections for the surplus in my budget are cautious and conservative."[8] On August 22, 2001, his CEA chairman, Glenn Hubbard, wrote in the *Wall Street Journal* that the tax cuts would not affect the U.S. budget surplus: "Budget surpluses are the result of the economy's underlying strength, not the other way around."

These people—the economists, lawmakers and Greenspan—were clearly deceptive, because within a year after the passage of the tax reduction, the federal budget turned from a small surplus into a huge deficit. They had made flagrantly optimistic forecasts—$5 trillion in surplus!—just to reduce taxes that largely benefited the rich. Why did the projected surplus disappear so fast? It was not because of the "unforeseeable" events of September 11, as some have claimed. It was because there was no real surplus to begin with. It had resulted mostly from the Social Security trust fund's net income and taxes on booming capital gains from the soaring stock market, which was beginning to crash in 2000. In fact, by the time the president introduced his tax cut in early 2001, the NASDAQ composite index had already plummeted. So there was no longer any reason to expect high tax revenues from capital gains. But that did not stop Bush's economic advisers; they continued to mislead, using phony figures to back their budget estimates. Their expected surplus of $5 trillion has now turned into an expected *deficit* of $5 trillion over ten years. Already the president has accumulated deficits of some $1.5 trillion. Our future is very dark because these same economists, who repeatedly deceived us about budget projections, continue to shape the government's economic policy.

But the economic elite have no shame. Even after Bush's first tax cut turned the budget surplus into a big deficit, even after the whole world could see how ridiculous their projections had been, Bush advisers insisted on another tax cut in 2002. With the Republicans in control of the

Senate and the House, the new proposal also became legislation. This plan favored corporations that already had plenty of loopholes and had seen a huge decline in their tax bill since 1981.

At the end of 2002, the president introduced yet another tax plan, which aimed at lowering the tax on dividends. This one was pushed mainly by Mr. Hubbard to stimulate business investment, and was enacted in early 2003. So now if someone works hard and earns a good wage, he or she has to pay an income tax rate of as much as 35 percent. But if someone makes money over six months from the stock market by earning dividends and capital gains, the tax rate is only 15 percent. The same thing happens if you get capital gains from the appreciation of real estate investments. Such a tax policy is the best way to move people away from work and turn them into stock and property speculators.

The current tax system discourages hard physical and intellectual work, and encourages idle speculation in asset markets. Billionaires are its biggest beneficiaries, because they earn vast sums in dividends. They enjoy low tax rates, while millions who toil hard, literally doing the economy's heavy lifting, are burdened with higher tax rates.

The handiwork of our elite economists does not stop there. Even after annually looting almost $80 billion from the Social Security trust fund, the federal government still expects $400 billion deficits annually for years to come. Although the tax cuts were passed on the basis of deceptive statistics, the president now wants to make his cuts permanent. Why? So that the nation can continue to enjoy a mediocre growth rate, while the vast majority of families see a falling real income? From the time Bush came into office until today, GDP growth has averaged no more than 3 percent.

Most economists call the Bush tax cuts pro-growth policies. This is puzzling, given that growth averaged over 4 percent per year in the 1950s and the 1960s, just when the top-bracket income tax rate—hold your breath—was as high as 92 percent. It averaged 89 percent during the 1950s and 80 percent during the 1960s. Even the oil-shocked 1970s, with an income tax rate as high as 70 percent, had a larger growth rate than the one prevailing since 1981. Crude oil prices jumped 1,000 percent in that decade, yet growth was higher. In reality, the Republican policies introduced by Reagan, and now carried on by George W. Bush, are pro-wealthy, anti-growth, anti-poor and anti-middle-class policies.[9]

We live in an era of colossal economic mismanagement. The government wants to borrow, borrow and borrow; it also wants people to borrow, borrow and borrow. The nation as a whole also wants to borrow, borrow and borrow—from other countries, yet. China, Japan and Saudi Arabia are now our major lenders. The government is happy borrowing money from them and passing the cash to our billionaires in the form of tax breaks. Our economists are busy singing the glories of this system, which they tout as free market capitalism. There is nothing free about it: How does a 15 percent tax rate for millionaires and 35 percent rate for middle-class families constitute a level playing field? What the United States has is monopoly capitalism. The economists turn a blind eye to all the governmental and corporate manipulation of the system, which now needs over $2 billion per day in loans from the rest of the world to stay afloat.

DAMNED LIES BEHIND DEFLATION

The trillion-dollar surplus was not the only outrageous forecast of the new millennium. There were many more, such as the projected outburst of deflation. In September 2005, the consumer price index (CPI) jumped 1.2 percent. Such numbers were last seen during the late 1970s and the early 1980s. We are currently paying a lot for food, gasoline and electricity. But, believe it or not, in 2003 there was a lot of talk from experts about deflation, the phenomenon in which prices actually *fall*: another bogus projection, which was also used to scare people into accepting pro-rich economic policies. Deflation spells depression. The last time it hit the world was in the 1930s, when the CPI fell as much as 25 percent in the United States. It frightens people, because a persistent fall in prices leads to large-scale unemployment.

On May 6, 2003, Alan Greenspan warned that there was some risk of deflation in America. He said the Federal Reserve was ready to lower the federal funds rate even below its level of 1.25 percent to fight the risk. He forgot that the CPI had been rising since 1940, that is, for more than 60 years. On May 15, a government report showed that wholesale prices had declined by 1.9 percent in the previous month, which tended to confirm some economists' worst fears. Two days later, another report said the CPI fell 0.3 percent. At this point, the race was on. Who was going to be the first to issue dark warnings of prolonged deflation? Economist and columnist Paul Krugman took the bait and wrote a column on May 24, 2003: "Deflation can be both a symptom of an economy sinking into the muck, and a reason why it sinks even deeper . . . *and the risks look uncomfortably high*" (my emphasis).[10]

Krugman scared a lot of people. He feared the world was moving into a Japanese-style quagmire, and supported the Fed for slashing interest rates swiftly and sharply. He wrote: "The Fed has taken these conclusions to heart. Once the U.S. economy began to falter, it cut rates early and often, trying to get ahead of the problem." He suggested the federal funds rate could go down as low as 0.75 percent, because the economy still remained weak. He even called on central banks in Europe to follow the Fed's lead and reduce interest rates drastically.

For once, Princeton University Professor Krugman and Greenspan were on the same side. They inspired many other economists to write about the fearful scenario. Fearing deflation, interest rates in financial markets fell even further. The 30-year fixed mortgage rate neared a lowly 5 percent and then fell below that level. When interest rates fall, bond prices move in the opposite direction. So bond investors reaped huge gains. However, elderly retirees suffered greatly, because many of them live on their interest incomes, which plummeted.

Krugman was not alone; he was supported by the International Monetary Fund (IMF) and its large team of economists. They were worried about a Japanese-style stagnation overtaking the world. But they ignored the fact that prices in America had not fallen in almost five decades, and given the huge budget deficits run by most nations, they could not fall much. After all, such deficits add to the nation's demand, and thus are a check against falling prices. But Krugman was not persuaded by history. He warned that "few analysts saw the Japanese quagmire coming either, and there is now a significant risk that we will find ourselves similarly trapped." He wanted the Fed to print even more money, which would further stimulate the housing market. Greenspan, of course, lowered the funds rate further—to 1 percent—but not to 0.75 percent, the level suggested by Krugman.

We don't know when the duo of Krugman and Greenspan stopped worrying about deflation. The Princeton professor did write another article on the subject on July 25, 2003, but none after that.[11] That was the extent of his fear of the prolonged period of deflation—May to July, barely three months—but the alarming tone of his first article suggested another great depression in the making. As Donald Luskin of the *National Review Online* described it on May 28, 2003: "As you might expect, Krugman tried to make it seem that imminent cataclysmic catastrophe is looming. But of course, only he and a few other really smart people can see the danger."[12]

Krugman's deflation forecast apparently contributed to a further decline in interest rates that occurred in the month his column appeared. To that extent he had an impact on the housing market. He bears some responsibility for the housing bubble that resulted when interest rates fell sharply. According to figures from the *Economic Report of the President*, the deflation threat lasted all of two months in 2003—from April to May. From June the CPI started to rise, while the year ended with a price gain of 2.3 percent compared to just 1.6 percent in 2002. How Professor Krugman saw deflation in this data is beyond my understanding. The year of 2003, when the professor sounded his deflationary alarm, actually turned out to be inflationary relative to 2002.

It did not take long before inflation began to pick up again, and then, of course, Krugman changed his tune. In less than 24 months the celebrated economist flip-flopped from worrying about deflation to worrying about inflation. He even began to express his concern about the housing bubble, to which he had contributed. Having first pushed Greenspan into lowering interest rates sharply to avoid deflation, Krugman criticized the Fed chairman for creating a housing bubble. Clearly, he wanted to denounce the chairman any way possible. In 2003, Krugman wanted the Fed to flood the markets with liquidity to avoid a deflationary trap, and as Greenspan dutifully followed that policy and lowered the funds rate further, the housing market boomed and turned into a bubble (see chapter 2). But you can't have it both ways.

Krugman is just as blind to the wreckage of outsourcing as are other economists. For instance, he wrote on February 24, 2004: "First and foremost, we need more jobs. U.S. employment is at least four million short of where it should be. Imports and outsourcing didn't cause that shortfall."[13] Now if outsourcing did not cause that shortfall, then what did? In five years, from 2001 to 2005, the economy generated only 700,000 private-sector jobs, or 140,000 per year—18 times fewer than in the Clinton years.

Some people blame Bush's sluggish job growth on the stock market crash of 2000 that sapped business morale and hence investment. But they forget that Greenspan lowered interest rates so drastically in 2001 and 2002 that his actions caused a housing boom and a strong pick up in residential investment. The overall level of investment, business plus residential, did not change much, if at all.

As regards annual GDP growth, it was about 4.2 percent during Clinton's presidency. Bush generated a similar growth performance, 3.8 percent to be exact, from 2003 to 2005. So the question is: Why does a 4 percent growth annually generate 2.6 million private sector jobs under Clinton compared to just 1.1 million under Bush? The answer is obvious. Under Clinton such growth came from U.S.-based increases in employment, whereas under Bush, a similar level of real GDP growth has arisen from a foreign-based expansion of jobs. In other words, outsourcing is the main culprit behind the Bush job stagnation.

Exploring this matter further, let's divide Clinton's annual job creation of 2.6 million by his annual growth rate of 4.2 percent. This comes to about 620,000, which means that a 1 percent increase of real GDP created 620,000 jobs under Clinton. Now let's repeat the exercise for George W. Bush, that is, divide 1.1 million by 3.8 percent. This comes to about 290,000. This means that under President Bush, 1 percent of real GDP growth generated just 290,000 jobs.

Let me add that this is the most generous way of evaluating Bush's economic performance. If you look at the president's record from 2001 to 2005, the average real GDP growth has been only 2.9 percent, netting private job creation of 140,000 per year. Here then, for each growth percentage, the economy has generated just 48,276 jobs. Is this a giant jobs machine?

Outsourcing need not crimp American GDP growth by much, but it crushes American job growth. U.S. output still rises, but not from substantial hiring of Americans; it comes from strong hiring of foreign-based labor. To be sure there are many other factors accounting for Bush's sluggish economy, but outsourcing is the most negative factor. After all, since Bush succeeded Clinton, not much could have changed in the private economy. However, as late as March 6, 2006, when more evidence of job stagnation appeared, Krugman opined, "Am I saying that we should try to stop outsourcing? No."[14]

ECONOMISTS AS TRICKLISTS

Few economists would admit to being supply-siders. But the material they teach, the papers they write, all smack of supply-side dogmas. For instance, it is an article of faith among macroeconomists today that low tax rates on high incomes offer an incentive to work hard and invest, and thus stimulate economic growth. Pick up any text used at top schools and you find this "incentive effect." Martin Feldstein, a George F. Baker Professor of Economics at Harvard University, Robert Barro, a Paul M. Warburg Professor of Economics at the same school, and two Nobel laureates, Robert Lucas and Finn Kidland, are among the influential exponents of this view. This idea is so commonplace that a front-page article in the *Wall Street Journal* made copious reference to it.[15]

The main premise of these distinguished economists is that everyone is free to make a choice between work and leisure. Rational individuals seek to maximize their happiness or utility within the limits of their income and wealth. Happiness comes from leisure and consumption, but work generates unhappiness, for which a person must be compensated in terms of money. The benefit from work is the wage income, and the loss is the unhappiness resulting from labor. A person works to the point where the benefit just offsets the discomfort of an extra hour of work.

In general, people seek a raise to forego extra leisure and either work longer hours or join the labor force. For this reason, marginal income tax rates—that is, rates that go up with income—are a strong deterrent to the work effort, because a rise in such a tax reduces the after-tax real wage and makes leisure more appealing. Other type of taxes such as the sales tax or the Social Security tax, which are low and have fixed rates, may have some negative impact on the work incentive, but the income tax rate, which is higher for some people, has the maximum deleterious effect. Therefore a rise in the income tax rate reduces people's work incentive and thus crimps their productivity. The end result is a decline in real GDP or output growth. Similarly, an income tax cut stimulates work effort and hence economic growth.

Such is the logic of supply-side economics—a garbled logic at best. You can easily see it is designed to please the wallet of a billionaire, who stands to benefit the most from its policies. Let's first examine its logic; later I will look at its historical underpinnings.

First of all, does the theory make sense? People's incentive to work hard comes mainly from their incentive to eat, to live in a house—that is, not be homeless—to be educated and receive health care, and, in general, to afford the necessities of life for their families. If the income tax rate goes up, few will stop working or trim their effort, unless they are independently wealthy. An exceptionally small minority of the fabulously rich may need a tax incentive to work, but not a common person belonging to the lower or the middle class.

It is noteworthy that jobs, as anyone who has ever had one knows, are not as infinitely elastic as the model assumes. You don't just work until your incentive goes down, and then simply walk off the job! Not if you want to work the next day. The bus driver doesn't stop the bus and walk away the moment his incentive for leisure takes command. The model assumes a social vacuum, where there is no coercion of hunger.

The distinguished professors mentioned above typically assume a representative consumer, who behaves like an average person, consumer or worker. Does an average worker have free choice between leisure and work? Clearly, this type of freedom requires an employee to have a thick cushion of savings. A 1995 report published by the U.S. Bureau of the Census discovered that at any moment the median American family had a financial net worth of about $1,000.[16] This means that half of all Americans had less than $1,000 and the other half had more. This was when the economy was booming. Since the median family income has not changed much since 1995, we can safely assume that the bank account of the median family is also the same. What is a $1000 today? Enough for a month's rent in a small city, perhaps.

The median American certainly resembles an average worker. According to the august economists mentioned above, the average American worker, armed with $1,000 in his possession, is free to exercise a choice between consumption and leisure. He can quit his job at will, postpone the work effort until some propitious time in the future and live in dignity without a care in the world. The average employee worries not for food, apartment rent, clothes and health care. The average employee is either a retiree or a multimillionaire.

This carefree average worker, according to some celebrated economists, is also motivated by a rising interest rate. If the interest rate increases, he rushes to work hard to earn more, in order to save more. Never mind that the average rate of saving in America has been sinking since 1981, and currently hovers around a laughable zero percent.

In fact, an average worker, as portrayed in the economists' models, is constantly thinking about the future. He keeps a keen eye on his future productivity, future rate of interest, future consumption, future investment, future money supply, future taxes, future jobs, future government debt and so on. With a whopping saving rate of 0 percent, the average worker cares more about future income than current income, because if the current paycheck and the income tax rate is not to his liking, he will quit in a huff, thrive on his wealth and wait until his $1,000 is used up to find a better job.

According to this scenario, the income tax infuriates the average American worker, and if it goes up, he will not work hard; his productivity will suffer and GDP growth will take a hit. The average worker doesn't mind paying a high sales tax, a high Social Security tax, a high property tax, a high excise tax, a high Medicare tax; but woe betide if you were to raise his income tax, he would quit his job and exercise his birthright for leisure. His action will then show up in statistics of high unemployment. It matters not that the average income level is mostly exempt from the income tax bite. He suffers vicariously when he sees the wealthy pay the tax.

The average worker also dislikes the capital gains tax and the tax on dividends (which tax kinds of income he doesn't have), but readily accepts other levies that hurt him—perhaps to do his patriotic duty for the nation. Such is the average American employee in this fantasy, which has unfortunately driven U.S. economic and tax policy for the last 25 years. Which of you can identify with this fictional worker?

There was a time when most celebrity economists vehemently opposed the government budget deficit, but in support of President George W. Bush and his multitude of tax-cut plans, they have mellowed and abandoned their passion. They now favor an income tax reduction regardless of the cost to future generations, who will have to pay off the government debt.

Our distinguished economists are so blinded by their self-interest that in their zeal to please the billionaires they even withhold key information from their students and the public. Professor Barro, for instance, has written a textbook on macroeconomics.[17] In this 866-page tome, he does not offer a single line about the income tax rates that prevailed in the 1950s and the 1960s, when GDP growth averaged over 4 percent per year. These were the banner years for American growth, which, as noted, coexisted with a top-bracket income tax rate as high as 92 percent. His theory calls for low income taxes to stimulate the economy, but he does not inform his readers that American history reveals just the opposite.

Then there is our Professor Lucas, a Nobel laureate at the University of Chicago, and regarded as the most influential macroeconomist today. Does he explore the income tax history in any of his voluminous works? Not to my knowledge. He admires the Bush tax cuts for the wealthy, but see what he offers the worker. He believes that all unemployment is voluntary. His like-minded peers declare with a straight face, "All joblessness is by choice," because of their premise that everyone is free to choose between work and leisure. So if someone is jobless, then that is their choice. There is no suffering involved, because the unemployed are enjoying leisure.

The voluntary unemployment syndrome is not just a matter of semantics. It has profound policy implications. If people choose not to work, why should the government do anything for them? The elite economists have chosen their words with care. They are dead set against state intervention on behalf of the unemployed. That is why they permit no layoffs in their analyses. Nobody ever gets fired in their world, so no one deserves government help in finding a job. In *Models of Business Cycles*, Professor Lucas argues that the "decision to model unemployment as voluntary is subject to ignorant political criticism."[18] I guess it is ignorance to believe that some employees do get fired from their jobs.

In the supply-side view, only the employers—the job creators as they would call them—need and deserve state help in terms of low taxes on their earnings, capital gains and dividends. In their view, such a tax policy promotes work effort, saving, investment and economic growth. Professor Samuel Morley explains the tricklist's logic in this way: "After all, they argue, if the labor force would accept a reduction in the money wages . . . there need be no involuntary unemployment."[19] In other words, a manager who is laid off from Enron can always go to work at McDonald's for $6 an hour. He or she need not be jobless, and those who don't jump at this opportunity are voluntarily unemployed.

These economists have no sympathy for the plight of the worker, who is never even fired in their models! If this is not a damned lie, what is? But looking at it from their vantage point, how can one be against outsourcing, when the American worker is jobless by choice? He didn't lose his job; he gave it away.

THE INCOME TAX AND FREE TRADE

It is an old habit of elite economists to suppress inconvenient information. Pick up any text on international economics written by economic wizards, and you will find the same tale: free trade eliminates the tariff, and so benefits the consumer with lower prices of imported goods. Absolutely no mention is made of how the government makes up for the loss in tariff revenue so it can still operate. Nor do the authors tell you that when free trade was first introduced in the United States in 1913, the income tax was also introduced at the same time so that the government would not have to live on air.

For much of American history, the tariff was the main source of state revenue, accounting for as much as 75 percent of federal tax collection. So when free trade was introduced in 1913, cutting tariffs, a constitutional amendment to levy an income tax was also passed.

As import duties fell during the 1910s, the income tax rates soared, so much so that the top-bracket rate climbed to 70 percent by 1918. World War I also had something to do with the jump in rates, but wars had been fought before without the need for a permanent income tax.

A free trader does not like to reveal this information to his students or the public, for then the benefit to the consumer from the tariff cut becomes dubious. In fact, most consumers, given the choice between the tariff and the income tax, would opt for the tariff, because they can avoid spending on imports, but they cannot avoid the call of the Internal Revenue Service.

Take, for instance, a very popular text by Paul Krugman and Maurice Obstfeld. They have a section on U.S. tariff history, but it starts from 1920, not 1913 when the income tax began replacing the tariff. In any case, the 795-page oversized volume makes no mention of the fact that the income tax is the everlasting gift of free traders to Americans. The nation went as far as passing a constitutional amendment to quash the opposition to the income tax replacing the tariff, yet the event is suppressed from the Krugman-Obstfeld tome.[20] The same is true of almost all texts on international trade.

Why is such information withheld? The reason is that economists want to brainwash students to believe that free trade has no negative effects at all. The CEO loves free trade, because it has fattened his wallet as never before, so the economist suppresses any inconvenient information that could challenge his theory.

Personally, I am also in favor of free trade—as long it occurs among nations with similar wage rates; when wages differ substantially among nations, then the workers of the high-wage nation are bound to suffer, especially in a world where technology is virtually the same everywhere. I will say more on this subject in chapter 11. For now, let me note that the suppression of inconvenient facts is an age-old disease among intellectuals. Today's intellectuals act out of their own self-interest, and create material and intellectual poverty for others in the process. The truth may not set us free just yet, but it is essential to understand what is going on.

CHAPTER 8

THE MUSLIM CIVILIZATION

Until now my focus has been on the U.S. economy and Western society, both of which are now creating economic and political conditions that could soon lead to financial chaos around the world. But the Middle East, as usual, is in ferment, and the growing Muslim rage against the West, especially Israel, could also play a crucial role in our future, just as it did in the breakup of the Soviet empire because of the Soviet entanglement in Afghanistan. The ongoing carnage in Iraq and our leaders' follies there demonstrate that we need to examine that area with the fresh approach offered by the law of social cycle.

This is not the first time our authorities have been caught off guard in their dealings with Muslims. In the fall of 1981, as I taught at Vanderbilt University, war broke out between Iran and Iraq. Two Nashville newspapers interviewed me, asking for a comment on the State Department statement that the war could last no longer than two months. Of course, they didn't believe my words that the conflict would go on for seven years.

In the early 1990s, I had the honor of addressing a group of naval officers based in Norfolk, Virginia; I talked about the social cycle and the role the army was then playing in the West. One officer asked what was the biggest danger facing the United States abroad. He probably expected me to name the Soviet Union or China. To the great surprise of the audience, I said that the biggest foreign danger to American interests was Islamic fundamentalism. Few believed me then, but I still maintain that position.

The reason why our leaders constantly make errors in foreign policy is that either their actions are distorted by self-interest, or they ignore history and the lessons we can draw from it. They have the stale, old thinking that only current, visible events shape the future. This is not true, and the law of social cycle is a great aid in discerning the unknown.

We need to examine the evolution of Muslim society in light of this law, because there is hardly a burning question in the globe today that one way or another does not involve the Muslim world. From Russia to the United Sates to Europe to the Middle East to India, Australia, Japan and China, everyone is affected by events occurring in Islamic countries. In order to understand the nature of international problems, economic, social and political, it is necessary to understand how the Arabs and Persians look upon the surrounding world of the West, Russia, India and China. Similarly, global poverty cannot be examined properly without a study of the crosscurrents affecting the Muslim lands, some of which are among the least industrialized nations in the world. Sudan, Morocco, Ethiopia, Bangladesh and even Pakistan are Muslim-majority countries that are mainly agrarian and suffer from extreme poverty.

There are over one billion Muslims today spread across the planet in all nationalities, races and ethnicities. They inhabit vast areas of Asia and Africa, and live as minorities in Europe, Russia, Canada and the United States. In order to comprehend how Muslims in different countries react to global events, we first need to study the history of Islam.

THE SOCIAL CYCLE IN ARAB LANDS

Since I have tackled this subject in detail elsewhere, here I will present a brief history of Islam, and focus primarily on whatever new I have to say on the subject.[1] Almost every great civilization has been associated with a monotheistic religion, and Muslim society is no exception. Its religion, Islam, was founded by a prophet named Muhammad, who was born in Mecca, Arabia, around 570. The city was then inhabited by nomadic tribes, suggesting that the region was either in the laborer age or in the tribal phase of the warrior age; one vast desert, Arabia with its hostile climate forced its inhabitants to move from one place to another in search of food and water. Life was generally hard, and petty feuds among the tribes were common.

At the age of 40, or a little earlier, Muhammad felt a great restlessness in his heart. He became increasingly interested in a reclusive life, and began to spend much of his time in a cave on Mount Hira just outside town. His people practiced paganism and idol worship, which he instinctively detested. But he yearned for the truth, and spent many days, at times weeks, in seclusion at the cave. On one of these occasions, in the year 610, Muhammad was deeply absorbed in contemplation when the archangel Gabriel appeared and revealed to him the truth. He realized that the angel was the messenger of God, or Allah, a singular being who had created the world. Allah had no equal, and was omnipotent and merciful. Muhammad subsequently set out to share his divine experience with his relatives and friends.

Muhammad preached the equality of human beings and the unity of God. Such words were anathema to the nomadic society in which he lived. As happens with every prophet, at first he faced much ridicule and hostility. Mecca's pagans, believing in many gods and idols, could not accept the idea that their deities were useless or subordinate to Allah, or that their slaves were equal to them in status.

"Islam" means "submission to God" in Arabic. Muhammad's teachings, which were no less than revolutionary, alarmed the ruling aristocracy, who began to make his life increasingly difficult. He was frequently insulted and at times pelted with stones. Undaunted, Muhammad continued to preach his message. Tensions in Mecca reached such heights that his adversaries began to plot his death. Muhammad then decided to leave Mecca and move to Medina, a town about 300 miles away.

Muhammad's departure for Medina is known as the Hijra, and occurred in 622, a year that marks the beginning of the Muslim calendar. Mecca's aristocrats, however, haunted by the Prophet's magnetism, feared his power even when he was in a distant town (where indeed he had been received with open arms). They began to incite the neighboring Bedouin tribes against him and his followers. A long conflict ensued, and the new faith, despite tremendous odds, won out. By 630, Muhammad had consolidated his position in Medina, and even captured Mecca itself.

The conquest of Mecca marks another watershed in Islamic annals. It resulted in the quick acceptance of Islam by most of the Arabs in the peninsula. Muhammad died in 632, two years after his Meccan triumph.

THE IMPERIAL WARRIOR AGE

Less than a decade after his arrival in Medina, the Prophet had been able to unite the nomadic Bedouin factions under the banner of Islam. This was an unprecedented event in Arabia and spelled trouble for its neighbors. The Bedouin were already fierce warriors, and now they were imbued with the zeal of a new religion that called upon the faithful to expand its influence and convert others. At least, this is how the Prophet's followers looked upon their role.

In a matter of seven years (634–641) Syria, Palestine, Iraq and Iran fell to the tiny but mighty army of Islam. The success of such a small force against entrenched enemies was simply stunning. Historians have ascribed such victory to various causes. The Arab soldiers believed that, live or die, they could not lose. For victory would bring them earthly rewards, whereas death in the cause of Islam was a shortcut to paradise. Islam's message of equality was also welcomed by minorities persecuted inside the vanquished nations.

There is also a deeper reason for the quick spread of Islam. Its founder had been brutally persecuted by the ruling aristocracy. It was his force, courage and lofty message that even after his death continued to inspire Muslims to perform amazing feats in battles. A similar evolutionary course of persecution followed by triumph had earlier greeted the movements of prophets like Zoroaster, Buddha and Christ.

Muhammad's successors were known as caliphs, and they were at first elected. The first four Muslim rulers, the direct disciples of the Prophet, have been regarded as the righteous caliphs, of whom Abu Bakr was the first and Ali the last. Ali deserves special mention. Some Muslims regarded him as the most qualified successor of the Prophet, who had personally designated him as his heir.

Ali was eloquent and well versed in the knowledge of Islam. A great schism followed his assassination in 661. His enraged followers broke away from other Muslims, called Sunnis, and started their own version of Islam, Shia. They believed that the Caliphate, or Imamate as they called it, belonged only to Ali and his descendants, for the Prophet himself had chosen Ali as his successor. The imam, according to the Shiites, was infallible. He alone could truly comprehend the teachings and sayings of the Prophet. By tradition, therefore, the Shiites follow only their imams in their religious practices. Obviously their beliefs

were subversive of the caliph's authority, and they were viciously persecuted over the years.

The Shia-Sunni schism is now a big factor convulsing Iraq, and it is
likely to play a major role in the world's future. It suggests that the two
factions are not likely to compromise easily, because their conflict has
deep roots in the past.

Following Ali's death, the Caliphate became hereditary, starting with
the Umayyad dynasty, and the capital city moved from Medina in Arabia
to Damascus in Syria. The caliph also became an absolute ruler of a vast
empire that included Arabia, Syria, Egypt, Iraq and Persia, among others. This was the imperial warrior age of Muslim society. Since the army
generals had brought laurels to their people, it should not be surprising
that the warrior mentality dominated Muslim polity soon after its birth.
The Arab commanders constituted the ruling aristocracy. They had
earned their high status and prominence; a career in the army was eagerly sought. Muslim theologians called ulema were also well respected,
just as during the Christian Middle Ages prelates were accorded respect
along with lords and kings. The ulema are also known as mullahs or
imams in some Muslim countries, and even today they play a major role
in shaping the foreign policy of their nations, especially toward Israel
and the United States. Their sermons can instigate or pacify crowds in
dealing with foreign countries.

THE AGE OF INTELLECTUALS

At the midpoint of the eighth century, in the year 750 to be exact, the
Umayyads were overthrown and replaced by the Abbasid dynasty. The
capital city then moved from Damascus to Baghdad, which had important consequences for subsequent social evolution.

The Caliphate now emerged with a new meaning. Immediately following Muhammad's death, the caliph was called the successor of the
Messenger of God. Later a militaristic and secular notion was attached
to the title, and the caliph became the Commander of the Faithful. The
theologians had always looked upon the Caliphate as divinely inspired,
and the glory of the caliph's rule, in their view, depended on whether or
not it conformed to sharia, which is the Islamic law laid down by the
Prophet's teachings in the Koran. Muslim clerics regard sharia as divinely sanctioned law.

In order to win general support and legitimacy for their overthrow of the Umayyad rule, the Abbasids set themselves up as champions of Islam. In theory at least, they accepted sharia as the basis of their rule. They also used the religious sentiment to glorify their own conception of the Caliphate. The caliph was now regarded as the "shadow of God on earth." So far he had been an absolute ruler in practice, now he became an absolute ruler in theory as well.

The birth of a vast empire defended by a large and standing army brought peace to the once warring tribes and lands. Muslim energies now found outlet in economic development. The Abbasid rulers created a vast system of irrigation that led to flourishing agriculture, which in turn led to growing industry, scientific progress, craftsmanship and home building. The Muslims also engaged in trade with their colonies, Egypt, Syria and Iran. This led to huge economic expansion, international commerce and prosperity. People in general, especially the elite, were affluent.

As long as the Abbasid caliphs were strong, they kept the ulema under their control. Later, as the political power of the caliph declined, the religious basis of the Caliphate acquired increasing prominence and heralded the dawn of the intellectual age. To the average Muslim, the caliph came to acquire the same aura of reverence that the pope had acquired earlier in Western society. Thus began the intellectual era of Muslim civilization, wherein the clergy and the educated came to dominate the warriors as well as other classes.

At this time, there was yet another way in which men of intellect came to rule the Islamic world. With the movement of the capital to Baghdad, which was once part of the large Persian Empire, top administrative positions went to Iraqis and Iranians. Later this administrative system gave prominence to the office of vizier, or the prime minister, who at times overshadowed the power and prestige of the caliph himself. One of the most illustrious rulers of the Abbasid dynasty was Harun-al-Rashid, who wanted to appoint intelligent and honest individuals to assist him in his administration. He created the office of a *wazir* (vizier). The first *wazir* was Yahya, who belonged to a prominent family of Barmak. Within a short time the *wazir* became so powerful that he outshone the caliph. In historian P. K. Hitti's words, "Yahya, who died in 805, and his two sons al-Fadd and Jafar practically ruled the empire from 786 to 803."[2]

A *wazir* is basically an intellectual, and so are the bureaucrats whom he heads. The *wazirs* were well educated and distinguished themselves in many ways. In theory the caliph represented the highest office in Muslim society. In reality, the administrative faculties and superior intellect of the prime ministers enabled them to be the real sovereigns. They brought such dignity to the office that even when the vizirate passed into the hands of other families, the *wazir* continued to make most decisions on his own. He would consult the caliph on important matters, but the latter generally accepted his advice.

Harun Rashid is much more famous than his advisers, but the fact remains that much of the financial and administrative efficiency of his empire was attributable to the skills of his *wazirs*. Similarly, Ronald Reagan and George W. Bush may get top billing in the history books a hundred years from now, but Alan Greenspan will have his mention, too, as the mind behind the policies, just as Niccolo Machiavelli and Alexander Hamilton are household names.

Even after the death of Harun Rashid, the *wazir* continued to be prominent. In fact, the prime minister at one time had become so influential that a Muslim historian, Hilal as-Sabi, devoted a book entirely to the *History of Wazirs*.[3] Many *wazirs*, and the families connected to them, became fabulously rich, a practice that started with the Barmak family members, who lived in luxurious palaces in Baghdad. In Hitti's words: "Fabulous fortunes were amassed by members of the Barmak family. Even what they saw fit to bestow on their clients, panegyrists and partisans, was enough to make such protégés wealthy."[4] While the intellectuals controlled the government toward the end of the eighth century, they were also much respected in society. Recall that the Abbasids had tacitly consented to base their rule on sharia, which holds that the government should be run on the basis of Koranic principles. This tacit consent of the Abbasid rulers led to the rise of what British historian W. M. Watt calls a "religious institution," which came to acquire considerable influence in society.[5]

FEUDALISM AND THE ACQUISITIVE AGE

Every epoch plants the seeds that subsequently sprout into a new age. In the process of trying to learn what kind of future we are sowing for our descendants with our actions today, it is helpful to look at past epochs, their rise and fall. Some societies have been able to change and adapt, even to correct their own worst excesses; others, like the Mayans, have died because of their tragic myopia. In Muslim society under the Abbasid Caliphate, after the age of intellectuals started around 786, the economy began a slow but steady decline. Some of the remote provinces, like Egypt, Morocco, eastern Persia and Syria, declared independence. Others, no longer afraid of the weakening Caliphate, reduced their annual gifts of precious metals. With the loss of money and declining revenues, it was no longer possible to maintain a large standing army. That is when the caliph began to grant land as fiefs to army officers in exchange for military service.

These fiefs were called *iqta*, and at first were granted only to the caliph's relatives and governors. But the caliph al-Mutawakkil, ruling from 847 to 861, began making land grants to generals and meritorious soldiers to keep them interested in the army. The generals were also given certain administrative functions such as collecting the land revenue for the central treasury. The *iqta* system, as in other societies, led to the rise of feudalism.

Once started, the *iqta* system gradually spread to most regions of Muslim society, including Egypt and Spain. By the end of the ninth century, the economy had entered the phase of sharp decline. The *wazir* had become tyrannical, and a caliph maker. The empire also kept shrinking. The caliph was reduced to a figurehead, and played mostly a symbolic role as the religious head of state.

A major event took place in 945, when an army commander from eastern Iran took control of Baghdad and founded the Buyid dynasty. The caliph now became a puppet in the hands of the Buyid rulers, but he remained the supreme sovereign of Islam. The general public continued to look upon the caliph as God's emissary on earth.

The *iqta* system expanded further. The Buyid army depended even more on land grants to military officers. The Buyids controlled enough territory to qualify as an empire. Under their dominion the Muslims regained their prosperity. The trade routes that had been abandoned or lost before were reestablished. Yet the prevailing affluence was not enough to meet the profligacy of the caliph and his vast entourage. The treasury still did not have enough revenue to support a standing army. So the power base gradually shifted into the hands of the distant overlords who owned the fiefs and nurtured soldiers needed in times of riots, wars and emergencies. Land, or wealth, became the main source of political power. The overlord himself bought military service through grants of land.

Around 1050, the Buyids were overthrown by another Persian dynasty, the Seljuks, who assembled an even larger empire. But the Seljuks only expanded the *iqta* system, and feudalism took deeper roots in their domains. Until then the fief holders had been authorized only to collect taxes from their peasants, use the revenue to meet the expenses of the local administration and pass the rest on to the central treasury. These were known as farming *iqtas*, and their purpose was mostly to produce revenue for the government. Purely military *iqtas* had also existed, but the farming *iqtas* were the rule. Under the Seljuk sultans (or kings), as these rulers were called, the military *iqta* expanded manifold. As historian Bernard Lewis writes:

> A notable development under the early Seljuqs was the militarization of the *iqta*. In the district assigned, the beneficiary retained all the revenues collected, and the only duty he owed to the central government was personal service in the army. . . . Generally speaking all powers of government were in the hands of its [*iqta's*] holder.[6]

This is exactly what was happening at the same time in the West, with the landed magnates assuming government powers because of their control over land. The holder of the military *iqta* was known as the amir, which literally means wealthy; some amirs possessed vast areas of land and were encouraged by the caliph and the sultans to form their own armies. This they did by parceling out a part of their fiefs to brave soldiers. Lewis writes:

> A full muster of the sultan's army included the great amirs with their contingents, which were themselves made up of the permanent force maintained by that amir, together with the men to whom he had assigned land or revenue within the greater *iqta* which he himself held of the sultan.[7]

With land as the main source of prestige and power, the amirs were constantly on the warpath, ready to grab estates of other amirs. The same system prevailed in all Muslim lands during the eleventh and the twelfth centuries. The amirs were thus acquisitors with vast influence in society. Few personally knew how to fight, but they had sizable armies under their command. Money in the form of precious metals and coins was in short supply. Therefore educated bureaucrats were also frequently paid in the form of iqtas, which made feudalism even more pervasive.

More and more people became interested in agriculture, the main fruit of land ownership. Urban centers and industries declined as a result. The business of farming made businessmen out of soldiers, who became increasingly mercenary. The sultan and the amirs had to promise them booty and plunder as rewards for victory in any war. Slowly the acquisitive mentality infected the entire society and led to the laborer age. As Lewis puts it: "Even the warrior of Jihad was often moved rather by consideration of earthly profit than of heavenly reward."[8]

Jihad, of course, was crucial for Muslims at the time, because they were entangled with Christian armies in the battles of the Crusades. Seljuk sultans did their fair share of checking the advance of the Christians, and even their largely feudal armies were able to win some victories.

THE LABORER ERA
AND SOCIAL REVOLUTION

At the end of the twelfth century, the vast Seljuk empire began to disintegrate. By then the sultan had made the *iqta* system hereditary. No longer did amirs need formal appointment or a letter of investiture from the king. Many declared independence from the central government and started their own dynasties. The amirs became acquisitive rulers, but they depended on the military service provided by warriors and even laborers, most of whom had been reduced to serfdom.

The fief holders became increasingly exploitative of their peasants and serfs. Riots among the poor became common. Statelets emerged within states, princedoms within provinces. Political authority was increasingly corrupt and decentralized, with amirs openly disobeying orders from the caliph and the sultan. Violent crime became rampant; petty warfare among amirs over land became common; poverty, famine and pestilence became the order of the day. British historian M. A. Rauf describes such dark days as follows:

> There was much terror, devastation and misery in the latter part of the
> reign. The rivalry between the Arabs, Persians and Turks, the disputes

between factions within each of these groups, constant quarrels between sects and schools of thought, the attacks of the Mongols and the
Crusaders—all brought misfortune and misery to millions and millions
in the world of Islam.[9]

This anarchic state of affairs could have lasted for a very long time, as it
did in the West. But a fortuitous event changed the Islamic world forever. Muslim society collided with Mongolian barbarians.

At the dawn of the thirteenth century when the Caliphate was already gasping for breath, a momentous event that a little later virtually
shook the foundations of all civilization occurred in distant Mongolia.
Around 1206, the fierce Mongolian nomads dwelling on the periphery of
northern China were united under the chieftainship of one Temuchin,
later known as Chingis Khan (or Genghis Khan). After conquering
northern China, he invaded the neighboring lands, and within a few
years commanded one of the largest empires ever known.

But Chingis Khan died in 1227, before his marauding armies could
reach Baghdad. This task was left to his grandson, Hulagu, who was invited by the caliph's *wazir* to march onto Iraq. The *wazir*, Ibn al-Alkami,
a Shiite, was fed up with the caliph's incompetence and tyranny. He
wanted to bring an end to the near anarchy that convulsed most Muslim
lands at the time. So he communicated with the Mongols and invited
them to invade Baghdad, and in the process launched a social revolution.

In their march, the Mongols destroyed the eastern centers of Muslim learning and culture. Thousands of innocent civilians were decapitated and their properties set afire. In 1258 the caliph, along with many
members of his family, was slain. Thus ended the Abbasid Caliphate in
Baghdad, the way it had started.

MONGOL DOMINATION AND
THE NEW WARRIOR AGE

The collapse of the Abbasid Caliphate was a momentous event in the
history of Islam. It was not only a physical blow to Islamic hegemony
over vast territories of Asia but also a psychological blow to Muslims all
over the world. For more than 500 years, the name of the Baghdad
caliph had been mentioned in Friday prayers. For millions of Muslims in
far-flung lands, the caliph had been a unifying religious symbol. With

the political weakening of the Caliphate, its religious component had gained importance. All this was now gone. Muslims felt this spiritual loss more than anything else.

Following the Mongolian conquest, the main centers of Muslim civilization, such as Iraq, Iran, Afghanistan and Transoxiana, came under the iron grip of the Mongols. Warriors were supreme in Mongolian society, and they transplanted their institutions and ethos onto the vanquished Muslim world. However, the Mongols were eventually won over to Islam. The states they founded were purely militaristic in character. The ruler, supported by powerful generals and the army, was absolute in theory and practice. The Muslim ideology of sharia was now replaced by the Mongolian ideal of what is known as *Yasa*. While sharia preached the rule of law in accordance with Koranic principles and the Prophet's sayings, *Yasa* derived sanctity from the prestige of Chingis Khan as a world conqueror. *Yasa* tended to legitimize the dynastic and absolutist rule in the families of the great khan. As M. G. Hodgson, a student of history, points out:

> Yasa had three purposes: First, a legitimation of independent dynastic law; second, the conception of the whole state as a single military force; third the attempt to exploit all economic and high-cultural resources as appendages of the chief military families.[10]

With *Yasa* competing with sharia, the influence of ulema, the intellectual scholars, dissipated. The civilian bureaucracy, in terms of rank and remuneration, was also organized militarily, and thus the army emerged with the greatest honor. In short, as Hodgson remarks, "the whole upper realm of society was to be subject to military discipline."[11]

The one Muslim power that had stemmed the Mongolian tide was Egypt under the Mamluks, who thus acquired unprecedented prestige. The Mamluks gained further legitimacy by providing sanctuary to Ahmad Abu Asim, who belonged to the deposed Abbasid family and who had somehow escaped the massacre at Baghdad. The young Abbasid prince was installed as caliph in 1261, and the Mamluk sultan Baybars and the ulema took an oath of allegiance to him.

However, the caliph's name was printed on coins and recited in Friday sermons. This was a last-ditch effort to revive the Caliphate, which remained a mere phantom of its former self. The new Caliphate had little temporal authority, but even its religious authority was limited to Egypt. The caliphs at Cairo were mere puppets in the hands of Mamluk sultans. This was the rule of muscle, not intellect.

Another bastion of Muslim society during the thirteenth century was India, which until then had been inhabited mainly by Aryans in the north and Drawidians in the south. The Muslim contact with Indo-Aryans had actually occurred as early as the eighth century when the Arabs conquered the Sind, but it was not until the eleventh century that a long conflict between the two sides occurred. By the beginning of the thirteenth century, a sultanate had been established at Delhi.

In 1296, a warrior named Alaudinn Khilgi subdued the acquisitive princelings called rajas and established a centralized state over major parts of India.[12] Thus by the end of the thirteenth century, the Indo-Aryan society came to mirror the military organization of Muslim civilization. From then on the destinies of Muslims and Hindus began to move together, as the Asians, from Syria all the way to the Indian subcontinent, came under the sway of warriors.

The new military era of Muslim society lasted until the middle of the sixteenth century. By that time great political and administrative changes had occurred in the world of Islam. The bulk of Muslim lands, including Egypt, had come under the control of Turkish Ottomans, with Iran under the Safavids and India under the Mughals. The city of Baghdad, which had been the center of Muslim efflorescence for almost a millennium, lost its prominence in the process. Today, because of the ongoing war in Iraq, the city is capturing headlines again, and what transpires there could monumentally impact our future, even the fate of capitalism itself. The city seems destined to shape history.

The Ottoman dynasty was founded by a certain Uthman around the end of the thirteenth century in Asia Minor, which was later renamed Turkey. Uthman was a mighty warrior. Starting as a mere soldier in 1289, by the time of his death in 1326, when his son Orhan ascended to the throne, he established a miniature kingdom. Orhan and his successors maintained Uthman's triumphant tradition, and by the end of the fourteenth century their conquests had added many more domains to the Ottoman state, which was beginning to grow into a vast empire. In 1402, the Ottomons suffered a temporary reverse at the hands of another Turkish warrior, Timur the Lame, who defeated and imprisoned their sultan Bayzid I. This was a lethal blow to the prestige of the Ottoman dynasty, but its effects did not last long. Timur died in 1405, and the Ottomans quickly regained their prominence. By the time of Murad II, who ruled from 1421 to 1451, most, if not all, of their earlier domains were reunited with their empire. It is during Murad's reign that the Janissary Corps, an arm of the Turkish army, gained ascendancy in society. This military corps was to play an important role in the evolution of Muslim civilization.

The Janissaries did not come from Turkey but from subject Christian lands. Each year the Turkish recruits would visit the Christian communities, select muscular youths, convert them to Islam and then subject them to rigorous military discipline. The Janissary Corps was a fierce fighting machine, and its members acquired top army positions.

Early in the sixteenth century, the already vast Ottoman Empire was expanded further by the addition of Egypt. The Mamluks were defeated in 1517 and were forced to accept the status of a vassal. This way the foremost Muslim power of the time came under the control of the Ottoman ruler Selim, who also usurped the title of caliph. With the conquest of Egypt, the Ottoman Empire became the principal champion of the Sunni faith and clearly the predominant Muslim power in the region, a position it retained until the end of the nineteenth century.

THE SECOND INTELLECTUAL AGE

Following Selim's death in 1520, the throne passed into the hands of his son Suleyman, who is regarded by some as the greatest Ottoman sultan. In Europe, he came to be called the "Magnificent." Historians have frequently observed that when the state switches from territorial expansion to the task of efficient administration, effective political power gradually passes into the hands of the bureaucracy, its chief and his supporters— unless, of course, the warrior monarch responsible for assembling the empire is a keen administrator himself.

The chief legacy of the Mongols to successive empires was their absolutism. Until Suleyman, the Ottoman sultan did not share much authority with his *wazir*, who at times came from the army. While some *wazirs* had indeed distinguished themselves in the conduct of government, most had little say in crucial matters. However, Suleyman believed in a constitutional form of government. He brought about a revival of sharia, and granted extensive authority to the vizirate, which until then had played a somewhat circumscribed role.

Hodgson remarks that the *wazir* "had been given highest precedence under Mehmed II, but received comprehensive authority, to be shared with no one under Suleyman. He stood at the head of the whole apparatus: effective commander in chief in war and the master of the fiscal and even judicial services in peace."[13]

To be sure, the Ottoman monarch, called *padishah*, was still the absolute ruler, and, in theory, his influence exceeded that of the *wazir*, but the point is that he could not accomplish much without him. Nor did the *padishah* have the interest or the intellect to be an effective ruler—with the result that real power, for a long time, remained in the office of the vizirate. At times, the *wazir* successfully conspired to kill his *padishah*.

After the death of Suleyman in 1566, the vizirate came back into power, as did the intellectuals. Not surprisingly, along with the vizirate, the ulema also made a return. They had been ignored under the Mongols who preferred *Yasa* to sharia. They had also been neglected by the early Ottoman sultans who mostly patronized a new Muslim faith called the order of *dervish*. Many Ottoman rulers, starting with the dynasty's founder, had favored this order, much to the suspicion and disapproval of the orthodox Sunni ulema whose fortunes were connected with the respect for sharia. Most scholars had insisted that the ulema alone were entitled to interpret sharia from the Koran and the Prophet's sayings. Therefore the ruler's sanction for sharia meant an increased political role and influence for the intellectual class of Islamic theologians.

When Suleyman acknowledged the supremacy of sharia, the social prominence of the ulema was inevitable. An influential scholar in the early sixteenth century was al-Dawwani, who raised the ruler's absolutism to a lofty pedestal but sought to subordinate him to the rule of law as interpreted by the ulema. Historian A. K. Faruki remarks that "in al-Dawwani, the class-stratification taken from Greek and Persian thought . . . persists—the first being the men of knowledge (*ilm*) comprising doctors of theology and law, judges, secretaries, officials, geometricians, astronomers, physicians and poets, then the warriors or defenders, then the traders and artisans, and finally, the farmers."[14]

Faruki goes on to suggest that al-Dawwani's work enjoyed a wide following and had an important influence on the manner in which the Ottoman state organized itself and on later Ottoman writings. In general, intellectuals rule by praising warriors and trapping them unawares in the web of their theories. They support the absolutism of the ruler, and in reality enjoy its fruits. This is precisely what Dawwani did, justifying the absolute monarchy as the true Caliphate but granting soldiers a subordinate position. It is not surprising that his views were popular in the royal family.

WESTERN INFLUENCE AND
THE NEW ERA OF ACQUISITORS

From the second half of the sixteenth century to the dawn of the twentieth, the *wazirs* in administration and the ulema in society at large were, with inevitable vicissitudes, on top of the social hierarchy in most Muslim lands. They ruled with the help of sharia, which came in handy in controlling the warriors. However, in the first half of the twentieth century, owing to increasing contacts with the West, Muslim society gradually began to reflect the Western acquisitive spirit. After England, France and Portugal began to colonize the Muslim lands in the eighteenth and nineteenth centuries, the secular and relatively materialistic ideas of Western society began to penetrate the largely religious and otherworldly thinking of the Islamic world.

As a consequence, since the beginning of the twentieth century, social respect has been shifting away from the clergy and the ulema, who long maintained their influence by claiming to be the sole authorities on the Koran. Muslims in India were the first to move into the new era, for Indo-Aryan society evolved into the age of the acquisitive mentality at the turn of the nineteenth century. By 1803 the Mughal emperor had become a puppet of the British East India Company, a trading enterprise that initially entered India just for commerce, but eventually became the dominant military power on the Indian subcontinent.

During the nineteenth century the power base of the ulema was destroyed by a series of violent episodes beyond their control. The hub of Muslim society during the eighteenth and nineteenth centuries was still the Ottoman state. Under the influence of the ulema, who were supported by the military elite of the once-dreaded Janissary Corps, Ottoman military strength declined relative to that of the European powers. This is because the ulema, whose hegemony derived from their monopoly over ideas, resisted new ideas. While neighboring countries had made great strides in terms of military equipment by using new technology, the ulema and the Janissaries fought every effort made by the state toward economic and military modernization.

The ulema were apprehensive of the corrupting influence of Western innovations and ideas, while the Janissaries feared the loss of their elite status within the Ottoman army. The first thoroughgoing attempt at military reform was made by the Ottoman sultan Selim III, in 1807. In response, the chief ulema and religious authority, Shaykh-al-Islam, ordered the deposition of the sultan, who gave way to a new figurehead ruler named Mustafa IV.

This was the beginning of the ulema's fall, which finally broke their stranglehold and allowed the circulation of fresh ideas. While the theologians lost ground, another group of intellectuals, those acquainted with Western ideas and educated in Western ways, steadily gained influence in the bureaucracy.

However, the Ottoman Empire kept shrinking because of the reverses it continued to suffer at the hands of better-equipped European armies. As a result, the people, especially the youth, generally became demoralized, and tensions grew. Those adopting Western ways and culture attributed this general malaise to the absence of individualism and liberal ideas in Muslim society. Others blamed it on the lack of public representation in a government that had revolved around the monarchy ever since the birth of Islamic society. Regardless of which class ruled the nerve center of Muslim culture, its inspiration had always been the monarchical form of government.

The West appeared to provide an alternative—a constitutional government with popular representation. To some alienated youth, this alternative provided a ray of hope in the midst of growing internal tensions and economic dilemmas. They formed an organization named the Patriotic Alliance of the Young Ottomans in 1865. The Young Ottomans sought to change the absolute monarchy into a constitutional monarchy subordinate to a parliament. There was a role for the sultan in their thinking, but he could exercise arbitrary powers only in an emergency. However, they had little following at the time, and their efforts at reforms were abortive until World War I, in which the Ottoman state was humiliated by the Allied powers.

The victorious Allied powers appointed a puppet sultan to rule over the defeated state that had now shrunk to the area of Turkey. The Ottoman Empire had disappeared, and even Turkey was virtually under foreign dominance. In response to such humiliation, a nationalist movement began under the leadership of Mustafa Kemal-Attaturk. The movement steadily gained strength, and Kemal won a string of victories over the European powers, thereby freeing the area of what today constitutes Turkey. The sultan was deposed in 1922, and Turkey declared itself a republic the next year.

The Kemalist movement thus began to cut Turkish ties with the past. But the biggest change was yet to come. In 1923, Turkey abolished the monarchical sultanate, but the role of the sultan as the caliph of all Muslims was still retained. In 1926, even the Caliphate was abolished. Thus ended the last remaining vestige of the ancient regime that, one way or another, had unified the discordant fibers of Islam for more than 13 centuries. Following the sack of Baghdad by the Mongols, the Caliphate had never regained its former glory, authority and splendor, but it had continued to be the symbol of religious, though not political, unity to all Muslims.

The abolition of the Caliphate was a momentous event in Islam. It opened up a new chapter in the history of Muslim society. It symbolized the decreasing influence of the ulema and the steadily increasing influence of secular ideas (along with materialism) that had been infiltrating the tightly knit Muslim social fabric for some time. Ever since then, most Muslim nations have been steadily coming under the sway of the rich. Muslim society is currently moving through the acquisitive age. The fundamentalists headed by the ulema have lost their high status of the past, and they blame the West and its materialism for their plight. This is the chief source of the current conflict between Muslim jihadists and the Western world, especially the United States. Thus Western hedonism and materialism have now collided headlong with the theocratic bent of the mullahs, and never the twain shall meet. That is why this conflict is likely to persist till the bitter end. However, before we delve into the future, we need to understand the roots of this bitter discord.

CHAPTER 9

ROOTS OF THE CURRENT CONFLICT BETWEEN ISLAM AND THE WEST

Islam remains as vigorous today as at any time in its history. Religion dominates the Muslim world, and few Islamic nations are as economically developed as the West. They lag behind the United States, Japan, China and India in terms of industrialization and the development of new technology. But that could change soon.

The Muslim world, to say the least, is in ferment, reflecting a variety of crosscurrents among its people, who are torn between the demands of their religious tradition and the allure of Western materialism. Contrary to the West, where religion began to recede following the Renaissance of the fifteenth century, Muslim society has never seen a secular age of intellectuals. Even the second intellectual era of Islamic lands prevalent in the eighteenth and nineteenth centuries was dominated by the clergy, sharia and the Koran. It is much easier for secularists and atheists to believe in earthly ideas than it is for the believers in God. That is why the transition currently taking place in Muslim lands, from the clerical era of intellectuals to that of worldly acquisitors, is extremely difficult and problematic. And the breathtaking pace at which materialistic ideas spread in the world today further scares the fundamentalists and the faithful.

There is a vast gulf between the underlying beliefs of a theocracy and the materialism of an acquisitive polity. While theology preaches unquestioned acceptance of authority, materialism exalts a probing attitude that may even challenge authority. A religious lifestyle and an unbridled pursuit of money just don't mix well. This is perhaps the basic reason underlying the current conflict between Islamic fundamentalists and their detractors. The jihadists of Islam detest not just the United States but also Israel, western Europe and India. All their adversaries are in the closing phase of the age of acquisitors, in which supermaterialism prevails. The Islamic fundamentalists are not at odds with the authoritarian states of China, North Korea or Vietnam. They are at loggerheads with nations where money dominates politics. To some extent, the rage of the jihadists, who are also at war with the secularists in their own nations, reflects pan-Islamic nationalism, as in the struggles between the Arabs and the Jews for Palestine, and between India and Pakistan for Kashmir.

There is, of course, more to the conflict between the jihadists and their secular adversaries, and we need to go deeper into history to unearth the roots of this long-standing feud. This will also enable us to see where this conflict is headed.

Let's return to the Ottoman sultanate, the point where I left off in the previous chapter. Relative to the sultanate, Muslim society—the sum total of all the nations with a Muslim majority—is decentralized and disunited today. Gone are the days when a single monarch could command the allegiance of an entire people. As late as the turn of the twentieth century, most Muslim regions were knit, even though loosely, in the fabric of a vast empire. The Ottoman state provided the nucleus for Muslim literature and theology. Narrow nationalistic thinking was not popular. Muslims primarily thought of themselves as Osmanis or as members of a large confederation of disparate regions.

But today the main ideology is nationalism. Muslims now think of themselves as Turks, Arabs, Egyptians, Iranians and so on. Religion still provides a common bond among them. But the virus of nationalism has destroyed several aspects of that bond. Muslims today fly different flags; their states have even warred with each other. Thus, nationalistic sentiment now dominates the former pan-Islamic sentiment.

Turkey, the hub of the Ottoman Empire, is now a democracy, with an elected parliament, political parties, a prime minister and a president.

As in other democracies, those with money are generally able to influence the election process and the government. Thus Turkey, which for four centuries was the hub of Islamic society, is now ruled by a rich oligarchy. Secular ideas and materialism dominate Turkish thinking, although there is a strong minority that still follows the ideas supplied by the ulema and the mullahs, the former ruling intellectuals.

SAUDI ARABIA

The pre-eminent country in the Muslim world today is Saudi Arabia, which was formerly called Arabia. Because of vast oil deposits, the nation is now the richest among Islamic lands. What is the current source of its supremacy in Islam? Wealth. Not military might, nor brain power, but an abundant flow of money lubricated by oil. Note that in the theory of social cycle, all four classes coexist all the time, but only one dominates at any point. The Saudis still have Mecca and Medina, sites that attract a large number of pilgrims every year; their nation is still the center of Islam, but their prominent role in Muslim society derives from their wealth. If tomorrow its wealth were to vanish, pilgrims would still come, but Saudi Arabia would no longer hold the primary position among the Muslim lands.

Saudi Arabia had attained a similar position of dominance some 1,400 years ago, just after the death of the Prophet Muhammad in 632. But then the country was influential because of its military strength; today its influence derives from its wealth. While many Islamic nations, such as Egypt, Syria, Iran and Pakistan, are much stronger militarily than Saudi Arabia, they are not at the apex of Muslim society.

Saudi Arabia, even though the cradle of Islam, was barely touched by the blossoming of Islamic civilization that took place in Syria, Iraq and Egypt. For centuries Arabia's prominence was due to the fortuitous location of the holy cities of Mecca and Medina. The nation had been ruled by various tribes before Muhammad, and, but for a brief interlude during which the early caliphs were in power, the tribes continued to rule it afterward, while paying homage to one Muslim dynasty after another.

Things changed little even after the country was conquered by the Ottoman sultan in 1517. However, early in the eighteenth century, Arabia experienced renewed religious fervor in the form of the Wahabi movement, which sought to purify Islam by removing from it all the interpretations that Iranian, Indian and other non-Arabic scholars had given to the Koran and Hadith (traditions). The Wahabis emphasized the fundamentals of Islam and are therefore called Islamic fundamentalists. They regarded themselves as *muwahhidin* (monotheists), and opposed mysticism (Sufism), magical beliefs, ostentations and the veneration of saints. In short, they favored a puritanical way of life.

The Wahabi movement and its religious fervor, though starting with a handful of followers, quickly spread throughout the Arabian peninsula. By the end of the eighteenth century, it had won the loyalty of some tribal chiefs, who subsequently even captured Mecca. Then, however, it had to contend with the Ottoman power, which crushed it by 1818, thereby ending its first phase.

The second phase of Wahabism began in 1902, when one of its ardent followers, Abdul Aziz Ibn Saud, attacked and captured Riyadh. Thus began a new kingdom that has lasted to this day. After capturing Riyadh, Ibn Saud began to consolidate his position. His religious zeal and the Wahabi following won him the loyalty of many Bedouin tribes. By the end of World War I, he had become the master of a large area called Nejd. Another large kingdom, Hijaz, containing the cities of Mecca and Medina, existed side-by-side with Nejd. In 1926, Ibn Saud defeated the Hijaz king, unified the two kingdoms, and in 1932 named his domain Saudi Arabia.

The renamed nation began as a theocratic state, but its character began to change soon after oil was discovered in the late 1930s. The king was, and is, not only the ruler of a large territory, but also an imam (or the head) of the Wahabi religious movement. Ibn Saud considered his mission to be the spreading of what he declared the true interpretations of Islam. He was not an autocrat, however, because he had to rely on the continued loyalty of the tribal sheikhs. His laws and decrees were based on the Koran and sharia.

In 1953, Ibn Saud was succeeded by his son bearing the same name. Saudi Arabia then became what may be loosely called a constitutional monarchy. A Council of Ministers was established to head the administration. This, as historian Don Peretz notes, "was the first effort to define authority in terms other than the traditional system in which the monarch arbitrarily makes all important decisions. Now the king is more like a constitutional monarch; his decisions are based on consultation with the Council of Ministers."[1]

Since 1953 many more ministries have been added to administer the country and its economy. Ministries of education, agriculture, health and commerce, among others, have formed over the years. The administrative system is beginning to resemble Western structure and organization. But most ministries are headed by relatives of the royal family. Many ministers are ambitious merchants; they frequently abuse their positions to enrich themselves or their commercial enterprises.[2]

The discovery of oil in the 1930s and the tremendous surge in oil prices since 1973 have radically changed Saudi Arabia. Until oil's arrival, the Saudi economy was one of the most primitive and technologically backward in the Muslim world. It was predicated on the self-sufficient, independent units of the oasis, the village and the Bedouin tribe. The country suffered from poverty, illiteracy, disease and a shortage of capital. Its predominantly agricultural economy was on the verge of financial collapse because of declining world demand for its exports. The king had the prudence to invite Western companies to explore for oil.

Soon the country was transformed from the desert to an oasis of oil. Millions of dollars began to pour into the royal treasury every year. Ever since the 1930s, oil has become the mainstay of the Saudi economy, providing more than 75 percent of its national income. Without oil revenues, the Saudi kingdom would perhaps have remained the tribal economy it had inherited from its predecessor. But oil has changed all that. It has enabled the country to import Western technology and luxuries on a vast scale.

But the oil royalties, while transforming the Saudi economy, have also transformed the mentality of the ruling family, which became the chief beneficiary of the surge in incomes. The royal family is a rather large group of about 5,000 people, including the king, his children, their cousins, spouses, relatives by marriage and so on. Easy availability of luxuries and money has altered their former religious zeal into a zeal for material possessions. Describing the royal family's transformation that began with the discovery of oil, Peretz remarks:

No longer were the Sauds austere Wahabi desert sheiks. They now lived in oriental splendor surrounded by every conceivable luxury. Scores of royal princes purchased several high-priced American automobiles each and went on sprees of building palaces equipped with such modern amenities as air conditioning and swimming pools.[3]

In the past, the Sauds won the loyalty of tribal chiefs through their religious fervor. They controlled society because of their control over ideas. All this has changed since the 1930s. By the 1950s and 1960s loyalties were won by money, not ideas. In Peretz's words:

> Subsidies exacted by tribal leaders and allies throughout the peninsula drained off much of the oil income. These payments helped lessen the complaints against the high style of living and strengthened ties with the central authorities. They were necessary if the Sauds were to retain the loyalty of numerous tribal leaders.[4]

Even after the discovery of oil in the 1930s, Saudi Arabia did not immediately become the dominant Muslim country. It had a small population and a one-sided economic base, which, over the past 70-plus years, has shifted dramatically from agriculture to industry. In the second half of the twentieth century, Egypt, under President Gamal Abdul Nasser, was perhaps the most influential country among Islamic lands.

However, in 1973, Saudi Arabia, along with some other OPEC members, imposed an oil embargo on the world. Soon oil prices rose fourfold from $2.50 per barrel to about $10 per barrel. Since then the flow of oil revenues to the Saudi economy has been truly staggering.

The world is now beholden to this new power, whose strength lies not in military might, nor in ideas, but in control over a natural resource. Many countries, from the left to the right sides of the political spectrum, have been trying to court the Saudi government for economic assistance or loans. The financial stability of the whole world depends on the economic policies of a relatively small group of people—the Saudi royal family. On them rests the fate of all economies that have an unquenchable thirst for oil. Today, Saudi Arabia has indeed become a wealthy giant and a financial superpower.

UAE AND KUWAIT

Besides Saudi Arabia, the Arabian peninsula is home to two other countries that are immensely rich because of their oil deposits—the United Arab Emirates (UAE) and Kuwait. The UAE was established in 1971 when the British decided to withdraw from their colonies in the Persian Gulf. The UAE consists of seven principalities, of which Abu Dhabi and Dubai are the best known.

Of the two UAE principalities, Abu Dhabi was, and is, the richest and most populous territory, followed by Dubai. The remaining five are not as rich in mineral and human resources. The UAE is a federation of which the presidency has usually been reserved for the sheikh of Abu Dhabi and the vice presidency for the sheikh of Dubai. The country is governed by the Supreme Council in which the cabinet seats are allocated according to the population of the territories. The National Federal Assembly, which has 40 seats, is formed in the same manner.

The UAE is a replica of Saudi Arabia on a miniature scale. Its oil wealth and sparse population of less than one million give it perhaps the highest per capita income in the world. As with Saudi Arabia's, the UAE's wealth has earned it international prestige and influence, exemplified by the Abu Dhabi Fund for Arab Economic Development, which has extended loans worth billions of dollars to some Arab and developing countries. Similarly, key government posts in the UAE are held by members of the ruling families, most of whom are rich merchants.

Kuwait is another oil-rich Muslim state. In terms of society, government and wealth, the nation is also a mini Saudi Arabia, except that in Kuwait democratic institutions such as a free press, national assembly and independent judiciary are somewhat more advanced than in any other Arab nation. Until 1961, Kuwait was a protectorate of England. When the British withdrew, the nation gained independence and adopted a constitutional monarchy with the ruling family, al-Sabah, holding important positions in the army, bureaucracy and government. The ruling sheikh is advised by a National Assembly, which consists of 50 members, who are chosen in elections held every four years.

In 2005, Kuwait gave women the right to vote, starting with the municipal election in 2006. The country now has a female cabinet minister, Dr. Massouma Mubarak, which is a big breakthrough for women's rights in the Persian Gulf region. However, the affluent oligarchs still dominate in Kuwait.

CENTRALIZED GOVERNMENTS

Muslim society is currently divided into more than 25 nations. In many, some sort of centralized rule prevails. This category includes Pakistan,

Libya, Syria, Egypt, Sudan and Algeria. Pakistan, until 1947, was part of Indo-Aryan society. Pakistan has been frequently under military rule ever since its independence. There, as elsewhere, the rich enjoy the highest prestige in the nation. Most people want to be businessmen rather than become intellectuals or join the army. Similarly, governmental policies serve the interests of the wealthy.

As regards Egypt, Syria, Algeria and Libya, the social and political fabric is mixed. These four nations are in a phase of transition, although at present the military is the mainstay of their regimes. Their present structure of bureaucratic administration and government came into being because of military coups against monarchies or constitutional democracies. Yet each of these nations has had a colonial past during which they were heavily influenced by England or France. Some of their intellectuals acquired Western education, secular ideas and a preference for Western lifestyles. Similarly, their societies have absorbed Western ideas of secularism and materialism. Some of them have even changed their names to separate themselves from their monarchic past. They call themselves republics to emphasize their commitment to socialist ideas of equality and public welfare. Thus Egypt is now the Arab Republic of Egypt; Sudan is now the Democratic Republic of Sudan. Yemen is the Yemen Arab Republic, and so on. Such names should not be taken to imply that democracy prevails in these countries; only that they have gone out of their way to deemphasize the centralized basis of their regimes. Yet there is no denying that the military is supreme in at least Libya, Syria, Egypt and Sudan.

Recent Colonialism

Let us now reexamine the colonial period in recent Arab history if only to see why some Muslim nations are still under the control of warriors. Almost all the Muslim territories that fell into British, French and Italian hands had been parts of the Ottoman Empire. The first territory to fall was Algeria, which was occupied by France in 1830. Next came Tunisia, which was also seized by the French. In 1875, Egypt was on the verge of financial bankruptcy and sold its shares in the Suez Canal to England, which, in order to protect its investment, occupied Egypt in

1882. By the turn of the twentieth century, Sudan was also added to the British Empire.

In 1911, Italy occupied Libya, and a year later Morocco became a French protectorate. By 1916, Syria and Lebanon fell to France, and Iraq, Palestine and Jordan to England. Thus by the end of World War I, almost all of the Arab world had fallen to European powers.

Both England and France claimed to be bringing light, modernity and civilization to what they regarded as primitive and backward areas of the world. They transplanted their own educational and administrative systems to exploit the colonial economies as much as possible. No European power, however, granted human rights to its colonial subjects, rights that were enjoyed by its people at home. Nevertheless, they brought modern technology and secular thought to the occupied lands.

Because of their British or French connections, many Muslim lands experimented with constitutional government or democracy. Egypt did this as early as 1882, when a two-chamber parliament, with advisory powers, was introduced in the country with the approval of King Tewfik, who formally acknowledged the sovereignty of the Ottoman sultan. But the real power rested with the British Consul General, a fact that stirred Egyptian nationalism. Such sentiment found expression in a political party called Wafd, which enjoyed mass support because of its anti-British views. The party won favor with a number of groups, including the middle class, merchants, students, landlords and businessmen.

Until 1922, Egypt was a British protectorate, a status that was terminated that year when the country formally reverted to the reigning monarchy of Sultan Ahmed Fuad. A new constitution was introduced in 1923, giving extensive powers to the king, who could appoint ministers, veto any legislation and dissolve the parliament at his whim. Yet the real power continued to rest with the British High Commissioner.

As Britain continued to meddle in Egypt's affairs, various political parties were elected to power. But none, including Wafd, championed the land reforms that were badly needed to eliminate poverty. The king was content in his own palace, while the wealthy landlords controlled the parliament.

Meanwhile, the influence of the ulema had declined because their monopoly over thought had been successfully challenged by the imported Western ideas that were basically secular and anticlerical. The

Wafd, which was anticlerical and strictly nationalistic, enjoyed mass support. However, the rich landlords, making up 0.4 percent of the population but controlling 37 percent of arable land, held the levers of power.

It is in the wake of such oppression of the masses that an army colonel, Nasser, staged a coup in 1952 and overthrew King Farouk. Nasser suspended the constitution, abolished the political parties and appointed a provisional government. In 1956 the country adopted a new constitution proclaiming Egypt an Islamic Arab state with a democratic form of government. Nasser was then elected president, a position he retained until his death in 1970.

Sweeping economic and social reforms were introduced in postrevolutionary Egypt. Ceilings were placed on landholdings, and the surplus land was widely distributed among landless peasants. At the same time, education was made compulsory for all children between the ages of 7 and 12.[5]

Ever since the 1952 revolution, the pendulum of power has swung toward the army, with army officers holding many cabinet posts. Following Nasser's death, another military official who had participated in overthrowing the monarchy, Anwar Sadat, was elected as president, although he was later assassinated. Since 1981, the presidency has belonged to an air force commander named Hosni Mubarak. Thus the military has ruled Egypt ever since 1952, the fateful year of Nasser's revolution.

Let us now examine the societies of Syria and Iraq, both of which can be analyzed very briefly, because their development, in terms of the law of social cycle, closely resembles that of Egypt. Both Syria and Iraq experimented with democracy and were dominated by rich landlords until the military coups that brought the warriors to power. Both had been infiltrated by Western acquisitive and secular ideas because of their long contact with European powers. And while both have advanced economically—Iraq more than Syria because of its oil—the power base of the landed interests and the rich remains intact.

In the period following World War II, both Syria and Iraq, unlike Egypt, experienced political instability. Coup after coup occurred, but the power effectively remained with the army. Syria still remains under military rule, but Iraq, currently under American occupation, is experimenting with democracy. We will come back to Iraq in the next chapter.

IRAN

Iran, another oil-rich state in the Persian Gulf, is one country that currently offers a radically different profile among Muslim nations. It is predominantly Shia, as is Iraq, its neighbor to the west. Most other Muslim lands are Sunni, and have been in conflict with the Shiites for over a thousand years. Iran's sudden entrance into the priestly era occurred in February 1979, when the reigning monarch, Shah Muhammad Reza Pahlavi, fled and moved into exile. This was a culmination of months of violence, bloodshed and turmoil in which thousands of Iranians, protesting the tortuous regime of the shah, were killed by the police and army. The Iranians were responding to the call of a little known mullah named Ayatollah Ruhollah Khomeini, who himself had been exiled by the government some 15 years before. How did the ayatollah rise to quick prominence? More important, how was he able to force the once mighty shah to abdicate his throne?

Reza Shah

The revolution of Iran was a long time in the making. The shah belonged to a dynasty that had been in power since 1921. His father, Reza Shah, had ascended the throne in a nationalist uprising against his predecessor. Reza Shah's actions and ideals are comparable to those of Kemal Attaturk in Turkey. Both ruled their respective countries with an iron hand, and came to power at about the same time. Both had undying faith in the superiority of Western institutions over those prevailing in their nations, and both sought to eliminate the influence of the clergy.

Reza Shah attempted to unify the nation by focusing on Iran's pre-Islamic days. In order to reduce the influence of the mullahs, he proclaimed Zoroastrianism as the state religion along with the Shiite faith. The sun and the lion, symbolic of the great Achaemenid and Sasanid empires, were introduced with much publicity and fanfare. The ancient religion had few followers left, but Reza Shah glorified it anyway. He called his dynasty Pahlavi, a name he borrowed from the Parthians of ancient Persia. Iranians were frequently reminded of the splendor of their pre-Islamic heritage, going as far back as the prophet Zoroaster and the emperor Cyrus the Great. In short, Reza Shah tried to create a nationalist sentiment by focusing not on religion, which he regarded as a hindrance to progress, but on Iran's ancient glories. Thus, in various ways, Reza Shah limited the influence of the clergy, the former ruling class, over society.

With Reza Shah's ascension, Iran rapidly launched a program of industrialization and Westernization. Factories, communications, railroads, hospitals, schools and universities were set up in quick succession, all based on European models. State industries were built in the areas of textiles, sugar refining and chemicals. At times, such ventures failed, because they had been introduced without regard to the availability of natural resources and markets.

A law in 1929 tried to encourage the use of Western clothing; European hats were introduced in 1935, and in 1936 women were required to discard their veils. Reza Shah, while copying Attaturk in many ways, was much more autocratic than his Turkish counterpart. While Attaturk had encouraged individual initiative, no such attempt was made in Iran. All changes, good or bad, were imposed by official decrees. Quite often opponents to the shah were simply murdered. For several years, Iran remained under a reign of terror, while the shah seized his people's property at the slightest excuse and amassed a huge fortune.

Shah Muhammad Reza Pahlavi

In the 1930s, Reza Shah, himself a dictator, entered into alliance with another dictator—Adolph Hitler. He did this in part to counteract the influence of Russia. However, he chose the wrong ally, and was caught in the web of international conflict leading to World War II. The British and Russian forces occupied Iran in 1941, and Reza Shah was forced into exile.

After the shah's abdication, the crown passed to his son, Muhammad Reza Pahlavi, who was 21 at the time. The new shah was not as autocratic as his father, at least not at the time of his coronation. Later he would become as ruthless as his predecessor, but in 1941, when he ascended the throne, he had different ideas. Like his father, he championed Westernization of the economy and society; unlike his father, however, he believed in individual initiative and in sharing a modicum of power with others.

There were two lasting effects of the 16-year rule of Reza Shah. First, the clergy were weakened. At least in big cities the Western system of education, secular outlook and imported technology tended to erode the influence of clergymen—mullahs and ayatollahs. Second, industrialization gave rise to a middle class and a group of rich merchants, who, because of their wealth, commanded respect and influence in society.

The new shah ruled from 1941 to 1979. His regime may be divided into three periods. The first, lasting from 1941 to 1953, was the most liberalized period of his rule. Many political parties flourished during these years, and the government was run somewhat on the basis of a constitutional monarchy. Westernization and secularization of society proceeded apace, and the torture and terrorizing perpetrated by the previous government largely disappeared.

The second period began in 1953 when a national uprising briefly forced the shah to abdicate the throne, but he was quickly reinstated by a military coup instigated by the U.S. Central Intelligence Agency (CIA). The lesson of the unsuccessful revolt was not lost on the shah. He became a changed man, ready to assert his authority and virtually unlimited powers. Iranians' constitutional rights were severely curtailed, and the shah began to take an active role in politics.

In 1957, the shah sponsored a People's Party to fill the role of the opposition. A few months later came the pro-government Nation Party, thereby creating a two-party system. Both groups were composed of prominent merchants and landlords loyal to the shah. Thus, political power was effectively in the hands of acquisitors.

After the abortive coup of 1953, the shah took firm command of all political activity while maintaining a facade of democracy. In addition, he began to restrict individual rights by increasing the powers of his secret police, known as SAVAK. Thus, the relatively liberal government of the shah turned into a repressive regime; SAVAK began to spy on Iranians, both inside and outside the country. Its torture tactics became internationally known. During this time, ironically, the shah continued to enjoy the support of democratic governments, which are at least theoretically committed to the observance of human rights. As the shah turned repressive, the influence of his friends, relatives, merchants and landlords, who all controlled the legislatures, soared. The fruits of industrialization, made possible by rising oil revenues, went mainly into the coffers of the rich loyal to the shah.

The third period began in 1963, when the shah introduced land reforms and confiscated many properties that belonged to the clergy.

While police power was increased sharply, land reforms were implemented only halfheartedly. This period saw the beginning of the rise of
clerical opposition to royal authority and culminated in the final overthrow of the shah in 1979.

The oil price surge following the 1973 oil embargo made the rich
even richer. Oil revenues jumped, and the shah sped up his program of
industrialization and technical development. But prosperity continued to
bypass the needy. Acquisitors were ruling society, and they continued to
amass wealth despite their already high incomes. For this is the way the
rich behave: no matter how much they have, they want more.

The rising inequities in the distribution of income and wealth, cou-
pled with the massive bureaucratic corruption that always accompanies
them, began to generate resentment among the clergy and secular intellectuals. The opponents of the shah became vocal inside Iran and
abroad, and SAVAK became even more ruthless. Thousands of Iranians
were tortured in the "chambers of horror." Some were decapitated; others were given electrical shocks; still others were regularly beaten with
lashes; some were summarily executed. The result was that gradually
many sections of Iran became committed to overthrowing the regime.
They included priests, factory workers, liberal intellectuals, the peas-
antry and even small-scale merchants.

To all this may be added the speedy import of the Western lifestyle,
which did not go well with the masses, who still cherished their Islamic
values. The showpieces of modernization introduced by businessmen—
including casinos, prostitution houses, pornographic literature, nudity,
industrial monopolies, bars and the like—were resented by a large majority of the people. By 1978, the ruler had managed to alienate almost
all sections of society. A sudden eruption of their collective anger was
simply a matter of time.

And the eruption came—with a bang. It began with an innocent
protest by oil workers demanding higher wages to cope with inflation.
Trying to catch up with industrialists, bankers and monopolists, they
sought higher salaries, which the government could not afford to pay
without risking a further increase in inflation. The result was an impasse
that resulted in occasional violence. The labor protest became infectious.
Oil workers were joined by workers from other industries, which came
to a virtual halt. The government responded with force, initially at-
tempting to break up protest marches through arrests and tear gas.

Workers responded by throwing stones and burning cars and theaters. Police in turn started shooting, thereby initiating a cycle of violence that lasted for more than six months, and ended in the forced abdication of the shah in January 1979.

Ayatollah Khomeini

When the Iranian revolution began in early 1978, it had no focus, no leader. It was simply a protest against rich men's oppression, which had resulted in great inequities of income and wealth. But soon a cleric named Ayatollah Khomeini, who had been exiled to Iraq in 1964, became a symbol of the revolution. Throughout his exile, he had insisted that the shah must go. Even from outside the country, he commanded a large following within Iran. His simple and austere way of life stood in sharp contrast to the ostentations and corruption of the shah and his supporters.

Every entity in this world moves around a nucleus. The Iranian eruption was leaderless in the beginning. But when Ayatollah Khomeini, while in neighboring Iraq, began to urge his followers to struggle and fight to overthrow the shah, he became the nucleus, and the eruption turned into a revolution. Demonstrators began to wave banners bearing ayatollah's images in their marches; they began shouting slogans in his name.

Frightened, the shah pressured Iraq into throwing Khomeini out. In October 1978, the ayatollah was exiled to France, where he made his home just outside Paris. There, joined by close followers and other exiles, he began to broadcast his views via the Western news media. This was an unexpected boon to the revolution as Khomeini's words could be heard by Iranians on radios tuned to the British and French broadcasting stations. Upon his calls, his followers shut down factories, bazaars, banks, the postal service and above all the oil wells, which were the main source of foreign exchange and imports.

The shah responded by imposing martial law, but it did not help. It could not, because the oppressed people were prepared to accept bullets. There were regular protests and demonstrations, with hundreds dying every day. Finally, the police and the military joined the protesters, and the shah was forced into exile, once again.

On February 1, 1979, Khomeini returned from France after 15 years of exile. The Iranians gave him a hearty welcome, cheering that the holy one had come. The ayatollah settled at the holy city of Qum and appointed a provisional government. But the real power rested with a 15-man Revolutionary Council that he headed. Within a few weeks of his return, it became apparent that all power rested with the clergy. Priests had taken over the land, with the nation reverting to the rule of clerical intellectuals.

When the clergy returned to power in Iran, the concomitant return of numerous rules and regulations restraining individual behavior was inevitable. Such transformations had happened in Muslim society and all other civilizations before, and there was nothing to prevent its repetition in contemporary Iran as well.

Shortly after the revolution, the ayatollah issued a series of directives, imposing an austere way of life on all Iranians. Some directives were designed to root out lechery and the dilution of moral values. Thus prostitution houses, bars and casinos were closed. Other directives, such as the ban of all forms of music, were restrictions on individual freedom.

Women, of course, bore the brunt of these restraints. Under the shah, women had enjoyed many freedoms. They could participate in all social activities without having to cover themselves under veils (or chadors). With the rise of the clergy, however, a complex series of restrictions was imposed on female behavior. Women were now urged, though not forced, to wear chadors. They were barred from several professions, and were advised to confine themselves to household activities. Iranian women did protest at first, but there was nothing they could do to stem the priestly tide.

As the clergy returned to power, the economy began to sink. Soon after the revolution, banks and heavy industry were nationalized. Most government officers had no managerial expertise. As a result, since the revolution, Iranians' living standard has declined considerably. Similarly, the economy has suffered high unemployment and occasional bouts of inflation.

The revolution had occurred in February; by December, a new constitution was introduced to legalize and solidify the hold of the clergy. It was overwhelmingly approved in a referendum, turning Iran into a theocracy. The constitution provides for a president and a parliament (Majlis), but above them is a guardian council of Muslim theologians whose purpose is to ensure that the legislation of the elected government conforms with Islamic law as contained in the Koran and Hadith. Heading them all is a *faqih*, the foremost theologian, who towers over the government and can veto any legislation. The *faqih* commands the military and can even fire the president. Thus, since 1979 when the hold of the clergy over the country was formalized, Iran has been in the midst of the priestly age of intellectuals.[6]

CONCLUSION

I have argued in this chapter that Muslim society, made up of about 25 nations, is currently moving through an acquisitive age, in which political power and social prestige belong to persons of the acquisitive mentality possessing great amounts of wealth. This is the second acquisitive era of Muslim society, an era still in its infancy. Its beginning may be traced back to the abolition of the Caliphate in 1923.

The new acquisitive era is still very young and moving very slowly. For this reason, the Islamic society does not currently present a unified or homogeneous picture. Some of its member nation-states such as Egypt, Syria, Libya, Sudan, Somalia and Tunisia are currently under the rule of the warrior class even though prior to their respective army takeovers they had moved into the acquisitive age. Other member nation-states, such as Saudi Arabia, Kuwait, United Arab Emirates, Turkey, Lebanon, Malaysia, Morocco, Bahrain, Oman, Pakistan, Bangladesh and even India, which has a large Muslim population, are in the midst of the acquisitive age. By contrast, Iran, in the midst of an acquisitive age until the deposition of the shah in January 1979, is currently ensconced in the priestly age of intellectuals.

In spite of its great diversity, Muslim civilization as a whole may currently be regarded as moving through the acquisitive age because its most influential member, the kingdom of Saudi Arabia, derives its influence not from military power, nor from the force of ideas, but from its control over vast amounts of wealth. In most Muslim countries, materialism and acquisitive tendencies are slowly gaining ground. The rich are highly respected, much more than theologians or army officers.

However, the intellectuals, or the religious fundamentalists, headed by the ulema, mullahs or ayatollahs, who ruled during the preceeding age, are still a strong force in most Muslim lands. They blame their loss of power and prestige on Western ideas; they think materialism is the same as liberal values, the observance of human rights and democracy, in which they are, or could be, the biggest losers. That is why they are hostile to the West, especially the United States. They will be happy to embrace democracy if their fundamentalist ideas help them win elections. But time is now on the side of acquisitive ideas, and the fundamentalists are fighting a losing cause. Subconsciously they are aware of their obsolescence, and that is why they cannot, for instance, permit free and fair elections in Iran.

The inherent conflict, predicted by the law of social cycle, between the intellectuals who were previously in power and the emerging class of acquisitors is really at the root of the turmoil in many Muslim lands. It is also the source of the battle between Islamic jihadists and the West, which the fundamentalists consider a friend of Islamic acquisitors. The ongoing mayhem in Iraq ultimately reflects this basic rift between the intensely religious-minded intellectuals (Shias) and relatively secular-leaning acquisitors (Sunnis). Unfortunately, the United States seems to be allied with the Iraqi Shiites, and time is not on their side. The United States is fighting a losing battle, which could eventually threaten its own economy and social stability. This is the subject to which I now turn in the pages to come.

CHAPTER 10

OUR COMMON FUTURE

I t is time to revisit the original purpose of this book, which is to weave the various strands of economic and historical analyses together and see why there is so much poverty amid plenty in the world, and where we're all headed. In the next chapter, I will offer a variety of reforms that could shorten the time of troubles that I see coming. It will explore what we as individuals can do to minimize the likely aftershocks of current myopic U.S. policies and hasten the process of change necessary to eradicate poverty.

My focus in this book has been on a variety of cycles, because they reveal patterns that can be used to make forecasts. Generally, if a pattern has lasted for a long time, even centuries, and can be broken only by a calamitous event, then barring such an event, the pattern is likely to hold true for the future. For instance, the three-decade cycle of inflation shows that ever since 1750 inflation has peaked every third decade in the United States, except for the immediate aftermath of the Civil War, which has no parallel in U.S. history. It is reasonable to assume that absent a similar calamity, the cycle will continue to hold.

Another recurring pattern of history is the law of social cycle, which maintains that in every civilization the age of laborers is followed by the age of warriors, then by the age of intellectuals, then by the age of acquisitors, culminating in a warrior-led social revolution of the laborers. This completes one rotation of the cycle; another rotation begins with the same pattern, as warriors, intellectuals and the wealthy come to power by turn, and so on. The social cycle is common to all civilizations, and, to my knowledge, has never failed in all of recorded history. Even calamitous events generally fail to break this cycle; on the contrary, they actually move it forward. This suggests that all we have to do to read the future is to see where a society stands in terms of the social cycle, and then apply the law to see where it is headed. In any case, in the late 1970s I applied such an analysis to unfolding world events and trends and was able to make a variety of predictions, such as the downfall of Soviet communism, the rise of the priesthood in Iran and a violent collision between Islam and the West, starting around 2000. In what follows, I will use similar analysis to make forecasts about global capitalism, share and bond markets and a host of other variables and institutions.

WHERE WE STAND TODAY

Before we know where we are headed, we have to know where we stand in terms of the social cycle. Figure 10.1 compares where, according to my calculations, the world is today and where it was in 1980, when I wrote about Muslim civilization. At that time, Russia was near the bottom of its age of warriors, but moved into the early phase of intellectuals in the mid-1990s, following the demise of the Soviet empire. Japan was at the peak of its age of acquisitors but is now in the declining phase of that age; Muslim society was at the beginning of its acquisitive era and is still near that point. China was at the midpoint of its age of warriors but now sits close to its top. Finally, Latin America (L.A.), the West, including the United States, and India were a few years away from their social revolutions and are now closer than ever to that point.

Let's take another look at U.S. history, especially in our new millennium. I have argued before that the United States moved into the age of laborers or the acquisitive-cum-labor age around 1973–1974, when the Nixon-Agnew duo was dethroned. That was the time when the real wage for production workers, who constitute at least 75 percent of the workforce, began to sink. Official corruption and growing wealth concentration, along with the public's falling living standard, are the main features of the age of laborers, and after 1973 such woes started to afflict the nation with increasing virulence.

Figure 10.1. Eras in Various Societies

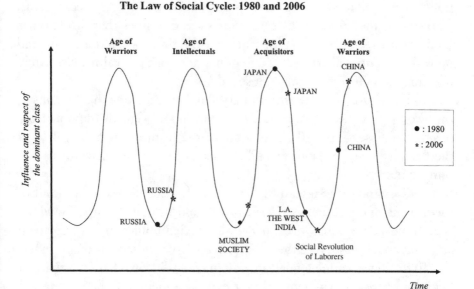

The Law of Social Cycle: 1980 and 2006

Everything that has occurred since then points to deepening degradation in society, something that I delineated in my book, *The Downfall of Capitalism and Communism*. Loose morals, family breakdown, a vanishing middle class, official arrogance, disobedient children, growing indiscipline, mushrooming poverty, sky-high debt, rampant crime, classroom cheating, a galloping tax burden on the destitute and above all the rich getting unabashedly richer at the expense of the poor are indicators of the last days of the acquisitive age.

Today, the United States is not far from where the Soviet Union was prior to its disintegration. The Soviet empire broke up right before our eyes. The U.S. business empire is next, because every age of laborers ends in a social revolution of the workers, who were previously warriors and intellectuals but, with the elite grabbing ever-increasing amounts of income and wealth, have to work harder and harder to maintain their lifestyle. Most of them end up in debt after providing heavy labor for lower pay.

In the West, people with the acquisitive mentality clearly dominate in every walk of life today, and they are almost single-minded in amassing wealth. They have become so obsessed with money that they are treating other classes with disdain. Real wages are sinking for teachers, policemen, soldiers, firefighters, salespeople, forklifters, technicians, clerks, auto mechanics and so on. Such are the times that, in Thomas Paine's words, "try men's souls;" such are the times when the public, fed up with the imperial arrogance and dominance of the wealthy, ultimately overthrows their regime through social revolt.

Today we are in a prerevolutionary stage, like the one that feudalism, the West's previous era of acquisitive-cum-labor, went through just before its collapse. Table 10.1 lists some of the features of the last days of the feudalistic age of laborers and compares them with those of its current capitalistic counterpart.

Let's examine these features one by one. Feudalism displayed all of them in its dying days from 1450 to the end of that century, by which time some warriors had overthrown the landed nobles in France, Spain and England. These were then Western society's prerevolutionary times.

To further examine feudalism, you may recall from chapter 5 that the living standard had risen sharply for everyone including the serfs in the feudalistic age of acquisitors. Serfs and peasants had even won their freedom from forced labor. But later, as wages went up, the landlords wanted

Table 10.1. America in a Prerevolutionary Stage: The Similarities between Capitalism and Feudalism

Feudalism	*Capitalism*
1. Landlords demand concessions from former serfs	1. Companies demand wage concessions from workers
2. Wealth concentration rising sharply	2. CEOs becoming billionaires and zillionaires
3. Rampant crime, near anarchy	3. Growing population of prisoners and criminals
4. Rising poverty among the people	4. Rising poverty among the people
5. People infuriated with feudal barons	5. People enraged by CEO scandals
6. An epidemic of official incompetence	6. An epidemic of official incompetence
7. Growing public unrest because of warfare	7. Iraq War killing soldiers, creating unrest and destroying army morale
8. Unusual natural calamities, especially drought and pestilence	8. Tsunamis, hurricanes, earthquakes piling upon the world
9. Black Death or plague	9. The spread of AIDS and the possibility of avian flu pandemic

to rescind their contracts and demanded that their former serfs provide hard labor on their farms. This led to peasant revolts, bloodshed and crippling poverty.

Something similar has happened this time around. The real wage went up for many, many decades in the United States; simultaneously, however, corporate barons began to demand free trade, and economic gurus, while theorizing and predicting that tariff cuts would trim real wages, supported these barons' demands. Thus the elite economists backed free trade in full knowledge that it creates poverty in America.

Following World War II, U.S. multinationals overwhelmingly dominated the world's industries, but they wanted more. They thought they could become even stronger through greater access to other markets. But the opposite happened, because other nations worked hard and began to outcompete the U.S. behemoths at their own game.

The economists' forecasts gradually came true, and for the first time in the nation's history, the real wage began to fall, from 1973 on, in spite of improving technology and rising productivity. During the 1990s, a new scourge arrived for workers in the form of outsourcing, which has been spreading like wildfire since 2000. Now U.S. companies are demanding increasing concessions from labor unions and older workers so the companies can compete with lower wages abroad. Not just lucrative wages, but health benefits as well as pensions are disappearing. Giant firms like Caterpillar and Delphi, a part of General Motors, that used to pay up to $30 per hour to their workers seek to pay only half as much. Sadly, American labor has little choice; if good jobs survive the company's potential or threatened relocation abroad, then they will be devoured by outsourcing.

Second, even though the workers are getting poorer, the CEOs are getting richer than ever. Feudalism went through the same phase, as more and more land became concentrated in the hands of fewer barons. CEOs are today's robber barons. As reporter Claudia Deutsch of *The New York Times* writes:

Animosity toward executives as a class, not just the institutions they work for, seems to be rising to a new level. . . . In a Roper poll . . . 72 percent of respondents felt that wrongdoing was widespread in industry; last year, 66 percent felt that was the case. . . . Only 2 percent checked off "very trustworthy" to describe the chief executives of very large companies, down from 3 percent last year.[1]

A mere 2 percent of Americans trust executives. People also detest corrupt congressmen and other lawmakers for being on the payroll of corporate barons. The Roper poll mentioned above implies that 72 percent of Americans view company executives as just plain thugs.

Third, feudalism was increasingly marred by violent crime, especially against women and the elderly. Today, nearly 3 million Americans are incarcerated because of rapes, murders and robberies. The only difference is that now criminals primarily use guns and pistols, whereas in the past they used knives, swords and machetes.

Fourth, people are becoming poorer, just as in the past, with America's poverty rolls soaring by a million every year.

Fifth, the public was fed up with the corrupt and ruthless barons during the fifteenth century; today, Americans, as just mentioned above, are increasingly furious with corporate crooks for financial swindles, as well as for their outrageous compensation that quite often has no connection with merit and performance.

Sixth, in the fifteenth century, official corruption was excelled only by official incompetence, which today reminds us of the Bush-Cheney Administration. Some polls taken in June 2006 put Bush's approval rating below 30 percent, and Cheney's at 25 percent. It seems that whatever the duo touches turns into a flop. The *New York Times* columnist Bob Herbert dubs its accomplishments, "a dismal record of failure after failure." He goes on to write: "The fiasco in Iraq and the president's response to the Hurricane Katrina catastrophe were Mr. Bush's two most spectacular foul-ups. There have been many others. The president's new Medicare prescription drug program has been a monumental embarrassment, leaving some of the most vulnerable members of our society without essential medication."[2]

Seventh, toward the end of feudalism, rampant crime was aggravated by warfare between England and France, and by civil war in Spain, with huge losses of money and life. Today, as in ages past when empires and stale social systems found themselves on the verge of collapse, we also have a demoralizing war on our hands. The Iraq War consumes billions of dollars of defense spending and thousands of lives. Iraqi deaths and destruction are much higher. Even some former generals such as Anthony Zinni, former chief of U.S. Central Command, are critical of the administration.[3]

Bush and Cheney's seeming contempt for the armed forces' men and women has become legendary. The administration's ruthlessness in this regard beggars description. Nixon and Agnew could not have done worse. They, too, were involved in an unpopular conflict—the Vietnam War. But unlike Bush and Cheney, they did not shortchange the soldier. They did not cut taxes in wartime. Now the soldier is making all the sacrifices, while the acquisitive elite enjoy galloping incomes and tax windfalls at the expense of the warriors' toil and blood.

The Bush-Cheney Administration, burdened by one of the worst budget deficits in U.S. history (which is primarily the product of their tax cuts), wanted to fight the war on the cheap. They did not send enough troops to the front, nor did they provide sufficient body armor for those they did deploy. Several thousand army men and women, not to mention the much-abused National Guard, have had to perform multiple tours, risking their lives and sanity—all so that multinational giants like Halliburton, Cheney's former employer, can profiteer from the war with no-bid contracts. The soldiers and their children, in the meantime, will be stuck with the debt burden in the future. It will be a war debt for which some gave up their lives.

Battle-weary troops, of course, want to get out of Iraq. In a Zogby poll conducted in March 2006, "72 percent of the respondents, serving in various branches of the armed forces, said the U.S. should leave Iraq within the next year, including 29 percent who said we should pull out immediately."[4] But how can they get out? One of the unstated reasons they were sent to Iraq in 2002 and 2003 was to secure cheap oil. The administration even predicted a price of $20 per barrel once the conflict was over. It had no idea at the time that its buddies, the oil tycoons and hedge fund managers, would take advantage of the war and use it as an excuse to raise the cost of gasoline, even while supplies remained plentiful.

That $20 oil, with prices hovering around $70 in 2006, appears a cruel joke on the Americans. What an irony: the soldiers' families have to face the same giant cost of gasoline that everyone else does, but the soldiers are dying or getting maimed for it. Such is the Bush-Cheney bequest to our military and to us. Poignant words from best-selling author Thomas Friedman, also a columnist for the *New York Times*, say it all: "These are people so much better at inflicting pain than feeling it, so much better at taking things apart than putting them together, so much better at defending 'intelligent design' as a theology than practicing it as a policy."[5] The army is now stuck with war, for if the troops were withdrawn, oil could skyrocket.

Internecine wars and grinding poverty were the principal reasons for the public's revolt against the barons at the end of feudalism. Today Americans face similar circumstances, and they could also rebel against their elite.

MY FORECASTS IN THE LATE 1970S

In what follows, in order to clarify how I develop predictions for the future, I will explain the thought process that underscored some of the forecasts I made between 1977 and 1980. Breathtaking events have swept the world since 1976, when I first started writing *The Downfall of Capitalism and Communism*. Those were the days of soaring oil prices and resultant economic malaise in the United States and western Europe. Nixon and Agnew had been recently ousted, and Western economies were beset by stagflation, an affliction that combines high inflation with soaring unemployment. The United States had also suffered humiliation in Vietnam, and communism, by contrast, seemed healthy and invincible. The Soviets dominated their satellite states, and were prospering from their oil exports at hefty prices. Communism was popular in the Third World. The system also had sympathizers and adherents in the United States. Any talk of the downfall of communism was tantamount to inviting ridicule and insults. At this time, one would need to be versed in the law of social cycle to see through the inner contradictions of the Marxist system and insist that it was going to collapse in a few years.

As I explored history, it appeared to me that Russia had been in the age of warriors ever since 1564, when Ivan the Terrible overthrew the rule of feudal landlords, known as boyars. So the Russian era of warriors was already more than 400 years old, and the system, reeling under despotism and veiled economic troubles, was due for a move into the age of intellectuals. The change could have occurred in 1917, around the Bolshevik Revolution, but at that time most Russians were illiterate; nor did their priests inspire confidence. The nation, lacking both clerical and secular intellectuals who could take on the mantle of leadership, could not move forward in terms of its social cycle.

Thus the bloodbath of 1917 did not alter the despotic nature of the Russian regimes. It ushered in communism, but the military rule remained. True, Lenin, an intellectual, came to power, but he died prematurely seven years later, with the government soon reverting to the warriors. But by the 1970s, Russia had become a nation of educators and intellectuals who could handle the administration if they were called upon to do so. So I felt that the massive change that could have occurred around 1917 was now due any time, and could erupt at the next moment of turmoil. All it needed was a spark to ignite a revolt of Soviet satellite states.

Downfall was published in late 1978; a year later the Soviets invaded Afghanistan, which seemed like the spark I was looking for; that is when, as described below, I became doubly convinced that the Soviet Union would break up before the end of the century, before 2000.

A tremor shook the world at the end of the 1980s, when the Berlin Wall fell on November 9, 1989, and thus started the process that led to the breakup of the Soviet empire. The Soviet Union was actually the USSR, the Union of Soviet Socialist Republics, and comprised 15 constituent republics, including Georgia, Armenia, Azerbaijan, Latvia, Ukraine and so on. It was a strongly centralized federation or union dominated by Russia. In addition, the USSR towered over a number of satellite states that included Czechoslovakia, Romania, Hungary, Poland and East Germany. All of them were in the age of warriors.

With the breakup of the Soviet empire in the 1990s, not only the satellite states but also the 15 constituent republics broke loose from the federation. While Russia still dominated its former republics, its rule was no longer absolute. This was the beginning of a decentralized authority that starts an era of intellectuals. The former Soviet Union and its constituents are now either in a transition stage or in the early phase of the new age. In some, like Czechoslovakia and Hungary, the intellectual age has been clearly established. For instance, the first post-Soviet president of Czechoslovakia was Vaclav Havel, a novelist; its second and current president, Václav Klaus, pursued an academic career at various institutes of science in Czechoslovakia, and is often addressed as Professor Klaus by his admirers. Similarly, recent Hungarian presidents, such as Arpad Goncz and Ferenc Mádl, also used to pursue academic careers.

East Germany was united with West Germany and is now part of the West's age of acquisitors. Russia, however, is in the transition stage of the era of intellectuals. That is why it displays features of both eras. Its president, as mentioned above, no longer has the absolute sway that he once had over all the republics, which are now semi-independent from Russia. In 1993, Russia adopted a new constitution and seemed to be moving toward further decentralization of authority, but the election of Vladimir Putin as president in 2000 halted this process and catapulted the nation toward a one-man rule.

Who rules Russia today? The army? No, because the army generals have been discredited and disgraced; their perks have vanished; the military budget is down; the public does not covet an army career. The uncertainty of the ongoing war in Chechnya and a reputation for incompetence and brutality have maligned the Russian army.

If the army doesn't rule Russia today, do acquisitors or the wealthy? No, because some billionaires are rotting in Russian jails on what may be trumped-up charges. Money does not reign in Russia. The Russian administration is run by educated bureaucrats, not by freely elected officials, who would need money for lavish campaigns. There is a lot of corruption in Russia today, but the acquisitive class is not dominant in politics.

Putin is a former KJB officer, the Russian equivalent of a detective or bureaucrat at the CIA. He used to deal with matters of intelligence; his niche was spying and analyzing, not fighting. He is also the former deputy dean of international relations at Leningrad University, from where he graduated with a degree in law in 1975. He is an intellectual, as defined by the law of social cycle, but he is taking the country back to dictatorship, which generally marks the warrior age. So Russia displays the features of the new era as well as those of the old; it is now (2006) in the transition phase of the new epoch, which should not be a surprise. When a powerful empire like the Soviet Union breaks up, it goes through many ups and downs before settling into the new age.

The transitional phase of intellectuals is likely to vanish once Putin retires or when new turmoil hits him and his people. The Russian economy has prospered from the big rise in the price of oil, which, as explained below, is likely to crash around the start of the coming decade. That is when the era of intellectuals is likely to prevail in Russia, possibly bringing an end to corruption.

You may find it interesting that I did not predict the fall of Chinese communism, which was also in the warrior age in 1978. This is because

China's military regime was, and is, very young; a warrior named Mao Zedong (Mao Tse-tung) had overthrown the nation's feudal institutions as recently as 1949 in a laborer revolution backed by the peasants. So I expected China to thrive, not face another turmoil.

Regarding Iran, when workers' protests began in early 1978, I was in the process of researching my book on Muslim society; I was more than a cursory observer of the mounting unrest against the ruler. At first, I thought that the shah of Iran would pull through and pacify the protesters by at least partially meeting their demands. But he did not; he turned ruthless instead. His police and army became increasingly repressive in order to crush the protesters, who were fired upon by helicopter gunships and tanks.

When the protests continued for a few months, I felt that a major change was underway, and that the Iranian prime minister might have to resign. Then in October 1978, Ayatollah Khomeini began to broadcast his message from France, and the energized protesters found a fiery leader. By November, I became convinced that the ayatollah, increasingly popular with Iranians, would soon overthrow the shah and bring the clergy back to power. In November 1978, Dr. Eden Yu, an economics professor at the University of Oklahoma at Norman, invited me to give a public lecture on December 5. An Iranian student attending my lecture asked me about the future of his country. Without hesitation I said to him: "The shah will be overthrown in 1979 and the priests will take over the reins of government." Neither U.S. policy makers, nor the Western diplomats, historians and journalists, were prepared for this.

Next let's recap the relevant aspects of my previous predictions about the bloody conflict that is currently taking place between Islam and the West, especially the United States. This information is vital to new predictions that I will shortly make in these pages.

In making this forecast, I employed what may be called the law of reverse justice, which also deals with a pattern. There have been bloody wars among tribes, races, nations and religions as far back as one can go into the human past. Frequently, the initial victor has eventually been conquered by the vanquished, through the force of arms or by the allure of a new culture, by their subjects' armies or by relatively cosmopolitan thought and literature. This has happened time and again.

In the ancient world, for instance, the Egyptians were trounced by the Hyksos from Assyria (modern-day Syria). Two hundred years later, the Egyptians turned the tables on the Assyrians and captured their kingdom. In the West, the Romans colonized Europe and many parts of western Asia and northern Africa. Subsequently warriors from the defeated lands rose to overpower their former masters. Later these warriors were overwhelmed and assimilated by the relatively cosmopolitan culture of Christianity.

In the Muslim world, the Arabs conquered Iran, but were later overpowered by the rich Persian heritage. The Mongols destroyed the Baghdad Caliphate, but then squatted humbly in the mosques to accept Islam. Many other instances can be cited in history wherein the initial victor was later conquered or absorbed by the vanquished. This is the law of reverse justice that supplements the social cycle.

In order to apply this law to the modern world, you have to separate the victors from the vanquished during the nineteenth and twentieth centuries. We need to distinguish between the imperial powers and their colonies. In modern times, the West convulsed the world of Islam and India. At one point, Britain and France colonized or exploited almost all of Africa and Asia. The British yoke was at its deepest and most overwhelming in India. At the same time, Britain, France, Italy and even Russia seized or exploited the territories of the Ottoman Empire. Western Europe and Russia rocked the Indian subcontinent and Muslim nations from 1800 to the 1960s, by which time most former colonies had become independent

Even the United States, the land of the free, meddled in the internal affairs of Iran, especially in 1953, when the CIA, worried over the price of oil, foiled a coup against the shah. Using the law of reverse justice, I predicted in 1980 that "it is now the turn of India and Islam to cause upheavals in the Western world and Russia. It is the Orient that is now poised to determine the future of the Occident."[6]

These were my words in *Muslim Civilization*. Now let's look at how I timed this forecast. When I wrote that book, it was clear that the Islamic world was already convulsing the West, which crucially depended on the import of oil from OPEC, the petroleum cartel dominated by the Arabs. With oil prices jumping sky high and generating the misery of stagflation in Europe and America, even current events served to validate the law of reverse justice.

I had already predicted in *Downfall* that both capitalism and communism would unravel in the next thirty to forty years. But systems don't perish without fortuitous events (some of which are discussed in the chapters on Western and Muslim societies). The entrenched elite are usually so strong that absent an external catalyst to rattle them, their reign may never die. At the time of writing *Muslim Civilization* I felt that Islam was this catalyst that would trigger some fortuitous tremors and help bring about the downfall of both systems, starting around 2000. I selected this year as an approximation, which appeared to be consistent with generational cycles described in chapter 3.

Unlike the West, Russia, a major oil exporter, was not hurt by costly oil. That meant that something else from Islam was going to jolt that nation. In the late 1970s, I was vague about how this would happen, but when Russia invaded Afghanistan in 1979, the picture became clearer. So in *Muslim Civilization*, published in July 1980, I wrote:

> I am not sure how the law of reverse justice will strike at the Soviet government. But strike it will. The soviets will one day have to pay for their atrocities in Afghanistan. *And that day may come before this century is over.* Thus the changing face of Islam, which is now slowly destroying the roots of capitalism, will one day cause the downfall of totalitarian communism as well.[7]

The rest is history. As you already know, Afghanistan became Russia's Vietnam. The Soviets, demoralized and stung by huge economic losses from the war, withdrew in early 1989. A few months later, the Berlin Wall fell, and Soviet president Gorbachov, chastened by the debacle in Afghanistan, did not press his armies to halt the fall. Thus Islam started a process that helped lead to the breakup of the Soviet empire. Many now agree with me that the communist misadventure in Afghanistan was a major reason for the collapse of the Soviet Union.

In the same vein, I felt in the late 1970s that oil itself was not going to bring capitalism down, because crude is ultimately subject to the exigencies of demand and supply, and the oil prices could not stay high forever. I felt that, as with the Soviet Union, it would be a direct conflict between the West and the fundamentalists or jihadists of Islam that would be the undoing of the Western age of acquisitors. Oil would indeed be an important factor, but not the sole trigger. I chose my words carefully in *Muslim Civilization*. I did not write that the West would fight with Muslim nations, but with their fundamentalists. This is precisely what is happening now. The West, especially the United States, is not battling Saudi Arabia, Turkey or Egypt, the most influential Muslim nations. Both in Afghanistan and Iraq, the United States is in combat with al-Qaeda, which is a splinter group and a self-proclaimed savior of Islam. Prior to invading Iraq, George W. Bush managed to convince Americans that Saddam had al-Qaeda connections.

THE FALL OF THE U.S. BUSINESS EMPIRE

Like any other empire, the American business empire will also fall. The question is not if, but when. The capitalistic era of acquisitors is about to end, the same way Soviet communism collapsed right before our eyes. As nearly as anyone can predict these things, I expect that the beginning of the end will start around 2009.

This is perhaps the right time for me to detail the concept of the final-year syndrome first mentioned in chapter 1. Ever since 1929, an interesting pattern has governed the unfolding of geopolitical events. I described the final-year syndrome in my 1999 book, *The Crash of the Millennium:*

> Specifically, ever since the start of the Great Depression, we can see clear portents of coming catastrophes by looking at the last year of each decade. Between 1929 and 1989, there were seven such years, and not a single one went by without an epochal event somewhere on earth. Each time, a bloody revolution, an economic fiasco, or a war erupted to traumatize the world for most of the next decade.[8]

This is the final-year syndrome—that is, something happens in the last year of the decade to warn or prepare us about the nature of things to come for the next ten years. Thus 1929 saw the start of the Great Depression; 1939, World War II in Europe; 1949, the Chinese revolution; 1959, the Cuban revolution; 1969, inflation; 1979, the Iranian revolution; 1989, the fall of the Berlin Wall.

So what happened in 1999, the last year of the 1990s? Well, Greenspan began raising interest rates in June 1999 and did it through the rest of the year. This was then an ominous sign for the coming crash. Sure enough, the economy slowed, profit growth fell below expectations and the stock markets collapsed around the world from 2000 to 2002.

Even now the planet is not free from the side effects of that crash. Greenspan panicked in 2001, slashing interest rates sharply, spawning the housing bubble, which could prove catastrophic in the coming years. Thus the last year of a decade either starts off an epochal event or forewarns us about things to come over the next few years.

This final-year syndrome points toward 2009 or 2019 as the starting point of a major event such as the coming revolution. Given the current boiling rage against acquisitive CEOs and the incompetent government that represents them, given the rampant corruption among congressmen and their cronies, I don't think American voters will wait long to overthrow the rule of money in society. As we peer into the inscrutable future, we should focus on 2009, which is also pinpointed by the cycle of inflation as a difficult year of raging stagflation. This could start the fall of monopoly capitalism, just as the fall of the Berlin Wall spelled the end of the Soviet empire in 1989.

The U.S. business empire seems to be going the way of the Roman Empire in its final years. You may recall from chapter 6 how Rome had colonized many nearby and distant territories, extracting taxes from them to finance its trade deficit. Later, warriors from these areas began invading the empire. First, the peripheries fell, then the nearby provinces and finally the capital city of Rome.

The U.S. business empire is now being invaded by businessmen from the peripheries. They have already captured many markets inside the United States. The country no longer produces goods that it invented and pioneered—televisions, VCRs, consumer electronics, textiles and shipbuilding are some of the numerous industries that have succumbed to the assault of imports. Eventually, the import invasion could do to the American empire what the so-called barbarian invasions did to the Roman Empire. After the demise of Rome's domains, a new era was born. The same pattern is likely to unfold in the West, starting around 2009. This is then likely to be the year that the laborer revolution, spearheaded by some brave souls, begins in the United States.

The revolution will be the climax of the rage that the public now feels against CEOs and their stooge, the Bush Administration, which is likely to become even more unpopular. The economy will steadily get worse, with home prices falling and layoffs rising. Resentment against the government's pro-business and anti-people bias is likely to grow, until it reaches a boiling point by the end of this decade.

The revolution will occur at the ballot box, following the elections of 2008, as Americans demand honesty and integrity from politicians. It is not likely to be ultraviolent. But the acquisitive class will not hand power back on a silver platter. No one ever does. So, in view of the 7.5-year cycle examined in chapter 3, it could take seven long years, from 2009 to 2016, before the revolution succeeds and the rule of money is overthrown for good. All the election years until 2016 could be chaotic. The nation is in for a long period of chaos and internal turmoil between the haves and the have-nots. There could be real class conflict for the first time in American history. The period will be punctuated by interludes of calm, but each episode of tranquility will be followed by recriminations between the acquisitive class and the vanishing middle class. Over time, the heated accusations could turn into violent protests and demonstrations, but there will not be the kind of bloodshed that marked other revolutions, such as the French Revolution or the Bolshevik Revolution. Recent peaceful immigrants' rights protests and marches are a preview of things to come.

What exactly will be the first signs of this revolution is hard to tell. It could be extensive marches and demonstrations by the poor and the unemployed, the ousting of several prominent lawmakers, the election of a female or minority president, the breakup of mega corporations, a strong electoral debut by a third political party, effective campaign-finance reform, a steep recession combined with inflation—or simply a stunning event.

You perhaps are cynical of this prognosis, and wonder how this revolution is ever possible. Unless the electoral college is reformed, Americans will eternally have the choice between Republicans and Democrats. As both parties are indebted to corporations and the rich, who finance their campaigns, how is anything revolutionary going to happen?

Keep in mind the New Deal, which placed all sorts of restraints on the greed of Wall Street and the corporations. Was such a future program even conceivable during the 1920s? But the cataclysmic events of the 1930s made it possible. Poverty in America is only going to grow, and our economy could collapse by the end of the decade or soon thereafter; these, combined with the scars and wounds of the Iraq War, could make the revolution possible.

THE BURSTING OF THE TWIN BUBBLES

The world is now suffering from bubbles in the housing and oil markets. Since all bubbles have burst in the past, someday these two will as well.

When are they likely to burst? I can answer this question by referring to the shorter seven-to-eight-year cycle that I first mentioned in chapter 3. In normal times, patterns of money and inflation peak every 30 years. In a graphical display, the complete cycle requires a full rotation of 360 degrees in four quadrants, with each quadrant representing a shorter cycle. One fourth of 30 is 7.5; this may explain why major events last from seven to eight years. For instance, there have been countless seven-year wars in history. This is what led me to predict in 1978 that the forthcoming Iran-Iraq War would last at least seven years. It actually lasted from 1980 to 1988—that is, eight years.

After approximately seven to eight years, the variable in question reaches a turning point; depending on its momentum, it either reaches a peak, or accelerates to endure for a total of 15 years. The housing bubble appears to be a major event, which once had a lot of momentum but is now beginning to recede. Its starting point was 2001, when the interest rate started a panicky fall. It is likely to burst in 2008, give or take a year. The burst could start in 2007 and continue until 2009.

The oil bubble started in 2003, ironically soon after the United States invaded Iraq, presumably to bring the oil price down. It should burst in 2010, again give or take a year. The same pattern marked the oil bubble of the 1970s. Starting in 1973, it peaked eight years later in 1981, and then imploded in 1982 and thereafter. The current bubble could go on until 2011, and then crash in 2012; or it could peak in 2010 and then crash the next year. Could it crash before 2010? Possibly! This is because 2009 could be a pivotal year, due to the inflation cycle and the final-year syndrome. In any case, 2009 to 2012 will be crucial years for the oil balloon. The analysis also suggests that until 2009–2010, oil prices, with minor glitches, will keep rising or at least stay high. The hedge fund managers and oil barons will continue to take advantage of small supply disruptions and disproportionately raise oil prices whenever they can. They have done so even when supply has responded adequately to increased oil demand. If the supply shortage becomes real and crude inventories fall, oil prices will soar, again and again.

What could pop the housing bubble? The rising oil prices could kill investor confidence, and thus the home demand. People could be stuck with unsold homes bought for investment. That would then trigger a home price fall, at first slowly, and later sharply, until the market collapses.

The rising price of oil could also affect the housing market by raising interest rates. As inflation heats up from expensive oil, Ben Bernanke, the current Fed chairman, will raise interest rates to curb the price explosion. The Fed chairman needs to cement his image as an inflation fighter to have credibility with Wall Street. So as prices climb fast, he will do the only thing that he knows will curb inflation: he will raise interest rates, at least until his action slows the economy substantially and possibly causes recession. Rising interest rates in turn will bring down the housing market.

The right measure under the circumstances, of course, is to bring down the price of oil, which can be done easily by injecting competition into that industry. Since expensive oil is the source of inflation, action should be taken to cut its price; it makes no sense to raise interest rates, kill the economy in the process and then curb price gains. But like most economists, Bernanke is a friend of big business, and it perhaps would never occur to him that the oil behemoths should be broken up to restrain inflation.

THE WAR IN IRAQ

Let's now explore the ongoing war in Iraq, which began in March 2003. The first consideration is whether the conflict has enough momentum to last. The momentum is clearly there. The United States, especially the Bush Administration, has a lot at stake in victory and the cessation of hostilities. So does the rest of the world, but other nations seem to be paralyzed about the entire episode. Believing that it is a Bush-Cheney war, they want nothing to do with it, simply because their advance warnings about the conflict were ignored. However, the Iraq episode may now be regarded as a part of what President Bush calls the war on terror that started on September 11, 2001.

The U.S. war with terrorism is likely to last at least seven years. If 2001 is regarded as its starting point, then it would continue until 2008; however, if the Iraq War is considered in isolation, with 2003 as its beginning, then the war could endure until 2010 or 2011. Either way, it will not be easy for the United States to extricate itself from the Vietnam-like mess. I will return to this subject below in the context of the Muslim world.

INFLATION AND INTEREST RATES

American inflation peaked in 1979 at 13.3 percent but averaged around 2 percent in the last three years of the 1990s. Since then it has picked up some, but not by much. In the first half of the 2000s, inflation has averaged 3 percent, which is slightly above the end point of the late 1990s. This suggests that, while rising, inflation will remain subdued this decade. The main reason is the rocketing trade deficit and the flood of cheap imports hitting the nation. There are now two forces bearing on product prices: the high trade deficit tends to check price growth, while the high price of oil, along with low interest rates that raise monetary growth, tends to spur inflation. Since the two forces contradict each other, inflation remains under control.

The outlook for the rest of the decade is likely to be more of the same. Price growth will pick up some more, especially as we approach the end of the decade, but it is not likely to be near the highs seen during the 1970s. This suggests that the rate of interest, which closely tracks the rate of inflation, will also not reach the previous highs.

There is one scenario in which all bets are off, and that is if Mr. Bernanke makes good on his oft-cited remark made in 2002 that if we have to we should drop money from helicopters to prevent the possibility of deflation that could cripple the economy. If the Fed indeed prints vastly more dollar bills in response to emerging economic troubles, then we could see a return of the 1970s, with both inflation and interest rates soaring.

THE DOLLAR AND GOLD

The dollar is the wild card that defies analysis at this point. Many recent forecasts about the imminent demise of the currency have misfired. With the United States borrowing nearly a trillion dollars every year to finance its trade deficit, the greenback should be drowning in a sea of red ink; but the world economy acts as America's colony, and is so off balance today that it cannot survive without investing heavily in American assets. Nations with a trade surplus send their dollars back to the United States as fast as they acquire them, because if they don't, the dollar will plummet relative to their currencies. Then America's import surplus will fall sharply, sending shock waves through the economies of China, Japan and Europe.

In theory this process could endure indefinitely, because it is in the self-interest of the global economy to remain America's colony. But it is a house of cards that will only take a minor hit to collapse in a turbulent world. With Iraq, oil and housing as looming disasters, only a miracle will keep the dollar stable. It is more likely than not that the greenback will crash by the end of this decade, which will further stoke the fires of inflation. This is because each nation's goods are valued in its own currency. So if foreign currencies appreciate sharply, then the dollar prices of foreign goods will soar, as will U.S. inflation. If 2009 somehow escapes the dollar turmoil, then 2010 could see its collapse.

Foreign investors would be big losers in any housing slump. That could then trigger a stampede away from the dollar; foreign money could rush out faster than it rushed in, causing a global financial meltdown. There would then be a serious banking crisis in the United States and elsewhere, possibly culminating in a depression.

This brings us to the consideration of gold and precious metals. They all do well in uncertain times and in an inflationary environment. If the dollar collapses, gold will skyrocket. So will silver and platinum. Even without the dollar's crash, precious metals will appreciate with inflation. In the next decade, however, precious metals could lose some of their luster, especially after the oil crash and the resulting drop in inflation.

UNEMPLOYMENT, POVERTY AND DEPRESSION

If the current economic policies are not changed, real wages and family income will continue to fall, with poverty still on the rise. The rich will keep getting richer and the poor getting poorer; similarly, the middle class will continue to shrink.

With growing poverty and a vanishing middle class, overwhelming CEO greed and ruthlessness, mounting official corruption and incompetence and above all the demoralizing war in Iraq, voters could become furious enough to bring an end to the rule of money in society. Thus, a depression need not be a precondition for the coming revolution. Economic and political reforms can come about without such a catastrophe.

With world governments willing to print or borrow oodles of money, hurling their people into debt, depressions and joblessness can be avoided, but not the accompanying poverty and the public rage. This is not to say that a depression could not happen again; only that it is not necessary for the age of acquisitors to end. The economy could still face a steep recession because of rising oil prices, but avoid the calamity of a depression. Unemployment could rise to the level of 10 percent or more, but hopefully the world would not experience 1930s-style joblessness. However, a steep recession will feel like a depression because of rising consumer prices. During the 1930s, prices fell and eased the consumer's burden somewhat. This time we will most likely have stagflation, with both high unemployment and inflation, just as we did in the 1970s and the early 1980s.

SHARE MARKETS

The behavior of share markets is easier to predict than that of the dollar. In 1999, Greenspan raised the federal funds rate sharply, and then stock prices crashed the next year. Since the events triggered by the final-year syndrome normally last through the next decade, share markets are likely to be stagnant until 2009. Even following that year the outlook is gloomy and at best uncertain. There could be more stock market crashes from 2008 to 2011 or 2012. Share prices will not take a breather until the oil market crashes. In any event they are not likely to return to the mania of the 1990s. But oil and energy stocks could rise, as big money chases the oil market. Gold stocks are also likely to shine in the current decade.

EUROPE AND ASIA

Since the world economy is a colony of one large empire, a crisis in the United States will plague the globe, but some nations might not suffer stagflation. Nations with little foreign debt will perhaps see their prices stay in check in spite of rocketing oil prices. Among the Asian Tiger economies, Hong Kong (now part of China) and Singapore have already witnessed decelerating inflation, because they have little foreign debt.

The European Union, tied to the euro (except Britain), also has minimal foreign debt, although some of its members such as Italy indeed have large foreign obligations. The collapse of the dollar will force up the value of the euro, the pound and the yen. The Chinese yuan could also appreciate, even though it does not float freely. The EU, Britain and Japan need not suffer from high inflation, although they would not be able to avoid layoffs and perhaps falling real wages, depending upon the severity of the U.S. slump. Their elite and others will pay a harsh price for keeping the U.S. elite in power.

However, if the EU and Japan choose to pump money into their economies the way they did during the 1970s, then they could also ignite inflation along with high unemployment. But the ECB (European Central Bank) is very inflation conscious. If it lives up to its reputation, then high inflation need not happen.

Let's now take a look at China, which has been in the age of warriors since 1949. Over a 30-year period, Mao Zedong inspired the peasants to revolt against the feudal system led by its president, Jiang Jie-shī (Chiang Kai-shek), and finally overthrow the rule of acquisitors in a laborer revolution. This was a warrior-led rebellion and therefore resulted in massive bloodshed.

Mao founded a new age of warriors. History shows that the early phase of such an age, after a brief period of violence, takes society to new heights. People become disciplined and diligent, the preceding drug culture declines and the economy improves sharply. It is therefore not surprising that China has been generating a growth miracle since the 1980s. The nation is associated with high-quality and affordable products, with its growth rate routinely approaching 10 percent. Chinese goods are in demand everywhere in the world, especially in the United States.

America and China now stand in a bond of interdependence. Without America's markets, a good deal of China's industry would come to a halt, and without China's investment in American assets generating low interest rates, the U.S. economy would be stagnant. Only a generation ago, the Chinese influence on American markets was next to nothing. A major change has occurred in an extremely short time.

There was a time when Chinese rulers played second fiddle to U.S. presidents. The United States sided with the corrupt government of Chiang Kai-shek, who oppressed the workers and peasants. But now reverse justice has occurred, and China deals with America on an equal footing. In 2005, the U.S. import surplus with China was as much as $200 billion. America is now dependent on Chinese money for its continued prosperity.

THE MUSLIM WORLD

Religion still plays a strong role in the Muslim world, even though ac-quisitors are now dominant in this society. Its acquisitive age is young, and the acquisitive class has not yet established an unchallenged reign. The formerly ruling class of the clergy still has a significant following, and is strong enough to mount effective opposition to the new rulers. Thus the infancy of the Muslim acquisitive era means that there is likely to be a continued battle between the ousted forces of clerical intellectu-als and those of the oil-rich acquisitors, who tend to be more secular.

The two groups have been competing for the support of their peo-ple. The acquisitors have won out but the mullahs have not yet been trounced. This suggests that the clerics are likely to remain an effective force, opposing the introduction of Western ideas in virtually all Muslim nations.

The ayatollahs in Iran seek nuclear weapons for the same reason: to fight the newly emerging forces that believe in acquisitive ideas. They fear the might of Western thought, which tends to be materialistic and secular. They are afraid that true democracy could oust them from power. But if they have nuclear weapons, they can keep their masses under control and also spread their ideology to their neighbors without fear of retaliation.

For centuries, the Islamic world has been divided into two main branches—Shiites and Sunnis. In fact, every Muslim land has some split between the two factions. Iran, Iraq and possibly Lebanon have a Shiite majority, whereas almost all other Muslim countries have a Sunni plural-ity. In good and prosperous times, the two live like peaceful neighbors, but in bad times their divisions come to the fore.

It appears to me that times are now as bad as they can be. On the one hand, Saddam Hussein, a Sunni minority ruler, was ousted by the United States on April 9, 2003; subsequently, elections took place in Iraq and now the Shiite majority rules the country. Former Sunni army officers, freshly ousted from power, have resorted to terrorism. With support from al-Qaeda, they have started an insurgency against the Shiites and the U.S. armed forces stationed in the nation. They number just a few thousand, but they have a dedicated cadre of suicide bombers, and to-gether constitute a killing machine. They have been able to wreak havoc on the Shiite government and the entire American army in Iraq.

The Sunnis and Shias are now a world apart. Not a day goes by without scores of people from both sides dying. There are very strong signs that a civil war could break out between the battling factions. Far more American soldiers have died fighting the insurgency than fighting Saddam. The Sunni insurgency has been joined by al-Qaeda fighters from Saudi Arabia, Kuwait, Afghanistan and Jordan, and the Shiites, of course, have the support of Iran. A civil war in Iraq could quickly become a regional war, drawing in other nations. It would then become a wide and bloody conflict, lasting for years.

No one wants a regional war at this point; few, except perhaps the ousted militants, want a civil war in Iraq, either. Regional war is more than likely. As history shows, wherever religion is dominant and has two strong yet opposing branches, there is the risk of a religious civil war. When Europe was divided between Catholics and Protestants after the Middle Ages, a conflict between the two branches of Christianity could not be avoided. There were several wars of religion among European nations, lasting over a hundred years. Such a brutal war, to my knowledge, has never occurred between the Shiites and Sunnis. Nor do I hope it does. I am afraid, though, that the current momentum of the Iraqi insurgency against the Shiites and the United States will pull other nations into a wider regional war.

The Shiite and Sunni nations, and factions within nations, could also battle behind the scenes and not openly declare war. But more bloodshed in a sectarian conflict is likely, because hostile sentiment among warring Muslims is not going to vanish any time soon. The conflict could also entangle Israel in its tentacles.

WHAT TO DO ABOUT THE IRAQ WAR?

Cycles only anticipate the timing of an event; they don't condemn us to inaction. They point to the likelihood of events only if current and past trends are allowed to fester. But we can learn from the natural laws that the cycles embody, and take timely action to prevent a calamity.

What should we do about the Iraq War? I remember the day in the early 1990s when I told some U.S. naval officers that the biggest foreign danger to the United States was Islamic fundamentalism. I still hold that view. The Shia-Sunni conflict now escalating in Iraq could one day engulf the whole world. Western Europe, wanting to stay clear of this conflict because of the Bush-Cheney intransigence in 2003, will not come to the aid of the approximately 135,000 beleaguered U.S. troops in Iraq. But now that we are stuck with the war, we cannot simply walk away from the scene. Doing so would not only be the height of cowardice in the abandonment of helpless Iraqis, such a reversal of strategy could also prove suicidal to the globe. The only thing we can, and should, do now is to persuade NATO and Muslim nations to get fully involved with the conflict, and send in the same number of troops, about 350,000, that ousted Saddam from Kuwait in 1991 in the first Gulf War. This way law and order could be restored in Iraq in about six months. Then a proper constitution, respecting the human rights of all, including women and minorities, could be swiftly introduced in the country. Elections will follow and the Bush-Cheney mess will be properly resolved.

Without such massive commitment in terms of troops and resources, the Iraqi conflict is likely to simmer, draw in other nations, keep oil expensive, help Iran become rich and acquire nuclear weapons and eventually convulse the whole world.

If European and Muslim nations refuse to participate, then the United States should withdraw its troops and let the world face the consequences. It is not fair that American soldiers die and get maimed in containing the conflict to Iraq, while the planet reaps the benefits without paying a price. After all, for all his follies, President Bush has indeed done a great favor, at least to Iraq's neighbors, by getting rid of Saddam. At the very least, they should be grateful and shoulder some of the burden of the war.

Once the world faces the real prospect of American withdrawal from the battle scene, it is likely to come around and join the United States in pacifying the region. This could be done under the auspices of the United Nations or NATO. Most nations instinctively know that what happens in the region will impact the common future of us all, but they are content to let the Americans make all the sacrifices. They see it as a fitting punishment for Bush-Cheney follies and arrogance.

Do we need to remind the Europeans how many times the United States has rescued them from their own military follies in the past? When Hitler had nearly half of Europe under his thrall, it was America that came to the rescue of the continent and sacrificed its soldiers. If the Shia-Sunni conflict is allowed to spread, the oil fields in Saudi Arabia and Kuwait could be incinerated, and that would become a problem for the whole world. It is better to nip this war in the bud before it leads to a global depression or a terrorist conflagration.

U.S. efforts to restore peace and sanity to Iraq are further complicated by the ever-present sniping between Israel and the Arabs that occasionally escalates into a shooting war. Tensions in the Middle East from America's military presence in Iraq were already high when violence flared up in July 2006 between Israel and Hezbollah, a Lebanon-based Shiite faction armed by Syria and Iran. There was never any doubt who would win between the warring parties, but Hezbollah put up unexpected resistance and hit deep in Israel with rockets and missiles, while Israel practically destroyed southern Lebanon. Hostilities finally ceased in August, but the tempers and hatred between the parties remain, and could flare up into renewed skirmishes in the near future. Thus, the Middle East cauldron is likely to add to escalating economic and political chaos expected before the end of this decade.

PREPARING FOR THE FUTURE

Since we are moving toward a time of troubles that could arrive by the end of the decade and, depending on our voting behavior, last anywhere from three to seven years, it only makes sense that we as individuals prepare for it now, while there is still time. How our votes affect the outcome will be explained in the next chapter. We especially need to take steps that are not drastic, and are prudent in times good or bad. This type of advice applies anywhere in the world.

At the outset, it may be mentioned that all preparatory steps should aim at surviving the impending crisis rather that profiting from it. This is because the crisis itself will reflect the relentless greed not only of the CEOs but also of speculators and war profiteers, and any attempt to benefit from it is likely to backfire. Furthermore, in the bubble economy that marks the United States today, volatility tends to increase before the bubbles burst. It is very difficult to make the right choices in such a milieu. The recent stock market crash of 2000 should provide a sobering experience to the speculators.

Remember the hedge fund called Long Term Capital Management (LTCM) that went bankrupt in the Russian default crisis of 1998. It was managed by two Nobel Prize–winning economists who won acclaim for, of all things, risk management. They should have been cited for risk enhancement instead. That is the kind of behavior we should avoid.

The rate of saving in America is close to zero today, while debt is sky high. This is a recipe for individual and social disaster at any time, let alone in a time of troubles. You should formulate a savings plan as soon as possible, and lessen the use of credit cards. This should be done even if it requires changes in lifestyle; as much as possible, current consumption should be postponed to the future; the sacrifice will be well worth it, because money saved is money earned forever.

The use of plastic should be trimmed; it makes no sense to pay 20-plus percent interest rates on borrowed funds, at a time of growing political and economic chaos. If you have to make a choice between further study and taking a job, go for a job at this point. This will bring income, enable you to save some money and possibly avoid taking out a student loan. Unemployment is likely to rise in the near future, and could offer you plenty of time for further study. If you're planning to switch your job, you should think carefully about it. Job seniority at your current place of work may save your job in the future.

If you plan to start a business, then go for one that requires little investment of personal funds. A service company is preferable to anything that calls for substantial sums of money. Similarly, for those already self-employed, business expansion plans should be postponed, unless you're in an oil-related business, because oil prices are likely to stay high, and even rise further, until the end of the decade. But the oil industry could also become risky in the coming decade.

As regards investing your savings, the strategy should be very conservative. For a while, beginning around 2010, we could see a rise in both inflation and joblessness. There could be stagflation—that is, steep price increases in a stagnant or sinking economy. In the worst-case scenario, there could be a depression with severe unemployment. Financial markets are big losers in such a milieu. Both stocks and bonds fall. The safest assets then are bank CDs (certificates of deposit) or short-term treasury bonds, with a maturity of five years or less.

Bank deposits are insured by the FDIC up to $100,000, or $200,000 for a joint account in which either party can withdraw funds. Your financial institution will show you how to expand your account's insurance. For those blessed with money, bank diversification should be high on their priority. Don't exceed the insurance limit with any single financial institution, because there could be a severe banking crisis around 2010 and beyond. The Federal Reserve will do its best to keep the banking system solvent, but that could still impose severe losses on those with uninsured deposits. Bank diversification is desirable even if it is inconvenient, and you have to spread your money around into several banks.

Gold rises in an inflationary environment; if you can afford the glittery metal, then park a small part of your money, 5 to 10 percent, into its purchase. Gold is likely to appreciate, but even if it does not, it is a good hedge against uncertainty. Gold coins are preferable to bullion. They are easier to buy and sell and are not subject to fakery. My preferences are the American eagle or the Canadian maple leaf, but many others may be just as good.

The U.S. dollar is likely to collapse in the future, while the euro, the British pound, the Swiss franc and the Canadian dollar are likely to appreciate. In fact, most other currencies will perhaps do well against the dollar. Some purchase of nondollar assets, especially diversified bank savings accounts or safe short-term government bonds, is then desirable.

In short, the investment and consumption strategy for the coming time of troubles has to be cautious and prudent. One should do the following:

1. Spend less, save more.
2. Take a job as soon as possible and, preferably, avoid job switching.
3. Avoid risky stocks and bonds, or avoid stocks and bonds altogether.
4. Avoid real estate, because the current housing bubble is likely to burst by 2009.
5. Diversify bank deposits and park the money in bank CDs up to the FDIC insurance limit.
6. Buy some gold.
7. Avoid business expansion unless it is an oil-related business; even oil could be risky after 2010.
8. Avoid speculation and stay away from hedge funds.
9. Buy some foreign currencies, preferably the euro.

Of course, this is my general advice to the public for facing the future, and may not apply to everyone; individual circumstances differ, and my exhortations may not suit your interests. You should follow my advice only if it seems right and prudent for your own circumstances.

The forecasts made here are not rosy, and the circumstances will hurt for a while; but with the help of proper economic and political reforms we will be able to turn adversity around and, for the first time in history, bring about the golden age that usually follows each era of acquisitors.

Since the 1920s every decade has ended or started with a recession. However, it should be noted that the bad times I am predicting need not be inevitable. I have never written a book without offering economic and political reforms that could prevent the anticipated calamities. But given the endemic governmental corruption, given the economic and political chaos now in the making, it would take heroic efforts on our part to escape from impending troubles. That kind of effort, along with the golden age, is what the next chapter describes.

CHAPTER 11

ERADICATING GLOBAL POVERTY: A CALL FOR A VOTER'S REVOLUTION

In spite of the surge in global economic growth since the early 1980s, poverty, destitution and occasionally hunger continue to affect a vast area of the world. Even in America, people live from paycheck to paycheck, from one loan to another. The great motto of the American Express Card, "Don't leave home without it," virtually defines Americans' lives. People literally live off plastic, desperately trying to sustain their lifestyle. A recent study contends that 43 percent of Americans spend $1.22 for every dollar they earn.[1]

American society as a whole practically saves nothing; the household rate of saving has varied from one to negative in recent years. Almost 39 million Americans, an all-time record, live below the poverty line. Under the relentless onslaught of tricklism, nearly 45 million have no health insurance; the minimum wage is $5.15 per hour compared to the inflation-adjusted figure of $8.00 in 1968. Nearly five million are homeless; an equal number go hungry everyday.

Real wages have been falling for almost three-fourths of the labor force ever since 1973, and even those who have lucrative jobs are buried deep under debt. Their autos, homes, appliances and furniture are mostly pawned to banks.

You would never know this from figures regarding the gross domestic product (GDP), which has grown faster than the population all through U.S. history. That's what is so sad about poverty in America; it exists amid plenty, at a time when the average American worker, empowered by computers, is the most productive ever. The productivity surge should have banished poverty a long time ago; instead, the ranks of the indigent swell every day.

Televised images of the poor scrambling but ultimately unable to escape the wrath of Hurricane Katrina finally exposed what most people heretofore regarded as mere statistics: namely, millions of Americans live below the poverty line and are unable to make ends meet. The hurricane revealed the human face of deprivation, which, as mentioned above, currently afflicts nearly 39 million people in supposedly the richest country in the world. At the time, some Republican lawmakers blamed the poor for their plight. The distinguished legislators exclaimed, why couldn't the hurricane victims get out of harm's way in their cars? This is blinding ignorance, revealing official ruthlessness and brutal corruption.

The legislators, spoiled by copious corporate money and junkets, wallowing in luxury, couldn't imagine that the poor had no cars. Such lawmakers—nay, lawbreakers—are now as much out of touch with reality as were the prerevolutionary French aristocrats. French masses overthrew their oppressors in the revolution of 1789. The same thing could happen in the United States.

The coming American revolution will not be as bloody as the French revolt, but, in terms of its power to effect a change in public psychology, tax reform and curing poverty, it will be swifter and sharper. The stale, decrepit old regime will vanish forever, heralding the dawn of a glorious new age. I will come back to this point later.

THE FUNDAMENTAL CAUSE OF POVERTY

Economists like to attribute poverty to a variety of superficial traits, such as the absence of capital, inefficient technology, poor education, lack of free trade, monopolized markets and a lazy workforce, among others. All these are just symptoms of indigence, not its fundamental cause. The experts miss a crucial point. The one fundamental cause of poverty, here and everywhere, is official corruption. Government malfeasance breeds cronyism, incompetence and other parasites that create destitution.

Let's first be clear about corruption. Its dictionary meaning is simple; corruption refers to dishonesty, bribery or a lack of integrity on the part of an individual. However, government corruption has broader implications. I define it as any policy that enriches the rich and impoverishes the poor and the middle class. This is because the rich beneficiaries of such policies essentially bribe government officials in the form of large campaign contributions, junkets and gifts. In general, when someone takes bribes or indulges in the abuse of political power for personal gain, there is corruption.

Let's take another look at the oil industry in the United States. The cost of gasoline has been skyrocketing since 2003; the product is a necessity, and its users can be easily exploited by giant firms with excessive monopoly power. Up to a point, oil firms can raise prices at will and impose them on hapless consumers. That is why many nations have antitrust laws to prevent corporate mergers and collusion that ultimately spawn exorbitant prices. The U.S. government should strictly enforce the antitrust laws, so that the indigent and the middle class are not victimized by business barons. If the government shirks this responsibility, then it is corrupt. If administration officials, for the sake of campaign donations and reelection, fail to uphold the antimonopoly laws, then their self-serving behavior makes them corrupt. High oil prices, of course, aggravate poverty. This is one example of how corruption breeds poverty.

When the government fails to fully enforce its antimonopoly laws, as it has since the early 1980s, it colludes in the collusive behavior of big companies. Such tolerance of merger mania not just in oil but also in other industries distorts the world economy. It is bad for other nations as well as for the United States. It gives rise to global imbalances that are likely to generate worldwide chaos by the end of the decade. It creates, among other things, a rising wage gap, a concept that I will explore shortly.

Tax policy is another example of government depravity. According to Adam Smith, the father of modern economics, who is constantly invoked by big business in defense of its obscene profits, taxes should be imposed primarily on those who can afford them. Thus the poor and the middle class should be taxed little and the rich should be highly taxed. This is known as the principle of progressive taxation, and when it is violated, poverty increases directly as well as indirectly. The direct effect is obvious, because low after-tax income can deprive the poor of the basic necessities of food, housing, clothing, education and health care.

But the indirect effect is to reduce consumer demand and hence economic growth, for no businessman likes to expand production and investment unless goods can be sold in the market. Thus if government leaders resort to regressive taxation, the opposite of the progressive structure, they engage in legalized corruption, because they please the rich to further their own reelection.

Let's now examine the minimum wage, still stuck at a pitiful $5.15 an hour. The Republicans argue that when the minimum wage rises, the unemployment rate also rises. If this is the case, why was the jobless rate only 3.5 percent in 1969, when the minimum wage peaked in terms of buying power? Furthermore, how is it that employment went up each and every time the minimum wage in money terms was raised from 1950 to 1997?

The Republicans also contend that any attempt to raise the minimum wage to keep up with rising prices is inflationary. But then why is it that lawmakers raise their own salaries year after year? Why is that not inflationary? The Democrats are usually in favor of raising the minimum wage and have offered such legislation time and again, with little apparent success in a Republican-dominated government. However, the Democrats, too, have been happy to pocket salary increases while the destitute grow poorer. No Democratic senator has ever filibustered lawmakers' own wage increases. If this had been done, all self-serving Republican arguments against the minimum-wage rise would have vanished in a hurry. The point is that the Democratic lawmakers are not innocent, but only less corrupt than the Republicans. Still, in a two-party political system, our main hope for economic reform, at least for now, rests with the honest and semi-honest leaders of the Democratic Party. I will say more on this later.

The minimum-wage decline is by far the biggest cause of growing poverty in America. But there are others as well, such as unmitigated globalization. Today the economic profession is united in its advocacy of free trade, which was first championed by a well-known businessman named David Ricardo in the early nineteenth century. But as late as 1941, two famous economists, Paul Samuelson and Wolfgang Stolper, predicted that free trade between rich and poor nations would lower real wages and raise profits in the United States.[2] Samuelson went on to win a Nobel Prize for his various contributions to economics.

The so-called Stolper-Samuelson theorem was an instant success, and it appears in all modern texts on international economics. Every free trader is aware of it, but still insists that the real-wage fall experienced by U.S. production workers since 1973 is not the fault of free trade. In other words, economists are busy disowning a renowned forecast that came true. Even Samuelson and Stolper joined others in advocating free trade, although in 2004 Samuelson wrote against outsourcing.[3] Normally people brag about their forecasting prowess, but free traders are exceptionally modest in this respect. This perhaps will be the first and last instance in which someone runs away from their successful prediction.

Instead of free trade, modern economists including the Fed chairman Ben Bernanke blame computers for the real-wage debacle in the United States since 1973. In a coauthored book, he writes, "Computerization is another development that has in many cases increased the productivity of more skilled workers while squeezing out those without the education or training to use the new tool effectively."[4] This is the chairman's explanation for why the unskilled worker has suffered a real-wage fall. Of course, he fails to mention that some skilled laborers have met a similar fate. Of all the excuses made by free-trade buffs, attributing poverty to technological advances or automation takes the cake. New technology began raising productivity in the United States soon after the birth of the American republic in 1789, and real wages moved up decade after decade for all workers. And now automation is getting the blame for the real-wage blight.

The reality is that the real wage has plummeted since 1973, just as foreign trade soared. Globalization, including outsourcing, is the only visible cause of the U.S. real-wage loss; this is, of course, a superficial cause, the real reason being government corruption and elitist propaganda that hypes catchy free-market slogans and slights the facts.

Globalization in fact is big business' biggest boondoggle. It has spawned poverty in America and billion-dollar payoffs for CEOs, something that was unheard of prior to 1970, the starting point of trade liberalization. If the government continues to follow this policy, then it is nothing but corruption, because the policy ensures the continued en-richment of the rich and impoverishment of the poor.

Free trade among nations with similar wages is great for all parties, but between rich and poor countries it has been disastrous for the vast majority of workers in affluent nations. Even so, I don't advocate a revo-cation of the WTO (World Trade Organization), nor a return to protec-tionist measures like tariffs. This is because most nations are now so interdependent on global commerce that protectionism would destroy the world economy. I just insist on balanced free trade, a policy to which I will return.

THE RISING WAGE GAP

I have noted four main causes of poverty in the United States—the rising price of oil, low minimum wage, regressive taxation and globalization. All four of them relate to government policy and reflect official corrup-tion, because they all impoverish the general public while making the rich richer. Furthermore, they add to global economic imbalances and threaten to unleash financial chaos in the near future. As shown below, they have already caused mayhem in some economies, and need to be re-strained before major damage strikes again.

Official corruption threatens economic stability around the world, because it raises what may be called the wage gap, which simply is a mea-sure of the chasm between labor productivity and the real wage. For the sake of precision, the wage gap may be defined as worker productivity di-vided by the average real compensation of employees. An economy func-tions smoothly and efficiently only if this gap remains constant and small, but morphs into myriad imbalances if the gap grows, as it has since 1980. An economy is efficient if it maintains full employment with-out resorting to excessive debt, which, as explained below, is itself linked to the rising wage gap.

Anything that lowers domestic labor demand tends to raise the wage gap, because when labor demand declines, the real wage falls rel-ative to worker productivity. The rising price of oil, regressive taxa-tion and globalization all tend to trim domestic demand for workers, so they all increase the wage gap over time. The low minimum wage does the same, because salaries in many occupations are linked to that wage.

How is all this relevant to our economy? Wages are the main source of demand, and productivity the main source of supply. Over time, business investment and new technology lead to a rise in productivity and hence supply; if real wages keep up with productivity, consumer demand matches the growth in supply, so that the demand-supply balance is maintained in a natural way. Here the economy continues to function smoothly and efficiently. However, if real wages trail productivity growth and the wage gap rises, supply grows faster than demand. Many distortions then arise, and if they are allowed to fester, the end result is growing poverty, possibly economic collapse.

The first distortion is that debt must rise exponentially to increase demand, because this is then the only way to close the demand-supply gap arising from the growing wage gap. The borrowing may be incurred by consumers and the government, but not by cash-rich corporations. The quantum leap in budget deficits in the U.S. economy since the early 1980s is purely the result of this phenomenon. This is the first distortion, because the demand-supply balance is maintained artificially by ever-increasing debt creation and cannot be sustained forever.

The second distortion arises from a quantum jump in corporate profits; once the demand-supply balance is maintained through increased debt, then profits must rise sharply, because with wages growing sluggishly, the fruit of increased productivity accrues mainly to the owners of capital. So CEO incomes jump. The profit leap is a distortion, because it cannot be sustained without mushrooming debt.

The artificial rise in profits triggers an artificial jump in share prices and leads to a stock-market bubble, which must burst one day, because it is all supported by an exponential rise in borrowing. The moment debt growth slows, profits begin to fall and lead to a crash. This occurred in 1929 and from 2000 to 2002.

One distortion feeds another. As the market crashes, the government must do something to contain its aftershocks; for instance, it slashes interest rates to lure more people into borrowing. If it does not, a depression may result, as in the 1930s. But if it does, there will be a housing bubble, because exceptionally low interest rates generate big declines in monthly mortgage payments and thus raise the demand for homes. So the government avoids the depression, but only at the cost of future stability. This is why we now face a housing bubble around the world in the aftermath of the global stock market crash of 2000.

With the continued rise in the wage gap, the rich keep getting richer at a record pace. But the stock market crash puts them in a quandary: What to do with all that money? With the share market losing its lure, the rich look elsewhere. Owing to their acquisitive mentality, they cannot rest without investing their money at a decent return; they may be ultrarich, but they want even more. So their cash ends up in exotic assets such as hedge funds, especially those which discover new avenues of speculation like investing in oil. Rabid speculation from oil-related hedge funds, some of which are backed by the oil companies themselves, is one reason for soaring gasoline prices even though there has been no physical shortage of oil to date.

These are all distortions that have resulted from the rising wage gap in the United States. Let's now see what the growing wage gap in Asian economies does to the world. After all, productivity is also outpacing real wages in Japan, China, India and the Asian Tigers (including South Korea, Taiwan, Malaysia, the Philippines, Singapore, Indonesia and Thailand). All these have high trade surpluses with the United States, and some even with Europe.

In Asian economies, where people are somewhat averse to borrowing, the trade surplus is the inevitable result of the rising wage gap. How do you maintain the economic balance as output grows faster than domestic demand? By keeping your currencies artificially low so you can export much more than you import. The resulting trade surplus then absorbs the domestic output surplus. This is how China and, to some extent, the other Asian economies mentioned above have been able to sustain their high levels of growth. This is also how Japan has avoided major trouble in the aftermath of its own stock market debacle in 1990.

The U.S. trade shortfall, of course, is not the product of its growing wage gap, but is the result of unmitigated globalization that has practically destroyed American manufacturing. With few products "made in the USA," there is not much that the United States can export to match its bulging imports. Even then its trade deficit would be much lower if Asia's currencies were free to appreciate in response to the growing export surplus.

The United States is not the only nation that finds itself in trade trouble. The Australian and British economies are basically American clones. They also suffer from a rising wage gap, high debt and large trade shortfalls. New Zealand is in even worse shape than the United States, Britain and Australia.

Continental Europe, especially Italy, Germany and France, all face rising joblessness and a growing wage gap, although not at the same intensity as in the United States. However, the stock market crash of 2000 has landed them in a variety of troubles. They also have a housing bubble, as well as an oil bubble. Their real wages have not declined, but then they face larger unemployment. They suffer more from the consequences of the growing U.S. wage gap than from their own.

The moral of the story is that a wide variety of distortions are created in the world because of the growing wage gap observed around the globe. When the labor market is in imbalance, every other market is shaky. Any cure for worldwide poverty must aim at eliminating this fundamental cause, which in turn reflects political corruption.[5]

AN IDEAL ECONOMY

An ideal economy is one in which every job seeker has employment that pays at least a living wage and provides for the basic needs of life—food, shelter, clothing, education and health care. It is an economy in which everyone enjoys the fruit of new technology in terms of a higher living standard. When national productivity rises, it is only fair that all see a rise in their real wage. Even in today's world, where big business hates to pay higher wages to its workers except its executives, there are countries that meet the exacting requirements of an ideal economy. Sweden, Norway and Switzerland quickly come to mind. The living standard in these nations keeps rising for the vast majority of people. Perhaps we can learn something from their experience.

Historically, two types of economies have emerged in the world—a diversified one and a specialized one. Today's economies are highly specialized; that is, they focus on a few industries, export these goods and import whatever they produce insufficiently at home. Thus, the United States has lost much of its manufacturing to the new economic powerhouses of China, Japan, India and South Korea. It has specialized in a few high-tech products that require a high degree of skill that only intellectuals can master. Such jobs are best filled by engineers, doctors, MBAs, accountants and attorneys.

In *Greenspan's Fraud*, I argued that specialized economies are fundamentally unstable and prone to imbalances. Here I will offer another argument against them. Their main flaw is that they cannot provide jobs at a decent wage to the entire labor force. This is because, as I explained in chapter 4, there are basically four types of people in society, and not all are suited for a particular type of employment available from just a few industries. Those who are warriors work best in the armed forces, police departments, the sports industry and factories. For them, an adequate manufacturing sector is a must. Absent sufficient manufacturing, their services are not put to the best use, and the nation's productivity suffers.

Similarly, farming, as opposed to farm research, is essential for those who are not capable of developing advanced skills, whether physical or intellectual. Physical workers fare well in agriculture and low-skilled jobs. Acquisitors, by contrast, are good at becoming entrepreneurs and business managers. In order to provide decent jobs to all types of people, an economy has to develop a wide variety of sectors. In other words, only a diversified economy can be an ideal economy, where every worker can earn a living wage.

Free traders keep harping on the vast benefits of specialization for nations that concentrate on export industries, even as import-competing industries shrivel. They contend that this raises national productivity and, in the long run, benefits everyone, including those laid off in sectors facing import competition. But such benefits have been elusive so far to the factory workers in the United States. Those without college degrees have been especially hurt, so free traders would have everyone attend college and obtain a graduate degree. American economists want to impose higher education on those who are laid off in manufacturing, but not every unemployed person can develop high-tech skills. Louis Uchitelle, an economics writer for the *New York Times*, explains that regardless of extensive training, laid-off workers suffer intense psychological damage and lower wages.[6]

Factory workers obviously excel from their physical skills, and when they are forced to transfer to industries that require intellectual skills, national productivity suffers. If they were suited for high-tech work, most of them would have opted for that at the start of their careers. So specialization does not make everyone more productive. It cannot generate an ideal economy that provides living-wage jobs to all types of people—laborers, warriors, intellectuals and acquisitors. A nation must develop many areas of expertise and not neglect any important sector. Thus the industries of manufacturing, farming, services, housing and the like are all needed if a nation is to provide a decent occupation to every job seeker.

This is what most advanced economies did in their long growth experience; Britain, France, Germany, the United States, Canada, Australia and Japan, among many others, focused on a wide assortment of industries in the process of development. Their economies were diversified. Consequently, not only GDP but also real wages grew for everyone in society. But since the early 1970s, the advanced nations, especially the United States, have neglected manufacturing and have increasingly specialized in services and a few high-tech industries. The result is either sinking real wages, as in America and Australia, or surging unemployment, as in western Europe. Of course, the workers' loss is the CEOs' gain.

GROWING ECONOMIC CHAOS

As argued above, the ever-increasing wage gap around the world has generated a wide variety of distortions and imbalances. Some nations consume much more than they produce; others have the opposite problem. Consumer, government and corporate debt is mushrooming in the majority of nations; speculation proliferates even in industries producing necessities such as oil and medicines. Millions starve around the globe, while a tiny minority indulges in gluttony. The scary part is that no one sees an end to this growing chaos. Even those who are eternally optimistic concede that global imbalances are only going to fester over time; but like all the bungling experts in the past, they insist that debt-supported prosperity can last forever, simply because it is in no one's interest to disrupt the status quo. Thus nations such as China will keep parking their surplus dollars in U.S. government bonds, simply because it is in their self-interest to do so. For this argument to be valid, nothing can ever go wrong in our shaky world.

When was it ever in the self-interest of any elite to disrupt their cozy milieu? Yet it is always in the interest of those who suffer at their hands to disrupt it, and hence there have been major revolutions in the past that dethroned the rulers and their corrupt systems. The fall of the Soviet Union should open the eyes of those who believe that global imbalances can endure forever simply because they preserve the status quo. In spite of massive borrowing from abroad, American poverty is only going to grow over time, possibly at a rapid rate. We have to do something about it, and very soon. We have to take action before it is too late, economies collapse and the flames of revolution engulf the United States, and with it the whole world.

ECONOMIC REFORMS

Since the global economy is now organized under the umbrella of the U.S. business empire, any transformation in America will quickly benefit other nations. The following is a list of reforms that can raise the living standard in the United States:

1. Trim the Social Security tax to reduce the tax burden of the poor and to prevent the government from looting the people's trust fund.
2. Raise the corporate income tax rate from the current 34 percent to 45 percent, and eliminate the tax loopholes.
3. Raise the top-bracket individual income tax rate to 40 percent, and rescind the preferential treatment of dividends and capital gains.
4. Raise the minimum wage incrementally to $8 per hour—to $6 immediately, followed by a dollar rise per year until it reaches $8; furthermore, index the minimum wage to the GDP deflator, the price index incorporating all goods and services, so that this wage rises automatically with inflation.
5. Enforce the antitrust laws vigorously to break up giant conglomerates like Exxon-Mobil, Royal Dutch Shell, British Petroleum, General Electric, Time Warner and other profitable companies that absorbed their rivals through mergers in the 1980s and 1990s.
6. Persuade other nations to adopt free trade, so that the trade deficit is eliminated, and America has balanced free trade.
7. Change the health-care system so that it is not an undue burden on the people and on American manufacturers.[7]

These reforms will create an ethical and efficient economy. It may be noted that ethics and efficiency go together; they have never contradicted each other and never will. To me the fundamental precepts of an ethical economic policy are as follows:

1. A progressive tax system
2. A need-based minimum wage
3. Free enterprise
4. Economic fairness resulting in salaries rising roughly in proportion to national productivity.

These precepts are self-explanatory, and in view of the discussion above, need no further elaboration. During the 1950s and the 1960s, economic policy was indeed ethical, because taxes were puny for the middle class and practically zero for the poor, so the tax system was highly progressive. Corporate taxes were as much as 25 percent of the federal revenue, compared to less than 10 percent today, and the top-bracket income tax rate varied between 70 and 90 percent. The minimum wage was as high as $8 per hour in current dollars compared to $5.15 today. Markets were relatively free: Exxon and Mobil, for instance, competed with each other; in 1996 they became Exxon-Mobil. Finally, real wages, unlike now, kept pace with rising productivity.

As a result of such policies, GDP growth averaged more than 4 percent per year, poverty fell year after year, family income grew constantly, unemployment hit a low of 3.5 percent and, above all, the middle class flourished, needing very little debt to sustain its lifestyle. All this happened without the advantage of the computer revolution. Today, economic policy is so corrupt that even this wonderful new technology along with soaring productivity is unable to prevent the growth of poverty.

The move toward unethical policy started in the early 1980s with President Reagan and his world-famous economic adviser, Alan Greenspan. By now the tax system has become ultraregressive, with the burden shifting to the destitute and the middle class, the purchasing power of the minimum wage sinking every year and markets becoming increasingly monopolistic because of megamergers among profitable firms, while real wages fall for production workers, who constitute as much as 75 percent of the labor force.

The deleterious consequences of these developments are there for all to see, with GDP growth averaging a paltry 3 percent, family income declining, joblessness rarely below 5 percent and the public drowning in a sea of debt.

In addition, the United States is now the largest borrower in the world. It has to obtain over $2 billion per day from other countries to finance its mushrooming trade deficit and to sustain its dwindling living standard. Compare this to the 1950s and the 1960s, when America was the world's major creditor and had an annual trade surplus.

It may be that not all our economic troubles arise from unethical economic policies, but most of them do, and it is high time that we revert to the ethical measures of the past. Political corruption and unethical policy are precisely why the nation now lives with the paradox of booming productivity along with growing poverty and the vanishing middle class. America's own history shows that ethics erases poverty and the lack of ethics feeds it.

Among the seven reforms listed above, the first three measures will trim the tax burden of the poor but raise additional revenue to reduce the federal budget deficit. They will restore some degree of progressiveness in the tax system, and thus enhance consumer demand, which in turn will invite greater investment and production from companies. So GDP growth will expand. The fourth measure will alleviate poverty immediately, stimulate consumer demand, raise economic growth and thus create more jobs. Note, again, that the rate of unemployment was its lowest, at 3.5 percent, in 1969, when the minimum wage was at least $8.00 in today's prices.

HOW TO REDUCE THE PRICE OF OIL?

The fifth reform listed above will quickly bring oil and gasoline prices down. Unlike in the 1970s, when OPEC dominated the oil market, oil prices today are determined at NYMEX, the New York Mercantile Exchange, where oil tycoons and their proxies, the hedge fund managers, hold sway. The so-called experts, backed by the government, promptly blame "geopolitical uncertainties" stemming from the Iraq War for skyrocketing oil prices. Remember the analysts in the 1990s; didn't they extol the virtues of worthless companies and make millions in commissions during the NASDAQ bubble? The experts were self-centered then, and are self-centered now.

The analysts played the share-market game in the 1990s, and are now playing the oil-market game, all to bamboozle us into believing that the zooming cost of oil is the fault of violence and tensions in the Middle East. When was the last time you saw peace in that region? During the 1970s there was the Yom Kippur War, the 1980s saw the Iran-Iraq War, the 1990s saw the first Gulf War and the ongoing skirmishes between Palestinians and Israel, and now, of course, we have the Iraq War. Middle East violence is nothing new, and did not raise the oil cost during the 1980s and the 1990s. Why now?

By the end of April 2006, oil hit $75 per barrel, up some 25 percent from the start of the year. Analysts were quick to blame it on production cuts in Nigeria totaling 500,000 barrels per day. Daily oil consumption around the globe equals 84 million barrels, so the Nigerian shortfall amounts to 0.06 percent of the total consumption, which is just a drop in the oil bucket. This should not even cause a ripple in the market; yet the price jumped nearly 25 percent. Let's face it, it is not the supply disruption or the geopolitical uncertainty that has sent oil soaring ever since 2003; it is the boundless greed of the oil tycoons, who have cornered the market in the United States. Since America is by far the largest oil consumer in the world, gobbling up nearly 20 million barrels every day, the price set at NYMEX prevails around the globe. The oil behemoths don't need to control global production; they just need to dominate the American market and keep the analysts and oil hedge funds under their thumb.

If you want to cut the price of oil and gasoline sharply and swiftly, there is no better way than breaking up the oil monopolies. Such an action also has a well-known precedent, namely, the breakup of Standard Oil into 16 smaller firms in 1911. But who will do it? The government? In May 2006, with gasoline selling for over $4 per gallon in some parts of the country, the Senate Republicans finally said "enough is enough." They responded with a gutsy attack on Big Oil and offered a proposal to give a $100 rebate to most taxpayers. Not to be outdone, the Senate Democrats vowed to take even harsher measures; they offered to suspend the 18.4-cent federal gasoline tax for 60 days. Bravo! Comedian Jay Leno quipped, "Congress is furious. They want to know how oil company profits are so high, but their money under the table has remained the same."[8]

AN EXPORT EXCHANGE RATE
TO BALANCE OUR TRADE

The sixth reform noted above concerns the current policy of unmitigated free trade, which ignores the hemorrhage it is inflicting on American manufacturing and most Americans' standard of living. As suggested above, a diversified economy backed by manufacturing is crucial to the revival of the American middle class. This is because only manufacturing pays reasonable wages to high-school graduates, not the service sector, which on average pays much lower salaries—although some service industries such as health care, legal assistance and information technology offer decent wages. Almost half of the U.S. labor force has no more than a high-school diploma. That is why declining manufacturing means rising poverty and a shrinking middle class.

The manufacturing debacle has resulted mainly because of the expansion of international trade. History shows that tariffs triggered U.S. industrialization as far back as 1816, and then led to America's industrial primacy between 1890 and the early 1970s. For much of U.S history, average tariffs, as high as 60 percent, ensured that our imports constituted no more than 5 percent of GDP. Today, they have tripled, exceeding 15 percent, and have created a mushrooming trade deficit, as much as 6 to 7 percent of the economy. Should we then bring the tariffs back? In the long run, tariffs could restore the living standard of the U.S. worker, although they would destroy some other economies. But in the short run, they would also wreak havoc with the American economy.

These are the days of globalization, and the whole world is interlinked by trade. Tariffs would start a trade war, and immediately impoverish everybody. Besides, they are not permitted by the World Trade Organization, to which our nation is committed. Furthermore, few politicians would vote for them because of intense opposition from academia, big business and the world. So tariffs are not practical today, but there is something else that we can do.

Many countries have fine-tuned the art of export promotion by setting their currency values low relative to the U.S. dollar. China, Japan, South Korea and Singapore, to name a few, maintain de facto fixed exchange rates that make their goods very cheap to Americans. So our imports keep rising faster than our exports, thereby killing our manufacturing industries. Why don't we join this crowd? Why don't we set an export exchange rate of our own?

The exchange rate determination is a two-way street. If they can set low exchange rates, so can we. This is what America can do unilaterally to ensure balanced free trade in which our exports rise to the level of our imports. The United States, like most nations, can tie the dollar to major global currencies, especially of those nations that have a large and persistent trade surplus with us, and use this rate only for its exports. Take, for instance, the case of the Chinese yuan, which has been basically tied to the dollar at a rate of 8 to 1 since early 2006. In other words, a dollar buys eight yuan.

Suppose the United States pegs the greenback at five yuan and makes this rate available only to foreign importers of manufacturing goods? This will cut our prices by almost 40 percent, and sharply increase Chinese imports from the United States, whose goods will become much cheaper in terms of the yuan. Instead of paying eight yuan to his central bank and obtaining one dollar, a Chinese importer would prefer to pay just five yuan to our Federal Reserve, and use the dollar to import American goods into China. The country would then import many more American cars, computers, airplanes, tractors, and so on.

The government of China should not oppose this policy, because Chinese exports to the United States would be unaffected, since a U.S. importer would still buy 8 yuan per dollar from the People's Bank of China and obtain Chinese goods as cheaply as before. Wal-Mart, Target and Sears, to name a few department stores, would still do the same amount of importing as before. In fact, China would be pleased, because it would no longer be under pressure to revalue its currency and thus hurt its own exports.

The United States could do the same thing with respect to other major currencies and revive its exports. Note that the pegged dollar rates would be available only to those companies that buy American goods and ship them abroad. The yen/dollar rate could be set at 80/1—that is, a Japanese importer could buy a dollar for only 80 yen, even though the government of Japan seeks to set a 110/1 rate. Similarly, the euro/dollar rate could be pegged at 1/1.5—that is, a euro could buy $1.50 instead of $1.25. This way the U.S. trade deficit could be trimmed and even eliminated without curtailing American imports.

The United States would then have a two-tier system of exchange rates. One set of rates, to be fixed by the Fed or the U.S. Treasury, would apply to foreign importers of American manufactures, and another, to be determined by the global market, would apply to all other international transactions such as U.S. imports, foreign investment and worldwide tourism. This way the United States would not restrict its imports through dollar depreciation, but would simply stimulate its exports to bring balance to its global commerce. The policy would expand, not curtail, overall world trade, and sharply cut our trade deficit, possibly eliminate it.

The dual exchange rate system proposed above will have to be managed by the Fed, not the Treasury, which has meager funds to support such a policy. The Fed will be able to buy foreign currencies from foreign importers or U.S. exporters, because there are no limits to its supply of dollars. At present these dollars are ending up with foreign exporters through their trade surpluses. But with the dual exchange rate system, our Fed will join the crowd of foreign central banks. They hold our currency, the Fed will hold theirs. They buy our assets, the Fed will buy theirs.

Will the dual exchange system be inflationary? Not really. Our companies will face the same amount of competition from imports as before. They will be unable to raise prices any faster than they do now. Our manufacturers will prosper and offer millions of lucrative jobs. Suppose it takes a company a maximum of $100,000 to create a high-wage job. The elimination of the trade deficit—more than $800 billion in 2005—will itself increase the U.S. GDP by $800 billion, which when divided by $100,000, yields 8 million. Thus the policy of balanced free trade will generate at least 8 million new and lucrative jobs. Even if the deficit is not eliminated, there will be a great industrial revival. If the deficit is cut just by half, 4 million new jobs will be created.

The world, especially Asian countries, have two advantages in their U.S. trade—cheap labor and cheap currency. While we cannot and should not do anything about their dirt-cheap wages, we can neutralize their currency advantage, revive our industries and eradicate our poverty. So they buy cheap, and we continue to buy cheap. But some lawmakers have to take the initiative and bring sanity to our economy, which today, as noted, must borrow more than $2 billion per day from the world to stay afloat. Until someone can come up with a better plan, the dual exchange rate is the only way to revive American manufacturing today.

HEALTH-CARE REFORM

The American health-care system is another example of greed run amok. The United States spends at least 40 percent more per capita than any other advanced economy on health care, yet delivers a relatively mediocre product. The nation ranks twentieth or lower in the world in terms of infant mortality, life expectancy and immunizations. There is nothing wrong with the quality of our doctors, hospitals and medical infrastructure. The problem, as usual, is with political corruption, as media analysts and politicians have been bought out by health industry lobbyists and corporate cash.

Drug manufacturers and doctors constantly reject any state effort to reduce medical costs. They flood newspapers and television with advertising to influence news coverage and editorials, which in turn mostly oppose government regulation to lower health-care expense. While most advanced economies tightly leash their medical industry, political corruption keeps the U.S. government from doing the same and helping its people.

The oil industry is not the only sector infested with corporate crooks. Much has been made out of how Lee Raymond, the Exxon-Mobil chairman, received a $400 million retirement package in 2005. What about William McGuire, the CEO of United Health Group, which is one of the largest health insurance companies? His annual salary is just $8 million, but according to the company's own records, in 2005 his unrealized gains on company-paid stock options were $1.6 billion. According to reporter George Anders of the *Wall Street Journal*:

> Dr. McGuire's story shows how an elite group of companies is getting rich from the nation's fraying health-care system. Many of them aren't discovering drugs or treating patients. They are middlemen who process the paper, fill the pill bottles and otherwise connect the pieces of a $2 trillion industry.
>
> The middlemen credit themselves with keeping the health system humming and restraining costs. They're bringing in robust profits—and their executives are among the country's most richly paid—as doctors, patients, hospitals and even drug makers are feeling a financial squeeze.[9]

Now you know why America's medical system is the costliest in the world. The middlemen are flourishing at the expense of the needy. Our nation spends the most on various illnesses, yet has 45 million people without health insurance. The system is bankrupting individuals as well as businesses. General Motors and Ford have to spend billions of dollars in the health management of their employees and retirees. Other nations, where health costs are much lower, have a decided competitive advantage over our firms. Thus, one way to strengthen our manufacturing and provide health care to all Americans is to follow the lead of nations that offer universal health insurance.

The prescription for America's health-care disease should then be obvious. Phase out and eventually abolish the private health insurance system, and organize it along the lines of the Social Security Administration (SSA). The federal government has been doing a masterful job of managing the retirement program at a minimal cost; it can do the same with medical care as well. In fact, the SSA itself can be expanded to do the job. No new agency need be created.

The SSA should create a new department of health security administration (HSA) to handle payments to health-care providers. Here's how the proposed system would work. The employers and employees will deposit the medical premiums, which are currently in vogue, with the HSA rather than private insurance companies. The HSA in turn will pay doctors, hospitals and other health-care providers for the treatment of patients. It will replace the functions of myriad insurance companies that now offer the same services with fat paychecks to their executives. Thus, the same care and medical benefits will be provided at a fraction of the administrative cost. There will then be a single health-care manager, the Health Security Administration as part of the SSA.

Just imagine the cost savings arising from this arrangement. The highest government salary belongs to the president, at $400,000 a year. Most other officers are paid less than $200,000. The private insurance companies, by contrast, pay millions in compensation and perks to their executives. Once the HSA takes over the health-care program, tens of billions of dollars will be saved annually. See what John R. Battista, an MD, and Justine McCabe, PhD, write on this topic:

> Single payer universal health-care costs would be lower than the current U.S. system due to lower administrative costs. The United States spends 50 to 100 percent more on administration than single payer systems. By lowering these administrative costs the United States would

have the ability to provide universal health care, without managed care, increase benefits and still save money. . . . Federal studies by the Congressional Budget Office and the General Accounting Office show that single payer universal health care would save 100 to 200 billion dollars per year despite covering all the uninsured and increasing health-care benefits.[10]

Similarly, a seminal article by a group of doctors belonging to Physicians' Working Group contends:

A National Health Insurance (NHI) Program is the only affordable option for universal, comprehensive coverage. Under the current system, expanding access to health care inevitably means increasing costs, and reducing costs inevitably means limiting access. But an NHI could both expand access and reduce costs. It would squeeze out bureaucratic waste and eliminate the perverse incentives that threaten the quality of care.[11]

According to the group's study released in 2001, the national health insurance program would save at least $150 billion annually. At today's (2006) medical costs the saving would be close to $200 billion. This cost reduction stems just from the elimination of middlemen, who pay themselves millions for just pushing paper. Additional savings may result from the fact that a single payer or manager can negotiate lower drug prices with pharmaceutical companies. Indeed the Veteran's Administration, a federal agency, receives discounts from drug companies for this very reason. Even doctors may offer discounts when they deal with a single agency rather than myriad insurance middlemen. The doctors themselves will face less paperwork and costs associated with bill collection.

The Canadians pay much lower prices for prescription drugs, which are manufactured by the same companies that do business in America. Why do our northern neighbors pay much less for the same medicines that we buy from the same firms? The answer, as usual, lies in political corruption. The Canadians have a single-payer system, while our politicians, fattened by the drugmakers, won't offer one to us.

Since the United States spends at least 40 percent more per capita than all other advanced economies on health care, the switch from the current system to the HSA program, modeled after that of other industrial nations, would save so much money that we could cover all those currently without insurance and still have some money left to offer discounts to employers. Taiwan offers a case in point. The nation switched to a single-payer plan in 1995. As a result, its insurance coverage soared from 57 percent of the population to 97 percent, yet the health care costs grew at a slower pace.[12]

America's high-cost manufacturing can certainly use some discounts in medical premiums, and a single-payer system is the way to go. The HSA plan will alleviate poverty, because it would provide health care, a basic need, to all.

ECONOMIC DEMOCRACY

The seven reforms listed above will ameliorate poverty in the short run but will not remove the fundamental cause of economic imbalances around the world, namely, the large and growing wage gap. The only way to eliminate financial frictions permanently is to institute economic democracy in which employees own a majority of company shares and have their representatives control the board of directors. Such firms function like self-employed businesses. If you have your own company, any productivity rise will raise your income proportionately; similarly, in employee managed firms, productivity gains resulting from new technology will accrue to workers as well as shareholders, which will keep the wage gap from rising. Once the wage gap is small and constant, an economy functions smoothly without having to resort to artificial supports like debt, fixing the exchange rate to ensure trade surplus and so on.[13]

THE COMING VOTER'S REVOLUTION

How are we going to materialize the eightfold reform described above to cure poverty and global imbalances? Even though I offer these measures for the U.S. economy, variants of them apply to all nations. Now the big question is this: How do we put these steps into action? The remedies are available, the prescription is crystal clear, but the pathway to legislation is not. The billionaires and multimillionaires will certainly oppose them. In our money-dominated system, which politician has the guts to stand up to corporate crooks and cronies, and bring about needed reforms?

No one immediately comes to mind. So we the people have to stand up and take action. Our constitution tells us in its preamble:

> We the People of the United States, in Order to form a more perfect Union, establish Justice, insure domestic Tranquility, provide for the common defence, promote the general Welfare, and secure the Blessings of Liberty to ourselves and our Posterity, do ordain and establish this Constitution for the United States of America.

These words are a clarion call to all Americans for action, because, with the political apparatus defiled by corporate money, many goals for which the Constitution was ordained can no longer be realized. The Republicans controlled Congress between 1994 and 2006, and many of them were, and are, incompetent and corrupt to the core. *The Nation* columnist Robert Borosage aptly describes the current state of American society as:

> Lethal incompetence and indifference in Katrina's wake. Republican House boss Tom DeLay indicted—twice. Senate Republican leader Bill Frist under investigation by the Securities and Exchange Commission. "Casino Jack" Abramoff's cynical cesspool of conservative corruption. Stagnant wages and rising prices. Quagmire in Iraq.[14]

On top of it all, the public is increasingly disenchanted with the president's reward-the rich, rip-off-the-poor economic policies, which manifest nothing but political payoffs. But the Democrats are adrift. They, too, have been silent or overt partners in the cesspool of corruption. While popularity ratings for President Bush were horrible in 2006, they were no better for Democratic bigwigs.

Political leaders are simply paralyzed. They seem to have no spine to confront well-financed lobbyists and corporate cash. The tycoons in myriad industries—oil, pharmaceuticals, health insurance, banking, housing, brokerage, to name a few—are picking people's pockets, yet nobody in the Democratic opposition has the guts to offer a coherent program to free the nation from political gridlock, cronyism and poverty. So we the people of the United States of America have to gird our loins; we have to restore economic justice and domestic tranquility to the Union.

How is it that a handful of corporate crooks can fool and exploit America, a republic of nearly 300 million people? Their formula is simple:

Divide and Rule. Their hired acolytes have split the nation into liberals and conservatives, insisting that the two groups have opposing interests. Mesmerized by their self-serving rhetoric, we the electorate vote as Democrats and Republicans, not as people united against corruption, degradation and exploitation. It is high time we woke up and heeded ethical principles rather than partisan slogans.

The nation's troubles afflict us all; they hurt Republicans as well as Democrats. When the purchasing power of the minimum wage sinks, it hurts nearly everyone, regardless of party affiliation. This is because wages for most blue- and white-collar workers are linked to the minimum wage, which is added to a skill premium to determine worker salaries. Poverty is galloping across the nation; while 39 million Americans subsist below the poverty line, another 54 million are the "near poor," those whose incomes are twice the poverty threshold but are just one injury or layoff away from joining the ranks of the destitute. In other words, 93 million, about a third of the nation, are either indigent or as a *New York Times* editorial calls them, "barely staying afloat."[15]

Poverty and debt are impartial; they plague a vast swath of Americans, including Republicans and Democrats. When illness strikes, we all wish we had health insurance regardless of our ideology. When politicians take bribes, inviting lobbyists and industry insiders to write legislation, it rankles us all regardless of our political beliefs. My point is that we should vote as a bloc against cronyism and sleaze and for honesty, courage and integrity. We should not remain divided. The Republican lawmakers and most Democrats kowtow to the wealthy because they need the money for reelection. They ignore us regular folks, because they feel that we will vote for ideology rather than the public good.

In a democracy, power and responsibility ultimately rest with the people. Let's use our ballot properly and fight injustices and deception. Don't think of yourself as a Republican or a Democrat; think of yourself as a victim of the misrule of acquisitors, because whatever you dislike today in society stems from the excessive greed and materialism of the acquisitive class. Regardless of party affiliation, we have a common enemy—the avarice of the ruling elite. You're cynical: What can I alone possibly do to dethrone the wealthy? With my low wages and high debt that keep me busy all day in my work, where do I find time to confront the powerful interests that have tons of money at their disposal to put me down? There is no doubt that fighting injustices needs courage and fortitude. But what choice do we have? If we don't take a stand, then the future, in fact the near future, will be horrible for us and our children.

All the symptoms that I expected to see before the start of an anti-acquisitive rebellion are now here. I anticipated many social and economic cancers, such as abysmal wages, growing poverty, rising homelessness, educational decline, family breakdown and loose morals. They are all here, so the revolution cannot be very far away. The law of social cycle, which has never failed in 5,000 years of recorded history, indicates that American society is about to evolve into an age of warriors, replacing the current stale era of acquisitors. According to this pattern, which proved true first for the fall of the shah of Iran and then for the collapse of Soviet communism, we are now on the brink of a major transformation.

The main characteristic of a warrior is courage. Those who display unusual valor in overthrowing the rule of wealth will be the new leaders; those who take risks in arousing people to oppose moneyed interests will steer the American ship of state in the near future. So time is now on the side of "we the people." We must make use of our meager resources and bring about a new age.

Today there seems to be little overt sentiment among the American public to launch a revolution, but this will quickly change; it will change as fast as Bush's once sky-high approval ratings plummeted. The public discontent has been rising already. As the economic and political chaos grows, the government and their acquisitive friends will lose all credibility. Their political ads and partisan propaganda will no longer sway the public.

In November 2004, George W. Bush won reelection with 50.7 percent of the vote. In May 2006, barely 18 months later, only 6 percent of those polled thought the economy was very good, while 66 percent disapproved of his handling of the economy. See how fast and intensely the acquisitors are losing public esteem? This is a preview of things to come.[16]

A social revolution is very close at hand. All "we the people" have to do is to muster courage and openly protest the shenanigans of billionaires. In fact, the coming economic turmoil will force us to do this.

What can we do singly and collectively? We have to adopt a voting strategy such that no congressman or senator feels that their seat is safe simply because they belong to a certain party. Until incumbents discover that no matter how much money they collect, their reelection is impossible unless they pass laws favoring the public interest, as opposed to the corporate interest, they will remain obedient to their paymasters. Once lawmakers realize they are not going to get votes unless they bring down the prices of oil and medicine, they will act in the public interest and shun big business. Only we the voters can teach politicians that amassing a campaign war chest is no substitute for honesty and integrity.

Let me state it candidly. Poverty will not be cured until there is a political revolution; the economic transformation of America requires a political transformation. There is no dearth of sensible policies; what is missing is a leader who has the guts to wage an election campaign without seeking a penny from moneyed interests.

THE VOTING STRATEGY

Who should we vote for? Vote for someone—a Republican, Democrat or independent—who sincerely promises to do the following:

1. Raise the minimum wage, and filibuster the annual pay raise in the Senate until the minimum wage is first raised piecemeal to $8 per hour and then linked annually to the cost of living.
2. Offer universal health insurance based on the HSA plan explained above.
3. Break up the giant monopolies such as Exxon-Mobil and Pfizer to bring down the price of oil and prescription drugs.
4. Adopt the dual export exchange rate to revive manufacturing, while preserving free trade.
5. Raise the capital gains, dividend and top-bracket income tax rates to the maximum 40 percent level that prevailed under Bill Clinton, who balanced the federal budget.
6. Reject campaign contributions from big business.

Our first priority should be to vote for someone who offers to uphold this six-point program. But politicians are very cunning and deceptive. They may not give us straight answers, or they may simply make empty promises. If their sincerity is doubtful, then we should simply vote against the incumbent. In fact, our votes can be a potent weapon against corporate sleaze and pollution. Could the challengers be any worse than today's legislators? An anti-incumbent voting strategy means that no incumbent will ever be safe regardless of how much cash they receive. In fact, we should base our vote on how much money a politician has amassed. Once the lawmakers discover that their reelection chances go down with the size of their campaign collection, they will shy away from big contributors.

Elections occur in America every two years. If a lawmaker breaks his or her promises, don't ever vote for them again, no matter what their excuse. We should also encourage independents to challenge incumbents by volunteering for them with our time, money and expertise. We must realize that only our voting behavior can end the rule of money in politics, and once this happens, the goals and ideals dear to the heart of both liberals and conservatives will be realized. Bear in mind that almost all the social, economic and spiritual travails that now bedevil the United States and the world are the result of the corrupt rule of wealth in society. After all, the public mostly follows its leaders.

Once money fails to bring power and influence, the public thinking will change. Money is important, but so are many other things, not the least of which are individual ethics and character. The sea change in leadership will divert the public from its mad pursuit of wealth. Materialism will subside; old-fashioned values like social service, politeness and caring for others, which guide some people even in the midst of the acquisitive age, will make a comeback.

At the federal level, voters exercise control over three institutions—the presidency, the Senate and the House of Representatives. As a general rule, unless candidates clearly commit themselves to the minimum six-point plan outlined above, we should split our vote between the two major parties regarding the executive and the legislature. That is to say, if our presidential vote is for a Democrat, then our congressional vote should be for a Republican. This way the government will remain divided between the two main parties, with each serving as a check on the depravity and arrogance of the other.

These are some of the rules that we should adopt as a voting strategy. They are my suggestions and should only be regarded as general guidelines. The main point is that we should not vote as Republicans or Democrats but as people working to uphold the fundamental principles of our

Constitution. This lofty document has been highjacked by the sleazy elite, because they have managed to divide us along party lines. As noted, the core economic interests of the liberals and conservatives are essentially alike; most conservatives, like liberals, belong to the middle class and would be unhappy to see their lifestyles evaporate. Once money no longer dominates politics, we will all be happy regardless of our ideology. For, no matter who we are, no matter what we are made of, we all have a common concern for honesty and integrity in public life. No one likes to be poor, and without ethical economic policies most of us will soon be stricken with poverty. So in our own interest, we should dethrone the acquisitors.

It is heartening that voices are building up at the grassroots level to oppose the prevailing ideas and rule of the intellectual acquisitors, who no longer command the respect they had in the past. Billionaire Martha Stewart was sent to jail in 2004 just for lying to the FBI, something that was unheard of in the past. Two of Enron's stalwarts, the late Ken Lay and Jeff Skilling, were convicted of financial fraud in May 2006 by a jury consisting of both Democrats and Republicans. What really struck the people was that the two white-collar convicts were brought to jail in handcuffs and treated like common criminals. In the past, someone of their stature would have been allowed to surrender quietly, outside the public view. As reporters Kurt Eichenwald and Alexei Barrionuevo write:

> There was a time when white-collar criminal prosecutions were delicate affairs, where prosecutors worked hard not to treat the wealthy and powerful defendants as anything as distasteful as, well, criminals. . . . Many of the techniques applied to drug cases and mob prosecutions have been brought into the once-genteel legal world for corporate wrongdoers.[17]

This is the sign of changing times and reflects the rage that the general public now feels toward the ruling elite. Republicans and Democrats alike are beginning to question the nonsense emitted by economists who support the elite. I know of three noneconomists, two Democrats and a Republican, who have written books that challenge the brutally exploitative orthodoxy. Michael Dorgan is a U.S. senator from North Dakota. His book is *Take This Job and Ship It*. Michael Blomquist is a real-estate businessman, whose book is entitled *The Housing Bubble: An American Dream or Nightmare*. Jim Cunningham is a Chemistry PhD, and former vice president of Advanced Micro Devices. His book is called *Hollowing Out: America's Flight from Manufacturing into a Perilous World of Economic Fantasy*. All these books, with their self-explanatory titles, make much more sense than what some Nobel laureate economists contend— namely, that no one is ever fired, or that people simply choose to be un- employed.[18] The point is that the public frustration with the status quo is rising, so much so that even noneconomists are beginning to question it and have gone to the extent of writing books about it.

Then there is Dick Alexander, the CEO of Global Shop, who has penned a manifesto entitled *Democrats: An America for All the People (Returning America to Greatness)*. He is extremely worried about Amer- ica's bleeding manufacturing industries, and is doing his utmost to bring my plan for an export exchange rate to the attention of key law- makers. He has been a great inspiration, as he writes, "We believe that America, at its best, is a kind and caring nation, which wants to pro- mote and promulgate its highest moral standards and values."[19] This is the kind of message that "we the people" need to hear and adopt in our voting behavior.

Other popular book titles that reflect the public rage are *The Buying of the President*, *The Buying of the Congress* and *How Much Are You Making on the War Daddy? A Quick and Dirty Guide to War Profiteering in the Bush Administration*, among others. As Frank Rich of the *New York Times* notes, "Americans are angry. The government has failed to alleviate gas prices, the economic anxieties of globalization or turmoil in Iraq. Two- thirds of Americans believe the country is on the wrong track."[20] But this is just the beginning. By the end of the decade, there will be more unrest, fury and chaos in society, and revolutionary change will appear as the only viable solution to restore sanity to the economy.

THE NEW GOLDEN AGE: A WARRIOR'S DEMOCRACY

The most common form of government until around 1700 was monar- chy, and a country's head was called a king or an emperor. India had its rajas and maharajas; Russia, its czars; Japan, its shoguns; Turkey, its sul- tans, and so on. The office of the monarch was more or less hereditary, and only close relatives of the king were entitled to help lead the nation. Regardless of which class dominated society, the form of government was mostly monarchical. Some rulers were powerful and absolute, some titular and feeble, but they were all royalty. Leadership transferred from warriors to intellectuals to acquisitors, but kings remained.

However, when Europeans began to migrate to North America, the migrants experimented with new forms of government, with governors and legislative assemblies ruling most colonies. Similarly, in England the parliament began to assert itself following the Glorious Revolution of 1688–1689, and political power gravitated toward the prime minister. This, you may recall, heralded the West's second age of intellectuals, during which the monarchy lost prestige and influence all over Europe.

Following World War I, monarchy all but vanished from the globe. Today Saudi Arabia is the only prominent country in which a hereditary king is more than a figurehead. The common form of government now is republican, where not only legislators are elected but also heads of state, as prime ministers or presidents. Monarchy has become obsolete following thousands of years of social evolution. Future governments will also be mostly republican, regardless of the character of the ruling class. Not that all polities will be democratic, because dictatorships, as the history of communism shows, can exist even in republics.

Democracy is commonly known as a government of the people, by the people, for the people. But this type of ideal has never materialized, and perhaps never will, because it is possible only if everyone is born equal in skill, vigor and intellect. In reality people are born unequal, so that there will always be some inequality in society. All we can hope to achieve is a social framework that offers equal opportunities to all. How people use these opportunities will still differ; some inequality will always remain, which means that one class will always be dominant over the other three even in republican governments and democracies.

Essential features of a democracy are elected officials; the basic freedoms of speech, media, assembly, location and religion; equality before the law, and a right to have a job affording the minimum necessities. Since of the four classes, only three take turns to rule, there can be three types of democracies: an acquisitor's democracy, an intellectual's democracy and a warrior's democracy. What is familiar to us is the acquisitors' democracy, in which money is indispensable to the electoral process. Here elected members of legislative assemblies and the executive branch are either affluent themselves or are supported by the wealthy. Without the backing of wealth, few even dare to contest elections.

The state machinery in an acquisitors' democracy operates to further the interests of the rich; as a result the latter grow richer and richer over time at the expense of other classes. Such is the form of government prevailing today in the West, India, Japan and much of Latin America.

Intellectual's Democracy

For a democracy to exist, it is not necessary that wealth play an important role in politics. People can get elected without the backing of money, as has been occurring recently in the formerly Marxist dictatorships of eastern Europe. Elections in Poland and the Czech Republic require little backing of the moneyed class. The Russian president and parliamentarians also need little support from the wealthy to get themselves elected. Of course, Russia does not have a democracy yet, but that could change, in about a generation.

A government in which a majority of the elected come from the class of intellectuals, where basic freedoms are respected and where money plays little role in the electoral process may be called an intellectual's democracy. In an acquisitor's democracy, top positions in government usually go to businessmen, bankers, merchants and landed magnates; but in an intellectual's democracy, poets, writers, lawyers, physicians, priests, professors, scientists, economists and the like hold the reins of government and the administration.

The British parliamentary system soon after 1689 was close to an intellectual's democracy, since the wealthy had no say in elections, and the legislative assembly was under the thumb of the prime minister.

Warrior's Democracy

An elected government in which money plays an insignificant role can also be a warrior's democracy. A republic, where the topmost positions of the president (or prime minister) and cabinet officers go to the class of warriors, where human rights and freedoms are honored and where wealth is secondary in the electoral process, may be called a warrior's democracy. As explained in chapters 4 and 5, the warrior mentality belongs to soldiers, policemen, firefighters, professional athletes and skilled blue-collar workers. Even in a warrior's democracy the majority of legislators may spring from the class of intellectuals, because the latter are mentally equipped to formulate laws and usually do so in all eras; but the executive branch of the state is mostly in the hands of people with martial qualities.

It is interesting to note that the first president of the United States, George Washington, was an accomplished warrior, and did not need the backing of the opulent to be elected. Similarly, when General Dwight Eisenhower became the president in 1952, money had little sway in his election. All this shows that warriors can get elected in the West without any help from the wealthy, while human rights are still respected. What democracy needs are a constitution, a free press and an educated public conscious of its rights as well as duties. The mentality of the ruling class need not matter in this regard.

The coming revolution will catapult the United States into a warrior's democracy. This is because the opponents of the prevailing acquisitive regime will have to display extreme courage and valor, qualities that belong only to warriors. Nobody surrenders power on a silver platter. The acquisitors and their cronies will fight tooth and nail before surrendering to the revolution, but their defeat is preordained by the law of social cycle. My calculations indicate that the laws of nature now favor the warriors; these laws will disrupt the status quo, unite the people and goad them into a ballot-box revolt, until the acquisitive regime is deposed.

The entire upheaval could last from 2009 to 2116, but if "we the people" strive hard, it could end sooner. When things are at their worst, greatness springs from the resilience of the human spirit. It is for us to turn the near-term adversity into lasting bliss. We will have to persevere in order to open a new chapter in the ever-flowing spring of civilization. Our success is assured, because history is about to repeat itself: after the downfall of the American business empire will come a global golden age.

When the ruling elite become brutal, corrupt and exploitative, then natural laws act to bring an end to their rule and put a new class in power in accordance with the social cycle. The acquisitors' orgy of greed grinds society down to such lows that a golden age must follow. The law of social cycle, the law of supply and demand, the law of reverse justice and so on, are all laws related to human nature. Such laws interact to bring about societal change in a rhythmic pattern.

In all civilizations, the golden age usually flourished in the ascending phase of the warrior eras. In Egypt, India, Japan, China, the West and the Caliphate, the golden era appeared when men and women of martial qualities held the reins. Today, China is in the age of warriors, and see how fast its economy is growing and its middle class emerging. Compared to where the nation was prior to the communist revolution of 1949, China may be said to be in the early phase of a golden era.

Note that a golden era, according to historians, does not signify a perfect society; it only means a rapid and previously unfathomable advance in many areas of a polity, including the economy, art, music, sports, literature and so on.

From the late nineteenth century until the 1949 revolution, China was known as the sick man of Asia. The nation had been humiliated in wars with Britain and Japan. Society was basically feudal, with much of the land owned by the rich, who ruthlessly exploited the peasants. Disease, destitution, drug addiction (especially to opium), prostitution, hunger and homelessness afflicted a large section of the populace. The life expectancy was a pitiful 35 years; the illiteracy rate was 80 percent; extreme corruption and lawlessness were common. All these are the hallmarks of the closing phase of the feudalistic age of acquisitors.

Then came a civil war in the late 1940s, culminating in a social revolution inspired by Mao, a warrior. A lot of bloodshed followed, which, however, was nothing new to China. According to the *Random House Encyclopedia*, "Unprecedented casualties were caused by the Taiping Rebellion (1850–64), two Muslim uprisings . . . and a north China drought in 1876–79 that led to famine." At least 25 million people, over 10 percent of the population, perished in the Taiping Rebellion alone. The famine devastated the countryside and claimed millions of lives.[21] The message of *Wikipedia*, the Internet encyclopedia, is much the same: "The large number of deaths during the period of consolidation of power after victory in the Chinese Civil War paled in comparison to the number of deaths caused by famine, anarchy, war, and foreign invasion in the years before the Communists took power."

Where is China today? Is it still the sick man of Asia? No, it is now the superpower of Asia. In fact, some describe it as the emerging superpower of the world. It has been the fastest-growing economy since the early 1980s; no longer are its citizens demoralized or addicted to drugs.

Its average life expectancy reaches into the 70s; its athletes routinely win gold medals at the Olympics. Its educational standards are second to none in the world. Above all, it holds hundreds of billions of dollars that give it an economic stranglehold over its former archenemy, the United States. Thus, compared to the prerevolutionary era, China has indeed entered the early phase of a golden period, and far greater achievements in the fields of science, technology, economics, arts, literature and music are yet to come. As two historians, R. Palmer and J. Colton, remark on the communist regime:

> The regime transformed life in many ways. . . . Impressive strides were made in public sanitation and public health. . . . Women, encouraged to reject traditional virtues of obedience and deference, received legal equality with men and could count on new opportunities. Old abuses like child marriage and concubinage were outlawed. . . . The Chinese Revolution refashioned the habits and ethos of a gigantic population, reaching remote villages and hamlets untouched for centuries. Within a generation an agrarian, semifeudal country was developing into a modern industrial society.[22]

There is, of course, a dark side to China's phenomenal progress. Corruption, judicial injustices, authoritarianism still afflict the land; but these social tumors are no worse than those in the past. It is hard to imagine even a single area in which the average Chinese was better off in prerevolutionary times.

China is not democratic; nor was the West in the aftermath of its own warrior-inspired revolution during the fifteenth century that overthrew the feudalistic era of acquisitors. One day China will indeed become a democracy, though not anytime soon. Already, the nation is the world's foremost industrial power. Such is the marvel of the ascending phase of the warrior age.

Modern China is just one example of how society shines in the early stage of the warrior era. History offers many more. A society's golden age may be regarded as a period in which there are significant strides in many walks of life—art, science, music, literature, philosophy. Peace and prosperity prevail at that time, which stands head and shoulders above the earlier, and possibly ensuing, times. Of course, the prerequisite for such a period is a prosperous and relatively "ethical" economy that gives people free time to pursue the finer aspects of life. The *Ency-*

clopaedia Britannica includes the following periods as golden ages in various societies:[23]

1. Athen's golden age ruled by Pericles
2. The golden age of Latin literature and jurisprudence under Augustus Caesar in the Roman Empire
3. Islamic golden age under the Abbasid dynasty and under Suleyman the Magnificent in the Ottoman Empire
4. Chinese golden age around A.D. 1000 under the Tang Dynasty
5. Spanish golden age under Isabella and Ferdinand
6. Britain's golden age under Queen Elizabeth I
7. Seventeenth-century Dutch golden age
8. The Gupta Dynasty's golden era in India
9. The golden age of Byzantium in the Byzantine empire

Of the nine periods mentioned in this list, all coincided with the age of warriors. Of great interest here is Athen's golden age in the fifth century B.C., which was presided over by Pericles, an illustrious army commander. According to the *Encyclopaedia Britannica*,

> The "glory that was Greece" reached its height then, in Athens, under the leadership of the statesman Pericles. He opened Athenian democracy to the ordinary citizen, he built the magnificent temples and statues on the Acropolis, and he created the Athenian empire.
>
> Pericles was first elected *strategos*, or general, in 458. Generals were elected yearly to devise and carry out the strategy necessary to manage the affairs of state at home and abroad. Pericles won reelection frequently for about 30 years. In a time of kings and tyrants as rulers, his policy at home was to place the state in the hands of the whole body of citizens under the rule of law. The Assembly made the laws, the Council of 500 executed them, and popular courts judged those who broke them.

Clearly, the Athenian polity under Pericles was a warrior's democracy, where army commanders were elected by an assembly of citizens. The assembly itself was an elected body, and anyone, regardless of wealth, could qualify for its membership. Pericles also made sure that money did not matter in the appointment of people to high public office. This is the kind of democracy I envision after the American social revolution, which will put an end to the rule of wealth in the United States.

Like most warrior eras in history, the U.S. warrior era will also blossom into a golden age; it will usher in the same kind of sea change in American society as occurred in China after 1949, except that it will be far more glorious and free from extreme bloodshed. This is because China started from a very low base marred by the feudalistic age of acquisitors; it had never tasted the bittersweet fruit of capitalism, nor the freedoms enshrined in democracy.

America's warrior age, by contrast, will start off from a lofty democratic foundation built on the general observance of human rights, a free press and an educated public extremely conscious of its rights. It will not have to go through the birth pangs that accompanied the Chinese revival following the 1949 revolution. It will be more like Britain's Glorious Revolution of 1689, in which a monumental change occurred without a shot being fired.

However, the intensity of the American renaissance will match China's recent surge. This is because in the final phase of the era of acquisitors, where the United States stands today, society sinks so low relative to its past that the upsurge has to be great.

The change will be especially beneficial to laborers and women. Today, both groups are victims of brutal economic and social discrimination. Women's wages are lower than men's; female poverty is worse than that of the general population. Whenever the warrior age replaced the era of acquisitors in the past, laborers and women breathed a sigh of relief. The living standard rose for all, while women scaled to new heights in political and social circles.

The near term is one of growing economic and political chaos, but there is a brilliant silver lining in a cloudy picture. Every new system in the past was better than the one it replaced. In fact, as described above, most eras of acquisitors were followed by a golden age. People were extremely happy after they got rid of the rule of money, and developed new economic, social, political and religious institutions.

Once money no longer dominated politics, social discipline returned; technology improved further and real wages jumped; crime and pornography receded, and old-fashioned ethical and spiritual values made a comeback, with the public becoming more honest and compassionate. Several economic reforms were instituted that trimmed the concentration of income and wealth. The tax burden of the poor and the middle class declined. This has happened all through recorded history, and will be repeated in the future as well.

The new golden age will be more effulgent than any seen before, not only because every new system has dwarfed its predecessor, but also because it will be built on a democratic pedestal. The revival of American society will be swift and stunning; soon the revival will infect the world, which is connected to the U.S. business empire.

The United States does not export much, but it does export ideas, which today mainly emit hedonism and materialism. A new standard exalting martial qualities and magnanimity will soon replace the currently dominant American ethos. It will also sound the death knell for tricklism, which is creating poverty around the world. America's revolutionary ideas will quickly captivate the globe; they will spread like wild fire and eradicate poverty within a generation. The Internet will make sure that the American renaissance spreads its fragrance all over the planet. Verily, for the first time in history, there will be a global golden age.

NOTES

CHAPTER 1

1. Anup Shah, "Causes of Poverty," www.globalissues.org.
2. The World Bank, *World Development Report, Attacking Poverty*, New York: Oxford University Press, 2000.
3. Shaohua Chen and Martin Ravallion, "How Have the World's Poorest Fared since the Early 1980s?" Development Research Group, World Bank, 2002.
4. Asian Development Bank, "Poverty in Asia: Measurement, Estimates, and Prospects," 2004.
5. J. Bradford Delong, "Estimating World GDP, One Million B.C.–Present," Department of Economics, U.C. Berkeley, 2002. Delong's estimates show that from 1980 to 2000, world per capita GDP grew annually at the rate of 2.5 percent; yet poverty went up around the globe.
6. Shah, "Causes of Poverty."
7. Asian Development Bank, "Poverty in Asia: Measurement, Estimates, and Prospects," 2004.
8. Bloomberg News, "One out of Every 100 Americans Is a Millionaire," *Dallas Morning News*, June 21, 2001, p. D3.
9. Thomas Friedman, "Saying No to Bush's Yes Men," *New York Times*, May 17, 2006, p. A23.
10. "Endorsement: Vote for Kerry and Replace Bush's Corporate-Driven, Inept Leadership," *Athens News*, October 18, 2004.
11. Spencer Hsu and Susan Glasser, "FEMA Director Singled Out by Response Critics," *Washington Post*, September 6, 2005, p. A1.
12. Molly Ivins, "Bush Makes Government Incompetence a Reality," *Buffalo News*, January 13, 2006, p. A9.
13. Claudia Deutsch, "Take Your Best Shot: New Surveys Show That Big Business Has a P.R. Problem," *New York Times*, December 9, 2005.
14. David Ploz, "Al Dunlap: The Chainsaw Capitalist," Slate.com, August 31, 2004.

15. Peter White, "Price of Peace Staggering; New Iraq to Cost U.S. Hundreds of Billions," *Atlanta Journal-Constitution*, April 17, 2003, p. 19A.
16. David Barlett and James Steele, "How the Little Guy Gets Crunched," *Time*, February 7, 2000, p. 38.
17. "Finance and Corruption in America," Socialscience.com.
18. Ravi Batra, *Greenspan's Fraud: How Two Decades of His Policies Have Undermined the Global Economy*, New York: Palgrave Macmillan, 2005.
19. Council of Economic Advisers, *The Economic Report of the President*, Washington D.C., 2006.
20. Ibid.
21. Department of Commerce, *The Historical Statistics of the United States*, Washington D.C., 1975.
22. Ravi Batra, *Muslim Civilization and the Crisis in Iran*, Richardson, Texas: Liberty Press, 1980.
23. Arthur Schlesinger, *The Cycles of American History*, Boston: Houghton Mifflin, 1986; reprint, New York: Mariner Books, 1999.
24. Ravi Batra, *The Crash of the Millennium*, New York: Harmony Books, 1999.

CHAPTER 2

1. Charles P. Kindleberger, *Manias, Panics, and Crashes*, New York: Wiley, 2000.
2. For a concise history of bubbles, see Ravi Batra, *Greenspan's Fraud: How Two Decades of His Policies Have Undermined the Global Economy*, New York: Palgrave Macmillan, 2005, chapters 3 and 4.
3. Greenspan, quoted in both Bloomberg.com and wsj.com.
4. Michael Blomquist, *The Housing Bubble: American Dream or Nightmare*, New York: Xlibris, 2007.
5. Dean Baker, "The Housing Bubble Fact Sheet," www.cepr.net, July 2005.
6. Ibid.
7. Blomquist, *The Housing Bubble*, chapter 6.
8. *The Economist*, June 16, 2005.
9. Christopher Palmeri, "T. Boone Pickens: Still Courting Controversy," *Business Week*, April 27, 2006.
10. "Gasoline Price Changes: The Dynamic of Supply, Demand, and Competition," ftc.gov, July 5, 2005.
11. Christopher Hope, "BP Chief Blames Oil Price Ramping," *Telegraph* (U.K.), April 26, 2006, p. 46.
12. "Oil Mergers Blamed for Higher Prices," www.consumeraffairs.com, April 2, 2004.
13. Tyson Slocum, Testimony before U.S. Senate Committee on Commerce, Science and Transportation, "Causes and Solutions for America's High Gasoline Prices," September 21, 2005.

14. Ralph Nader, "Stop Exxon-Mobil from Squeezing Us Dry," www.commondreams.com, July 29, 2006.
15. Slocum, Testimony before U.S. Senate Committee on Commerce, Science and Transportation.
16. Associated Press Financial Wire, "Oil Prices Rally; Gas Regains Some Ground," www.associatedpress.com, January 6, 2006.
17. Bill O'Reilly, "Oil Companies Fined for Manipulating Prices," *The O'Reilly Factor*, 8:28 P.M. EST, Fox News Network, January 13, 2006.
18. Ibid.

CHAPTER 3

1. Ravi Batra, *Common Sense Macroeconomics*, Richardson, Texas: Liberty Press, 2003, chapter 3.
2. Estimates of money supply can be obtained from Milton Freidman and Anna Schwartz, *A Monetary History of the United States, 1867–1960*, Princeton, N.J.: Princeton University Press, 1983; Ravi Batra, *The Crash of the Millennium*, New York: Harmony Books, 1999; and Council of Economic Advisers, *The Economic Report of the President*, Washington D.C., 2006.
3. Gilbert Fite and Jim Reese, *An Economic History of the United States*, Boston: Houghton Mifflin, 1973, chapter 10.
4. Arthur Schlesinger, *The Cycles of American History*, Boston: Houghton Mifflin, 1986, p. 30.
5. Ibid.

CHAPTER 4

1. Milton Friedman, *Methodology of Positive Economics*, Chicago: University of Chicago Press, 1953.
2. P. R. Sarkar, *Human Society*, part 2, Denver, Colo.: Renaissance Universal Press, p. 40.
3. Ravi Batra, *The Downfall of Capitalism and Communism*, London: Macmillan, 1978, and *Muslim Civilization and the Crisis in Iran*, Richardson, Texas: Liberty Press, 1980.

CHAPTER 5

1. E. M. Burns and P. L. Ralph, *World Civilizations*, New York: Norton, 1974; R. Palmer and J. Colton, *A History of the Modern World*, New York: McGraw Hill, 1995; and Ravi Batra, *The Downfall of Capitalism and Communism*, London: Macmillan, 1978, p. 390.
3. Burns and Ralph, *World Civilizations*.
4. E. H. Tuma, *European Economic History*, New York: Harper & Row, 1971.
5. Ibid.

6. V. L. Bullough, *The Subordinate Sex*, Urbana: University of Illinois Press, 1973, p. 179.
7. E. K. Hunt and H. G. Sherman, *Economics: An Introduction to Traditional and Radical Views*, New York: Harper & Row, 1975, p. 7.
8. Tuma, *European Economic History*, note 44.
9. W. K. Ferguson and G. Brunn, *A Survey of European Civilization*, Boston: Houghton Mifflin, 1947, p. 375. Also see John Merriman, *A History of Modern Europe*, New York: Norton, 2005.
10. Tuma, *European Economic History*, note 44.

CHAPTER 6

1. M. Rostovtzeff, *The Social and Economic History of the Roman Empire*, London: Oxford University Press, 1926.
2. Ibid.
3. Percival Griffiths, *The British Impact on India*, New York: Archon Books, 1965.
4. For a brief history of the dollar, see Ravi Batra, *Common Sense Macroeconomics*, Richardson, Texas: Liberty Press, 2003, chapter 3, note 35.
5. See Kurt Eichenwald, "Enron in the 90's: Arrogant and Reckless," *New York Times*, May 26, 2006, p. C1, and Bill Marsh, "Capital Alert: The Unfolding Story of Brent Wilkes," *New York Times*, May 21, 2006, p. A16.
6. Ravi Batra, *Greenspan's Fraud: How Two Decades of His Policies Have Undermined the Global Economy*, New York: Palgrave Macmillan, 2005, note 11.
7. Ibid.
8. Epinet.org.
9. Lawrence Orlowski and Florian Lengyel, "The Corner Office in Bangalore," *New York Times*, June 9, 2006, p. A27.
10. Jenny Anderson, "Atop Hedge Funds, Richest of the Rich Get Even More So," *New York Times*, May 26, 2006, p. C1.
11. Charles Lewis, *The Buying of the President 2004: Who's Really Bankrolling Bush and His Democratic Challengers—and What They Expect in Return*, New York: Avon Books, 2004.
12. David C. Johnston, *Perfectly Legal: The Covert Campaign to Rig Our Tax System to Benefit the Super Rich—and Cheat Everybody Else*, New York: Penguin, 2003.

CHAPTER 7

1. Scott Jaschik, "The Rich Get Richer," www.insidehighered.com, January 23, 2006.
2. Council of Economic Advisers, *The Economic Report of the President*, Washington D.C., 2006.

3. Ravi Batra, *Greenspan's Fraud: How Two Decades of His Policies Have Undermined the Global Economy*, New York: Palgrave Macmillan, 2005, chapter 6.

4. Lawrence Orlowski and Florian Lengyel, "The Corner Office in Bangalore," *New York Times*, June 9, 2006, p. A27.

5. David C. Johnston, "In the New Economics: Fast-Food Factories?" *New York Times*, February 20, 2004, p. C2.

6. Council of Economic Advisers, *The Economic Report of the President*.

7. Ibid. Also see Mike Allen, "Hastert Rebukes Bush Adviser: Speaker Challenges Mankiw's Statements on U.S. Job Loss," *Washington Post*, February 12, 2004, p. A17.

8. Jonathan Chait, "Deficit Reduction," *New Republic Online*, www.tnr.com, January 2, 2003.

9. See Batra, *Greenspan's Fraud*, chapter 6, note 11.

10. Paul Krugman, "Fear of a Quagmire?" *New York Times*, May 24, 2003, p. A15.

11. Paul Krugman, "Dropping the Bonds," *New York Times*, July 25, 2003, p. A23.

12. Donald Luskin, "Desperately Seeking Something—Anything!" www.nationalreview.com, May 28, 2003.

13. Paul Krugman, "The Trade Tightrope," *New York Times*, February 27, 2004, p. A27.

14. Paul Krugman, "Feeling No Pain," *New York Times*, March 6, 2006, p. A21.

15. David Wessel, "Wealth Effect—Capital: Behind Tax Debate, Issues of Ethics and Economics," *Wall Street Journal*, January 2, 2003, p. A1. The article mentions Professor Feldstein as one of the chief exponents of this view.

16. Joseph M. Anderson, "The Wealth of U.S. Families in 1995: A Report to Merrill Lynch," www.savingscoalition.org, June 1, 1998.

17. Robert Barro, *Macroeconomics*, 5th edition, Cambridge, Mass.: MIT Press, 2000.

18. Robert Lucas, *Models of Business Cycles*, Oxford: Basil Blackwell, 1987, p. 66.

19. Samuel Morley, *Macroeconomics*, New York: Dryden, 1984, p. 167.

20. Paul Krugman and Maurice Obstfeld, *International Economics: Theory and Policy*, New York: Addison Wesley, 2002.

CHAPTER 8

1. Ravi Batra, *Muslim Civilization and the Crisis in Iran*, Richardson, Texas: Liberty Press, 1980.

2. P. K. Hitti, *History of the Arabs*, New York: St. Martin's Press, 1973, p. 295.

3. P. M. Holt, *The Cambridge History of Islam*, Cambridge, U.K.: Cambridge University Press, 1977.
4. Hitti, *History of the Arabs*, note 83.
5. W. M. Watt, *The Majesty That Was Islam*, London: Sidgwick and Jackson, 1975.
6. Bernard Lewis, editor, *Islam: From the Prophet Muhammad to the Capture of Constantinople*, volume 2, New York: Harper & Row, 1974, p. 65.
7. Ibid., p. 67.
8. Ibid., p. 75.
9. M. A. Rauf, *A Brief History of Islam*, London: Oxford University Press, 1964, pp. 66–67.
10. M. G. Hodgson, *The Venture of Islam*, volume 1, Chicago: University of Chicago Press, 1974, pp. 405–406.
11. Ibid., p. 407.
12. Ravi Batra, *The Downfall of Capitalism and Communism*, London: Macmillan, 1978, chapter 7, note 11.
13. Hodgson, *The Venture of Islam*, p. 102, note 91.
14. A. K. Faruki, *The Evolution of Islamic Constitutional Theory and Practice*, Karachi, Pakistan: National Publishing House, 1971, p. 75.

CHAPTER 9

1. Don Peretz, *The Middle East Today*, New York: Holt, Rinehart and Winston, 1978, p. 437.
2. George Lipsky, *Saudi Arabia: Its People, Its Society, Its Culture*, New Haven, Conn.: Yale University Press, 1959, p. 120.
3. Peretz, *The Middle East Today*, p. 440, note 96.
4. Ibid.
5. Ibid., p. 216.
6. Elton Daniel, *The History of Iran*, Denver, Colo.: Greenwood Press, 2000.

CHAPTER 10

1. Claudia Deutsch, "Take Your Best Shot: New Surveys Show That Big Business Has a P.R. Problem," *New York Times*, December 9, 2006.
2. Bob Herbert, "A President Who Can Do No Right," *New York Times*, January 26, 2006, p. 23.
3. Sidney Blumenthal, "Revolt of the Generals: The Denunciation of the Administration's Handling of Iraq by Former U.S. Army Chiefs Is Unprecedented," *Guardian* (U.K.), April 21, 2006.
4. "U.S. Troops in Iraq: 72% Say End War in 2006," www.zogby.com, February 28, 2006.
5. Thomas Friedman, "Osama and Katrina," *New York Times*, September 7, 2005, p. A25.

6. Ravi Batra, *Muslim Civilization and the Crisis in Iran*, Richardson, Texas: Liberty Press, 1980, p. 196.
7. Ibid., p. 203.
8. Ravi Batra, *The Crash of the Millennium*, New York: Harmony Books, 1999, pp. 24–25.

CHAPTER 11

1. Danielle DiMartino, "Homeowners: Protect Yourselves," *Dallas Morning News*, May 9, 2006, p. D4.
2. Paul Samuelson and Wolfgong Stolper, "Protection and Real Wages," *Review of Economic Studies*, 1941.
3. Paul Samuelson, "Where Ricardo and Mill Rebut and Confirm Arguments of Manistream Economists Supporting Globalization," *Journal of Economic Perspectives*, Summer 2004, pp. 135–146.
4. Andrew Abel and Ben Bernanke, *Macroeconomics*, New York: Addison Wesley, 1995, p. 89.
5. For more on the effects of the wage gap, see Batra, *Greenspan's Fraud*, chapters 6 and 11.
6. Louis Uchitelle, *The Disposable American: Layoffs and Their Consequences*, New York: Knopf, 2006.
7. For more on these reforms, see Batra, *Greenspan's Fraud*, chapter 12.
8. Jay Leno, cited in "Laugh Lines," *New York Times*, April 30, 2006, section 4, p. 2.
9. George Anders, "As Patients, Doctors Feel Pinch, Insurer's CEO Makes a Billion," *Wall Street Journal*, April 18, 2006, p. A1.
10. John Battista and Justine McCabe, "The Case for Universal Health Care," http://cthealth.server101.com/contact_us.htm, 1999.
11. Physicians' Working Group, "Single-Payer National Health Care Reform," www.physiciansproposal.org, May 1, 2001.
12. Paul Krugman and Robin Wells, "The Healthcare Crisis and What to Do About It," *The New York Review of Books*, March 23, 2006.
13. For more on economic democracy, see Batra, *Greenspan's Fraud*, note 11.
14. Robert Borosage, "A Real Contract with America," *Nation*, October, 24, 2005.
15. Editorial, "Barely Staying Afloat," *New York Times*, May 10, 2006, p. A22.
16. Daniel Gross, "When Sweet Statistics Clash with a Sour Mood," *New York Times*, June 4, 2006, p. B3.
17. Kurt Eichenwald and Alexei Barrionuevo, *New York Times*, May 27, 2006.
18. Michael Dorgan, *Take This Job and Ship It*, New York: St. Martin's Griffin, 2005; Michael Blomquist, *The Housing Bubble: An American Dream or Nightmare*, New York: Xlibris, 2007; and Jim Cunningham, *Hollowing Out: America's Flight from Manufacturing into a Perilous World of Economic Fantasy*, New York: Protheous Books, 2007.

19. Dick Alexander, thedemocratsforamerica.com and Globalshop.com.
20. Frank Rich, "How Hispanics Became the New Gays," *New York Times*, June 11, 2006, section 4, p. 12.
21. *The Random House Encyclopedia*, New York: Random House, 2000, p. 1170.
22. R. Palmer and J. Colton, *A History of the Modern World*, 8th edition, New York: McGraw Hill, 1995, p. 916.
23. "Golden Age," www.EncyclopediaBrittannica.com.

INDEX